Intelligence

From Secrets to Policy

Second Edition

Mark M. Lowenthal

CQ PRESS

A Division of Congressional Quarterly Inc.
Washington, D.C.

CQ Press
1255 22nd Street, N.W., Suite 400
Washington, DC 20037

(202) 729-1900; toll-free, 1-866-4CQ-PRESS (1-866-427-7737)

www.cqpress.com

∞ The paper used in this publication meets the minimum requirements of the American National Standard for Information Sciences—Permanence of Paper for Printed Library Materials, ANSI Z39.48-1992.

Typeset by MidAtlantic Books & Journals, Inc., Linthicum, MD
Cover design by Berg Design

Printed and bound in the United States of America

06 05 04 03 02   5 4 3 2 1

LIBRARY OF CONGRESS CATALOGING-IN-PUBLICATION DATA

Lowenthal, Mark M.
  Intelligence : from secrets to policy / Mark M. Lowenthal.-- 2nd ed.
      p. cm.
Includes bibliographical references (p.   ) and index.
  ISBN 1-56802-759-1
  1. Intelligence service--United States. 2. Intelligence service. I.
Title.
  JK468.I6 L65 2003
  327.1273--dc21

                                        2002008409

For
Michael S. Freeman
1946–1999
Historian, Librarian, Friend

Contents

Figures and Boxes

FIGURES

BOXES

Preface

In years past, when academics who taught courses on intelligence got together, one of the first questions they asked one another was, "What are you using for readings?" They asked because there was no standard text on intelligence. Available books were either general histories that did not suffice as course texts or academic discussions written largely for practitioners and aficionados, not for undergraduate or graduate students. Like many of my colleagues, I long felt the need for an introductory text. I wrote this book to fill a gap in intelligence literature.

Intelligence: From Secrets to Policy will not turn readers into competent spies or even better analysts. Rather, it is designed to give readers a firm understanding of the role that intelligence plays in making national security policy and insight into its strengths and weaknesses. The main theme of the book is that intelligence serves and is subservient to policy and that it works best—both analytically and operationally—when tied to clearly understood policy goals.

Admittedly, this book has a U.S.-centric bias. I am most familiar with the U.S. intelligence establishment, and it is the largest, richest, and most multifaceted intelligence enterprise in the world. At the same time, readers with interests beyond the United States should derive from this book a better understanding of many of the basic issues in intelligence collection, analysis, and covert action and of the relationship of intelligence to policy.

This book begins with a discussion of the definition of intelligence and a brief history and overview of the U.S. intelligence community. The core of the book is organized along the lines of the intelligence process as practiced by most intelligence enterprises: requirements, collection, analysis, dissemination, and policy. Each of these aspects is discussed in detail in terms of its role, strengths, and problems. This structure allows the reader to understand both the overall intelligence process and the specific issues encountered in each step of the process. The book also examines covert action and counterintelligence in a similar vein. Three chapters explore the performance of U.S. intelligence during and after the cold war and the moral and ethical issues that arise in intelligence. Finally, this second edition contains entirely new chapters on intelligence reform and on foreign intelligence services.

Intelligence grows out of two courses that I have taught for many years: "The Role of Intelligence in U.S. Foreign Policy," at the School for International and Public Affairs, Columbia University, and "The History of U.S. Intelligence," at the Elliott School for International Affairs, George Washington University. As I tell my students, I provide neither a polemic against intelligence nor an apology for it. This volume takes the view that intelligence is a normal function of government: sometimes it works well; sometimes it does not. There is room for both praise and criticism of any intelligence service, including that of the United States. My goal is to raise important issues and to illuminate the debate over them, as well as to provide context for the debate. I leave it to professors and students to come to their own conclusions. As an introduction to the subject of intelligence, the book, I believe, takes the right approach, rather than asking the reader to agree with the author's views.

This introductory text is not meant to be the last word on the subject. It is intended instead as a starting point for a serious academic exploration of the issues inherent in intelligence. Each chapter concludes with a list of readings recommended for a deeper examination of relevant issues. Additional bibliographic citations and Web sites are provided in Appendix 1. Appendix 2 lists some of the most important reviews and proposals for change in the intelligence community since 1945.

Plans for a second revised edition of this book were already under way when terrorists attacked the United States on September 11, 2001. Inevitable changes in the practice of intelligence in the United States itself, as well as helpful comments from friends, students, and reviewers, prompted these initial revisions. Obviously, the onset of the war against terrorism necessitated further changes.

Given the dynamic nature of intelligence, any textbook on the subject runs the risk of containing dated information. This may be an even greater problem in the more fluid situation after the terrorist attacks, replicating the intelligence analyst's dilemma of needing to produce "finished" intelligence during changing circumstances. This risk cannot be avoided. However, I am confident that most aspects of intelligence—and certainly the main issues discussed here—are more general, more long-standing, and less susceptible to being outdated rapidly than the ever-changing character of intelligence might suggest.

The CIA's Publications Review Board has read the manuscript of this book to help eliminate classified information and raises no security objections to its publication. This review, however, should not be construed as an official release of information, confirmation of its accuracy, or an endorsement of my views.

Several words of thanks are in order: first, to my wife, Cynthia, and our children—Sarah and Adam—who have supported my part-time academic career despite the missed dinners it means. Cynthia also reviewed the text incisively and provided me with much help and support throughout the production of both editions. Next, thanks go to three friends and colleagues—Sam Halpern, Loch Johnson, and Jennifer Sims—who reviewed early drafts and made many important improvements. The following scholars also provided extremely helpful comments: William Green, California State University at San Bernadino; Patrick Morgan, University of California at Irvine; Donald Snow, University of Alabama; James D. Calder, University of Texas at San Antonio; Robert Pringle, University of Kentucky; and L. Larry Boothe, Utah State University. Richard Best of the Congressional Research Service helped me keep the bibliographic entries up to date for both editions. None of these individuals is responsible for any remaining flaws or any of the views expressed. Moreover, I have been most fortunate to collaborate with these editors: at CQ Press, Charisse Kiino, Jerry Orvedahl, and Elizabeth Jones and freelance editor Janet Wilson. Working with them has been most enjoyable. Thanks to the CIA for providing the "Star of David" photograph and to Space Imaging for supplying the series of overhead images of San Diego. Finally, thanks to all of my students over the years, whose comments and discussions have greatly enriched my courses and this book. Again, I am solely responsible for any shortcomings in this volume.

Chapter 1

Introduction—What Is "Intelligence?"

What is intelligence? Why is its definition an issue? Virtually every book written on the subject of intelligence begins with a discussion of what "intelligence" means, or at least how the author intends to use the term. This editorial fact tells us much about the field of intelligence. If this were a text on any other government function—defense, housing, transportation, diplomacy, agriculture—there would be little or no confusion about, or need to explain, what was being discussed.

Intelligence is different from other government functions for at least two reasons. First, much of what goes on is secret. Intelligence exists because governments seek to hide some information from other governments, which, in turn, seek to discover hidden information by means that they wish to keep secret. All of this secrecy leads some authors to believe that there are issues about which they cannot write or may not have sufficient knowledge. Thus, they feel the need to describe the limits of their work. Although numerous aspects of intelligence are—and deserve to be—kept secret, this is not an impediment to describing basic roles, processes, functions, and issues.

The second reason for treating intelligence differently is, in many respects, unique to the United States. The U.S. intelligence community is a relatively recent government phenomenon. Since its creation in 1947, the intelligence community has been the subject of much ambivalence. Some Americans are uncomfortable with the concept that intelligence is a secret entity within an ostensibly open government based on checks and balances. Moreover, the intelligence community engages in activities— spying, eavesdropping, covert action—that some people regard as antithetical to what they believe the United States should be as a nation and as a model for other nations. Some citizens have difficulty reconciling American ideals and goals with the realities of intelligence.

To many people, intelligence seems little different from information, except that it is probably secret. However, it is important to distinguish between the two. Information is anything that can be known, regardless of how it may be discovered. Intelligence refers to information that meets the stated or understood needs of policymakers and has been collected, refined, and narrowed to meet those needs. Intelligence is a subset of the broader category of information; intelligence and the entire process by which it is identified, obtained, and analyzed respond to the needs of policymakers. All intelligence is information; not all information is intelligence.

WHY DO WE HAVE INTELLIGENCE AGENCIES?

The major theme of this book is that intelligence exists solely to support policymakers. Any other activity is either wasteful or illegal. The book's focus is firmly on the relationship between intelligence, in all of its aspects, and policymaking. It is important to understand that the policymaker is not a passive recipient of intelligence, but rather actively influences all aspects of intelligence. The policymaker's role will also be examined fully. That said, intelligence agencies exist for at least four major reasons:

TO AVOID STRATEGIC SURPRISE. The foremost goal of any intelligence community must be to keep track of threats, forces, events, and developments that are capable of threatening the nation's existence. This goal may sound grandiose and farfetched, but several times over the past one hundred years nations have been subjected to direct military attacks for which they were, at best, inadequately prepared—Russia in 1904, both the Soviet Union and the United States in 1941, Israel in 1973. The terrorist attacks of September 11, 2001, are another example of this pattern, albeit carried out on a much more limited scale. (*See box, "The Terrorist Attacks on September 11, 2001: Another Pearl Harbor?"*)

Strategic surprise should not be confused with tactical surprise, which is of a different magnitude and, as Professor Richard Betts of Columbia University pointed out in his article, "Analysis, War, and Decision: Why Intelligence Failures are Inevitable," cannot be wholly avoided. (*See box, "Strategic versus Tactical Surprise."*) Tactical surprise, when it happens, is not of sufficient magnitude and importance to threaten national existence. Repetitive tactical surprise, however, suggests some significant intelligence problems.

TO PROVIDE LONG-TERM EXPERTISE. Compared with the permanent bureaucracy, all senior policymakers are transients. The average time in office for a president of the United States is five years. Secretaries of state and defense serve for less time than that, and their senior subordinates— deputy, under, and assistant secretaries—often hold their positions for even shorter periods. Even though these individuals enter their respective offices with considerable background in their fields, it is virtually impossible for

The Terrorist Attacks on September 11, 2001: Another Pearl Harbor?

Many people immediately described the terrorist attacks as a "new Pearl Harbor." This is understandable on an emotional level, as both were surprise attacks. However, beyond that superficial similarity, there are important differences. First, Pearl Harbor was a strategic surprise. U.S. policymakers expected some sort of Japanese move but not against the United States. The Soviet Union was seen as one possible Japanese target, but the greatest expectation and fear was a Japanese attack on European colonies in Southeast Asia.

The terrorist attacks were more of a tactical surprise. The enmity of Osama bin Laden and his willingness to attack U.S. targets had been amply demonstrated in earlier attacks on the East African embassies and on the USS *Cole*. Throughout the summer of 2001, U.S. intelligence officials had warned of the likelihood of another bin Laden attack. What was not known—or guessed—was the target and the means of attack. Second, Japan and the Axis had the capability of defeating and destroying U.S. power and our very way of life. The terrorists do not pose a threat on the same level.

them to be well versed in all of the matters with which they will be dealing. Inevitably, they will have to call upon others whose knowledge and expertise on certain issues are more extensive. A great deal of knowledge and expertise on national security issues resides in the intelligence community, where the analytical cadre is relatively stable. Stability tends to be greater in intelligence agencies, particularly in higher-level positions, than is the case in foreign affairs and defense agencies. Also, intelligence agencies tend to have far fewer political appointees than the State and Defense Departments do, although these two differences have diminished somewhat over the past decade.

TO SUPPORT THE POLICY PROCESS. Policymakers have a constant need for tailored, timely intelligence that will provide background, context, information, warning, and an assessment of risks, benefits, and likely outcomes. Their needs are met by the intelligence community.

In the ethos of U.S. intelligence, a strict dividing line exists between intelligence and policy. The two are seen as separate functions. The government is run by and for the policymakers. Intelligence has a support role and may not cross over into the advocacy of policy choices. Intelligence officers who are dealing with policymakers are expected to maintain a certain objectivity and not lapse into advocacy for specific policies,

Strategic versus Tactical Surprise

The following example puts in perspective the difference between the two types of surprise. There are two partners in a firm, Mr. Smith and Mr. Jones. Every Friday, while Mr. Smith is out at a regular lunch with a client, Mr. Jones helps himself to money from the petty cash.

One afternoon Mr. Smith comes back from lunch earlier than expected, catching Mr. Jones red-handed. "I'm surprised!" they exclaim simultaneously.

Mr. Jones's surprise is tactical: he knew what he was doing but did not expect to get caught.

Mr. Smith's surprise is strategic: he had no idea the embezzlement was happening.

choices, or outcomes. To do so is seen as threatening the objectivity of the analyses they present. If intelligence officers have a strong preference for a specific policy outcome, their intelligence analysis may display a similar bias. This is what is meant by "politicized intelligence," one of the strongest expressions of opprobrium that can be leveled in the U.S. intelligence community.

Three important caveats should be added to the distinction between policy and intelligence. First, the idea that intelligence is distinct from policy does not mean that intelligence officers do not care about the outcome and do not influence it. One must differentiate between attempting to influence (that is, inform) the process by providing intelligence, which is acceptable, and trying to manipulate intelligence so that policymakers make a certain choice, which is not acceptable. Second, senior policymakers can and do ask senior intelligence officials for their opinions, which are given. Third, this separation works in only one direction, that of intelligence advice to policy. Nothing prevents policymakers from rejecting intelligence out of hand or offering their own "intelligence" inputs—an action that they will likely see as being different from imposing their views on the intelligence product per se. This also politicizes intelligence, which is an accusation policymakers as well as intelligence officials hope to avoid, because it calls into question the soundness of their policy and the basis on which they have made decisions. (*See box, "Policy versus Intelligence: The Great Divide."*)

TO MAINTAIN THE SECRECY OF INFORMATION, NEEDS, AND METHODS. Secrecy does make intelligence unique. That others would keep important information from us, that we need certain types of information

Policy versus Intelligence: The Great Divide

One way to envision the distinction between policy and intelligence is to
see them as two spheres of government activity that are separated by a semipermeable membrane. The membrane is semipermeable because policymakers can and do cross over into the intelligence sphere, but intelligence
officials cannot cross over into the policy sphere.

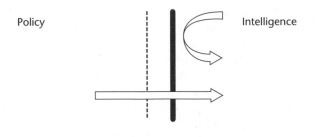

and wish to keep our needs secret, and that we have the means to obtain
information that we also wish to keep secret are major reasons for having
intelligence agencies.

WHAT IS INTELLIGENCE ABOUT?

When we use the word *intelligence,* we are largely referring to issues related to national security—that is, defense and foreign policy and certain
aspects of internal security.

The actions, policies, and capabilities of other nations are primary
areas of concern. But policymakers and intelligence officers cannot
restrict themselves to thinking only about enemies—those powers that
are known to be hostile or whose policy goals are in some way inimical.
They must also keep track of powers that are rivals, even though they may
be neutrals, friends, or even allies. For example, the European Union is
made up largely of nations that are U.S. allies. However, in the competition for global resources and markets, many of these countries are our
rivals. This is also true of Japan. Circumstances may also arise in which
we would need to keep track of the actions and intentions of friends. For
example, an ally might be pursuing a course that could involve it in conflict with a third party. Should this not be to our liking—or should it
threaten to involve us as well—it would be better to know early on what

this ally was doing. Adolf Hitler, for example, might have been better served had he known in advance of Japan's plans to attack the U.S. fleet at Pearl Harbor in 1941. In the late twentieth and early twenty-first centuries it has become increasingly important for the United States to keep track of "nonstate" actors—terrorists, narcotics traffickers, and others.

We want information about these actors, their likely actions, and their capabilities in a variety of areas—economic, military, societal, and others. The United States built its intelligence organizations in recognition of the fact that some of the information we would like to have is either inaccessible or being actively denied. In other words, the information is secret as far as we are concerned, and those who have the information would like to keep it that way.

The pursuit of secret information is the mainstay of intelligence activity. At the same time, reflecting the political transformation brought about by the end of the cold war, increasing amounts of once secret information are now accessible, especially in states that were once subject to or allied with the Soviet Union. Indeed, the ratio of open to secret information has likely shifted dramatically. Still, foreign states and actors harbor secrets that the United States must pursue.

Most people tend to think of intelligence in terms of military information—troop movements, weapons capabilities, and plans for surprise attack. This is an important component of intelligence (in line with avoiding surprise attack, the first reason for having intelligence agencies), but it is not the only one. Many different kinds of intelligence—political, economic, social, environmental, health, and cultural—provide important inputs to analysts. Policymakers and intelligence officials also must think beyond foreign intelligence. They must consider intelligence activities focused on threats to internal security, such as subversion, espionage, and terrorism.

Other than the internal security threats mentioned above, domestic intelligence, at least in the United States and kindred democracies, is a law-enforcement issue. This fact differentiates the practice of intelligence in Western democracies from that in totalitarian states. The Soviet Union's KGB, for example, served a crucial internal secret police function that the CIA does not. Thus, in many respects, the two agencies were not comparable.

What is intelligence *not* about? Intelligence is not about truth! If something were known to be true, states would not need intelligence agencies to collect the information or analyze it. Truth is such an absolute term that it sets a standard intelligence rarely would be able to achieve. It is better—and more accurate—to think of intelligence as "proximate reality." Intelligence agencies face issues or questions and do their best to arrive at a firm understanding of what is going on. They can rarely be assured that even their best and most considered analysis is true. Their goals are intelligence products that are reliable, unbiased, and honest

---

"And ye shall know the truth...."

Upon entering the old entrance of the CIA headquarters, you see on the left-hand marble wall the following inscription:

"And ye shall know the truth, and the truth shall make you free."

John VIII–XXXII

It is a very nice sentiment, but it overstates and misrepresents what is going on in that building or any other intelligence agency.

(that is, free from politicization). These are all laudable goals, yet they are still different from "truth." (*See box, "And ye shall know the truth."*)

Is intelligence integral to the policy process? The question may seem rhetorical in a book about intelligence, but it is an important question to consider. At one level, the answer is yes. Intelligence should and can provide warning about imminent strategic threats, although several nations have been subjected to strategic surprise. Intelligence officials can also play a useful role as seasoned and experienced advisers. The information their agencies gather is also of value by virtue of the fact that it might not be available if agencies did not undertake secret collection. Therein lies an irony, in that intelligence agencies strive to be more than just collectors of information. They emphasize the value that their analysis adds to the secret information, although equally competent analysts can be found in policy agencies. The difference lies in the nature of the work and the outcomes for which the two types of analysts are responsible: intelligence versus policy decisions.

At the same time, intelligence suffers from a number of potential weaknesses that tend to undercut its function in the eyes of policymakers. Not all of these weaknesses are present at all times, and there may be times when none are present. To repeat, they represent *potential* pitfalls.

The first of these weaknesses is that a certain amount of intelligence analysis may be no more sophisticated than current "conventional wisdom" on a given issue. Conventional wisdom is usually—and sometimes mistakenly—dismissed out of hand. But policymakers expect more than that, in part justifiably.

Second, analysis can become so dependent on data that it misses important intangibles. For example, a competent analysis of the likelihood that thirteen small and somewhat disunited colonies would be able to break away from British rule in the 1770s would have concluded that

Intelligence—A Working Concept

Intelligence is the process by which specific types of information important to national security are requested, collected, analyzed, and provided to policymakers; the products of that process; the safeguarding of these processes and this information by counterintelligence activities; and the carrying out of operations as requested by lawful authorities.

defeat was imminent. After all, Britain was the largest industrial power; it already had trained troops stationed in the colonies; colonial opinion was not united (nor was Britain's); and Britain could use the Indians as an added force, among other reasons. A straightforward political-military analysis would have missed several factors that turned out to be of tremendous importance.

Third, "mirror imaging," or assuming that other states or individuals will act just the way we do, can undermine analysis. The basis of this problem is fairly understandable. Every day we make innumerable judgments—when we drive, walk on a crowded street, or interact with others in our homes and offices—about how people will react and behave. Indeed, we assume that their behavior and reactions are based on the golden rule. These judgments are based on societal norms and rules, etiquette, and experience. It is all too easy for analysts to extend this commonplace thinking to intelligence issues. However, in intelligence it becomes a trap. For example, no U.S. policymaker in 1941 could conceive of Japan's starting a war with the United States overtly (rather than continuing its advance while bypassing U.S. territories), given the great disparity in the strength of the two nations. In Tokyo, however, those same factors argued compellingly for the necessity of starting war sooner rather than later. The other problem with mirror imaging is that it assumes a certain level of shared rationality. It leaves no room for the "irrational" actor, an individual or nation who may be completely irrational or whose rationality has a basis other than our own.

Fourth, and perhaps the most important weakness, policymakers are free to reject or to ignore the intelligence they are offered. They may suffer penalties down the road if their policy has bad outcomes, but there is no way to force policymakers to take heed of intelligence. Thus, they can dispense with intelligence at will, and intelligence officers cannot force their way (or their products) back into the process in such cases.

This host of weaknesses seems to overpower the positive aspects listed earlier. It certainly suggests and underscores the fragility of intelligence within the policy process. How, then, can we tell whether intelligence matters? The best way, at least retrospectively, is to ask: Would policymakers have made different choices with or without a given piece of intelligence? If the answer is yes, or even maybe, then the intelligence mattered.

What is intelligence? We return to the question posed at the beginning of this chapter. There are several ways to think about intelligence, all of which will be used throughout this book, sometimes simultaneously:

- Intelligence as process: Intelligence can be thought of as the means by which certain types of information are required and requested, collected, analyzed, and disseminated, and as the way in which certain types of covert action are conceived and conducted.
- Intelligence as product: Intelligence can be thought of as the product of these processes, that is, as the analyses and intelligence operations themselves.
- Intelligence as organization: Intelligence can be thought of as the units that carry out its various functions.

FURTHER READINGS

Each of these readings grapples with the definition of intelligence, either by function or by role, in a different way. Some deal with intelligence on its own terms; others attempt to relate it to the larger policy process.

Betts, Richard. "Analysis, War, and Decision: Why Intelligence Failures are Inevitable." *World Politics* 31 (October 1978). Reprinted in Klaus Knorr, ed. *Power, Strategy, and Security.* Princeton: Princeton University Press, 1983.

Hamilton, Lee. "The Role of Intelligence in the Foreign Policy Process." Essays on Strategy and Diplomacy. Keck Center for International Strategic Studies, Claremont College, 1987.

Herman, Michael. *Intelligence Power in Peace and War.* New York: Cambridge University Press, 1996.

Heymann, Hans. "Intelligence/Policy Relationships." In *Intelligence: Policy and Process.* Ed. Alfred C. Maurer et al. Boulder: Westview Press, 1985.

Hilsman, Roger. *Strategic Intelligence and National Decisions.* Glencoe, Ill.: Free Press, 1958.

Kent, Sherman. *Strategic Intelligence for American Foreign Policy.* Princeton: Princeton University Press, 1949.

Laqueur, Walter. *A World of Secrets: The Uses and Limits of Intelligence.* New York: Basic Books, 1985.

Shulsky, Abram N., and Gary J. Schmitt. *Silent Warfare: Understanding the World of Intelligence.* 2d rev. ed. Washington, D.C.: Brassey's, 1993.

Shulsky, Abram N., and Jennifer Sims. *What Is Intelligence?* Washington, D.C.: Consortium for the Study of Intelligence, 1992.

Troy, Thomas F. "The 'Correct' Definition of Intelligence." *International Journal of Intelligence and Counterintelligence* 5 (winter 1991–1992).

Chapter 2

The Development
of U.S. Intelligence

Each nation practices intelligence in ways that are specific—if not peculiar—to that nation alone. This is true even among nations that share a great deal of their intelligence, such as the United States, Britain, Canada, and Australia. A better understanding of how and why the United States practices intelligence as it does is important as the basis for much that will be discussed in the following chapters and also because the U.S. intelligence system remains the largest and most influential in the world—as model, rival, or target. The practices of several foreign intelligence services are discussed in chap. 15.

This chapter focuses on the major themes and historical events that have shaped the development of U.S. intelligence. It is not intended to be even a brief history of U.S. intelligence in outline form. Rather, these themes and events have been chosen because they played a significant role in forging U.S. intelligence and in determining how it continues to function.

A brief word is in order about the phrase "intelligence community," which is used throughout the book, as it is in most other discussions of U.S. intelligence. The word "community" is particularly apt in describing U.S. intelligence. The community comprises agencies and offices whose work is often related and sometimes combined, but who work for different clients and under various lines of authority and control. The intelligence community grew out of a set of evolving demands and without a master plan. It is highly functional and sometimes dysfunctional. One director of central intelligence, Richard Helms (1966–1973), testified cogently before Congress that, despite all of the criticisms of the structure and functioning of the intelligence community, if one were to create it from scratch, much the same community would likely emerge. Helms's focus is not the structure of the community, but the fact that the services it provides are multiple, varied, and not under one individual's complete authority. This approach to intelligence is unique to the United States, although others have copied facets of it.

MAJOR THEMES

THE NOVELTY OF U.S. INTELLIGENCE. Of the major powers of the twentieth and twenty-first centuries, the United States has the briefest history of significant intelligence beyond wartime emergencies. British intelligence dates from the reign of Elizabeth I (1558–1603), French intelligence from the sway of Cardinal Richelieu (1624–1642), and Russian intelligence from the reign of Ivan the Terrible (1533–1584). Even taking into account the fact that the United States did not come into being until 1776, its intelligence experience is brief. Not until 1940 was there the first glimmer of what might be called a national intelligence enterprise. Although permanent and specific naval and military intelligence units date from the late nineteenth century, a broader U.S. national intelligence capability began to arise only with the creation of the Coordinator of Information, the predecessor of the World War II–era Office of Strategic Services (OSS).

How do we explain this nearly 170-year absence of organized U.S. intelligence? For most of its history, the United States did not have very strong foreign policy interests beyond its immediate borders. The success of the Monroe Doctrine, articulated in 1823, abetted by the acquiescence and tacit support of Britain, solved the basic security interests of the United States and its broader foreign policy interests. The need for better intelligence became apparent only after the United States achieved the status of a world power and became involved in broader international issues at the end of the nineteenth century.

Furthermore, the United States faced no threat to its security from its neighbors, from powers outside the Western Hemisphere, or—with the exception of the Civil War—from large-scale internal dissent that was inimical to the form of government. This benign environment—so unlike that faced by all European states—undercut any perceived need for national intelligence.

Until the cold war, the United States had a well-established tradition of severely limiting expenditures on defense and related activities during peacetime. Intelligence, already underappreciated for the reasons noted above, fell into this category. (Historians of intelligence have noted, however, that intelligence absorbed a remarkable and anomalous 12 percent of the federal budget under President George Washington. This was the high-water mark of intelligence spending in the federal budget, a percentage that was never approached again. In 1999 intelligence accounted for roughly 1.6 percent of the federal budget, according to figures declassified by the director of central intelligence.)

Intelligence was a novelty in the 1940s. Policymakers in both the executive branch and Congress viewed intelligence as a "newcomer" to national security. Even within the Army and Navy, intelligence developed relatively late and was far from robust until well into the twentieth century. As a result, intelligence did not have long-established patrons in the government, but it did have many rivals among departments, particularly the military and the FBI, which were not willing to share their sources of information. Another result of its novelty was that intelligence did not have well-established traditions or modes of operation and thus was forced to establish these during two periods of extreme pressure: World War II and the cold war.

A THREAT-BASED FOREIGN POLICY. With the promulgation of the Monroe Doctrine, the United States assumed a vested interest in the international status quo. This interest became even more pronounced after the Spanish-American War in 1898. With the acquisition of a small colonial empire, the United States achieved a very satisfactory international position—largely self-sufficient and largely unthreatened. However, the twentieth century saw the repeated rise of powers whose foreign policies were direct threats to the status quo: Kaiserine Germany in World War I, the Axis in World War II, and then the Soviet Union.

Responding to these threats to the international status quo became the mainstay of U.S. national security policy. The threats also gave focus to much of the operational side of U.S. intelligence, from its initial experience in the OSS during World War II to its broader covert actions in the cold war. Intelligence operations were one way in which the United States countered these threats.

The terrorism threat in the late twentieth and early twenty-first centuries fits the same pattern of an opponent who rejects the international status quo and has emerged as an issue for U.S. national security. However, now the enemy is not a nation-state—even when terrorists have the support of nation-states—which makes it more difficult to deal with the problem. Indeed, one can argue that this refusal to accept the status quo is more central to terrorists than it was to nation-states such as Nazi Germany and the Soviet Union, for whom the international status quo was also anathema. Such countries can, when necessary or convenient, forgo those policies and continue to function. Terrorists, however, cannot accept the status quo without giving up their raison d'etre.

THE INFLUENCE OF THE COLD WAR. Historians of intelligence often debate whether the United States would have had a large-scale intelligence capability had there been no cold war. The view here is that the answer is yes. As will be discussed below, it was Pearl Harbor, not the cold war, that prompted the formation of the U.S. intelligence community.

Even so, the prosecution of the cold war became the major defining factor in the development of most of the basic forms and practices of the

U.S. intelligence community. Until the collapse of the Soviet Union, the cold war was the predominant national security issue, taking up to half of the intelligence budget, according to former director of central intelligence Robert Gates (1991–1993). Moreover, the fact that the Soviet Union and its subject allies were largely closed targets had a major effect on U.S. intelligence, forcing it to resort to a variety of largely remote technical systems to collect needed information. Unable to get close to the Soviet intelligence target, the United States learned how to achieve its collection requirements from a distance.

THE GLOBAL SCOPE OF INTELLIGENCE INTERESTS. The cold war quickly shifted from a struggle for predominance in postwar Europe to a global struggle in which virtually any nation or region could be a pawn between the two sides. Although some areas always remained more important than others, none could be written off entirely. Thus, U.S. intelligence began to collect and analyze information about and station intelligence personnel in every region.

A WITTINGLY REDUNDANT ANALYTICAL STRUCTURE. Intelligence can be divided into four broad activities: collection, analysis, covert action, and counterintelligence. The United States developed unique entities to handle the various types of collection (imagery, signals, espionage) and covert action; counterintelligence is a function that is found in virtually every intelligence agency. But for analysis, U.S. policymakers purposely created three agencies whose functions appear to overlap: the CIA's Directorate of Intelligence, the State Department's Bureau of Intelligence and Research, and the Defense Intelligence Agency. Each of these agencies is considered an "all-source" analytical agency—that is, they have access to the full range of collected intelligence, and all of them work on virtually the same issues.

There are two major reasons for this redundancy, and they are fundamental to how the United States conducts analysis. The first is the recognition that different consumers of intelligence—policymakers—have different intelligence needs. The president, the secretary of state, the secretary of defense, and the chairman of the Joint Chiefs of Staff do not have identical intelligence needs. Even when they are working on the same issue, each has different operational responsibilities. The United States developed analytical centers to serve each of their specific and unique needs. Also, admittedly, each policy agency wanted to be assured of a stream of intelligence dedicated to its needs.

Second, the United States developed the concept of competitive analysis. This is based on the belief that by having analysts in several agencies who have different backgrounds and views work on an issue, it is more likely that parochial views will be countered—if not weeded out—and "proximate reality" is more likely to be achieved. Competitive analysis should, in theory, be an antidote to "group think" and forced consensus, although this is not always the case in practice. Competitive analysis is not possible without multiple analytical agencies.

CONSUMER-PRODUCER RELATIONS. The distinct line that is drawn between policy and intelligence leads to questions about how intelligence producers and consumers should relate to each other. The nub of the issue is the degree of proximity that is desirable.

There have been two schools of thought in this debate in the United States. The "distance" school argued that the intelligence establishment should keep itself at some distance from the policymakers to avoid the risk of providing intelligence that lacks objectivity and favors or opposes one policy choice over others. Adherents of the distance school also feared that policymakers could interfere with intelligence in order to receive analysis that supported or opposed specific policies. This group believed that too close a relationship increased the risk of "politicizing" intelligence.

The "proximate" group argued that too great a distance raised the risk that the intelligence community would be less aware of policymakers' needs and therefore produce less useful intelligence. This group maintained that proper training and internal reviews could avoid politicization of intelligence.

By the late 1950s to early 1960s the proximate school became the preferred model for U.S. intelligence. But the debate was significant in that it underscored the early and persistent fears about intelligence becoming politicized.

In the late 1990s some people perceived two subtle shifts in the policy–intelligence relationship. The first was a greatly increased emphasis on "support to military operations," which some believed gave too much priority to this sector—at a time when threats to national security had decreased—at the expense of other intelligence consumers. The second was the feeling among some analysts that they were being torn between operational customers (see the next issue) and analytical customers.

THE RELATIONSHIP BETWEEN ANALYSIS AND COLLECTION AND COVERT ACTION. Parallel to the debate about producer-consumer relations, factions have waged a similar debate about the proper relationship between intelligence analysis, on the one hand, and intelligence collection and covert action, on the other.

The issue has centered largely on the structure of the CIA, which includes both analytical and operational components: the Directorate of

Intelligence (DI) and the Directorate of Operations (DO); the latter is responsible for both espionage and covert action.

Again, distance and proximate schools took form. The distance school has argued that analysis and the two operational functions are largely distinct and that housing them together could be risky for the security of human sources and methods and for analysis. They have raised concerns about the ability of the DI to provide objective analysis where the DO is concurrently running a major covert action. Will there not be pressure, either overt or subliminal, to have analysis support the covert action? This is not an abstract question. Such stresses existed between some analytical components of the intelligence community and supporters of the contras in Nicaragua in the 1980s, for example. Some analysts questioned whether the contras would ever be victorious, which was seen as "unsupportive" by some people involved in supporting the contras.

The proximate school has argued that separating the two functions deprives both analysis and operations of the benefits of a close relationship. Analysts gain a better appreciation of operational goals and realities, which can be factored into their work, and also a better sense of the value of sources developed in espionage. Operators gain a better appreciation of the analyses they receive, which can be factored into their own planning.

Although critics of the current structure have repeatedly suggested separating the two functions, the proximate school has prevailed. Indeed, in the mid-1990s the DI and DO entered what they called a "partnership," in which their front offices and various regional offices were located together.

THE DEBATE OVER COVERT ACTION. Covert action has always generated uneasiness in some quarters in the United States concerned about its propriety or acceptability as a facet of U.S. policy. Within that debate, another debate emerged, about the use of paramilitary operations—the training and equipping of large military units, such as the contras. Other than assassination, paramilitary operations have been among the most controversial aspects of covert action, and they have a very uneven record. The vigor of this debate has varied widely over time. There was little debate at all before the Bay of Pigs (1961), and then little further debate until the collapse of the cold war consensus and revelations about intelligence community misdeeds in the mid-1970s. The debate revived during the contra war in the mid-1980s. In the aftermath of the terrorist attacks in the United States in 2001, however, a broad consensus emerged for a full range of covert actions.

THE CONTINUITY OF INTELLIGENCE POLICY. Throughout most of the cold war, there was no difference between Democratic and Republican intelligence policies. The cold war consensus on the need for a continuing policy of containment vis-à-vis the Soviet Union transcended politics until the Vietnam War, at which point a difference emerged between the two parties that was in many respects more rhetorical than real. For example, both Jimmy Carter and Ronald Reagan made intelligence policy an issue in their campaigns for the presidency. Carter, in 1976, lumped revelations about the CIA and other intelligence agencies' misconduct with Watergate and Vietnam; Reagan, in 1980, spoke of "restoring" the CIA, along with the rest of U.S. national security. Although the ways in which they supported and used intelligence differed greatly, it would be wrong to suggest that one was "anti-intelligence" and the other "pro-intelligence."

HEAVY RELIANCE ON TECHNOLOGY. Since the creation of the modern intelligence community in the 1940s, the United States has relied very heavily on technology as the mainstay of its collection capabilities. A technological response to a problem is not unique to intelligence; it also describes how the United States has waged war, beginning as early as the Civil War in the 1860s. Also, the closed nature of the major intelligence target, the Soviet Union, required remote technical means to collect information.

The reliance on technology is significant beyond the collection capabilities it engenders, because it has had a major effect on the structure of the intelligence community and how it has functioned. Some people maintain that the reliance on technology has resulted in an insufficient use of human intelligence collection (espionage). There are no empirical data to support this view, but it has persisted since at least the 1970s. The main argument, which tends to arise when intelligence is perceived as having performed less than optimally, is that human intelligence can collect certain types of information (intentions and plans) that technical collection cannot. There is little disagreement about the strengths and weaknesses of the various types of collection, but such an assessment does not necessarily support the view that espionage always suffers vis-à-vis technical collection. The persistence of the debate reflects an underlying concern about intelligence collection that has never been adequately addressed, that is, the proper balance—if one can be constructed—between technical and human collection. This debate has arisen again in the aftermath of the terrorist attacks in 2001. (See chap. 12 for a fuller discussion of the types of intelligence collection required by the war on terrorism.)

SECRECY VERSUS OPENNESS. The openness that is an inherent part of a representative democratic government clashes with the secrecy required by intelligence operations. No democratic government with a significant intelligence community has spent more time debating and worrying about this problem than has the United States. The issue cannot be settled with finality, but the United States has made an ongoing series of compromises between its values—as a government and as an international leader—and the requirements for some level of intelligence activity as it has continued to explore the boundaries of this issue.

THE ROLE OF OVERSIGHT. For the first twenty-eight years of its existence, the intelligence community operated with a minimal amount of oversight from Congress. One reason was the cold war consensus noted above. Another was a willingness on the part of Congress to abdicate rigorous oversight. Secrecy was also a factor, which appeared to impose procedural difficulties in handling sensitive issues between the two branches. After 1975, as will be discussed below, congressional oversight changed suddenly and dramatically, increasing to the point where Congress became a full participant in the intelligence process and a major consumer of intelligence.

MAJOR HISTORICAL DEVELOPMENTS

In addition to the themes that have run through much of the history of the intelligence community, several specific events played pivotal roles in the shaping and functioning of U.S. intelligence.

THE CREATION OF COI AND OSS (1940–1941). As noted above, until 1940 the United States did not have anything approaching a national intelligence establishment. The important precedents were the Coordinator of Information (COI) and then the Office of Strategic Services (OSS), which President Franklin Roosevelt created. Both the COI and OSS were headed by William Donovan. In addition to being the first steps toward the creation of a national intelligence capability, COI and OSS were important for three other reasons. First, both organizations were heavily influenced by British intelligence practices, particularly their emphasis on what we would now call covert action—guerrillas, operations with resistance groups behind enemy lines, sabotage, and so on. For Britain this wartime emphasis on operations was the natural result of being one of the few ways the country could strike back at Nazi Germany in Europe until the Allied invasions of Italy and France. These covert actions, which had little effect on the outcome of the war, became the main historical legacy of the OSS.

Second, although OSS operations played little role in the Allied victory in World War II, they served as a training ground—both technically and in terms of esprit—for many of the people who helped establish the postwar intelligence community, particularly the CIA.

A final legacy of OSS was its difficult relationship with the U.S. military. The military leadership was suspicious of an intelligence organization operating beyond its control and perhaps competing with organic military intelligence components. The Joint Chiefs of Staff therefore insisted that OSS become part of their structure. This tension between the military and non-military intelligence components has continued, with varying degrees of severity or cooperation.

PEARL HARBOR (1941). Japan's surprise attack was a classic intelligence failure. The United States overlooked a variety of signals; U.S. processes and procedures were deeply flawed; and mirror-imaging blinded U.S. policymakers to a very different assessment in Tokyo. For U.S. intelligence, the attack on Pearl Harbor was most important as the raison d'etre for the community that was established after World War II. Its fundamental mission was to prevent a recurrence of a strategic surprise of this magnitude, especially in an age of nuclear-armed missiles.

MAGIC AND ULTRA (1941–1945). One of the Allies' major advantages in World War II was their superior signals intelligence, that is, their ability to intercept and decode Axis communications. MAGIC refers to U.S. intercepts of Japanese communications; ULTRA refers to British, and later British-U.S., interceptions of German communications. This wartime experience demonstrated the tremendous importance of this type of intelligence, perhaps the most important type practiced during the war. Also, it helped solidify U.S.-British intelligence cooperation, which continued long after the war. Moreover, in the United States the military, not OSS, controlled MAGIC and ULTRA. This underscored the friction between the military and OSS. It also secured for the military a major intelligence function, signals intelligence, which continues to this day in the National Security Agency, a part of the Defense Department.

THE NATIONAL SECURITY ACT (1947). The National Security Act gave a legal basis to the intelligence community, as well as to the position of director of central intelligence (DCI), and created a CIA under the director. The act signaled the new importance of intelligence in the nascent cold war and also made the intelligence function permanent, a step away from the previous U.S. practice of reducing the national security apparatus in peacetime. Implicitly, the act made the existence and functioning of the intelligence community a part of the cold war consensus.

Several aspects of the act are worth noting. Although the DCI could be a military officer, the CIA was not placed under military control. Nor was the CIA to have any domestic role or police powers. The legislation does not mention any of the activities that came to be most commonly associated with the CIA—espionage, covert action, even analysis. Its stated job, and President Harry S. Truman's main concern at the time, was to coordinate the intelligence being produced by various agencies.

KOREA (1950). The unexpected invasion of South Korea had two major effects on U.S. intelligence. First, the failure to predict the invasion led DCI Walter Bedell Smith (1950–1953) to make some dramatic changes, including putting increased emphasis on national intelligence estimates (NIEs). Second, the Korean War made the cold war global. Having previously been confined to a struggle for dominance in Europe, the cold war now spread to Asia and, implicitly, to the rest of the world. This broadened the scope and responsibilities of intelligence.

THE COUP IN IRAN (1953). In 1953 the United States staged a series of "popular" demonstrations in Iran that overthrew the government of Premier Mohammad Mossadegh and restored the rule of the shah, who was more friendly to Western interests. The success and ease of this operation made covert action an increasingly attractive tool for U.S. policymakers, especially during the tenure of DCI Allen Dulles (1953–1961).

THE GUATEMALA COUP (1954). In 1954 the United States overthrew the leftist government of Guatemalan president Jacobo Arbenz Guzmán because of concern that it might prove sympathetic to the Soviet Union. The United States provided a clandestine opposition radio station and air support for rebel officers. The Guatemala coup "proved" that the success in Iran was not unique, thus further elevating the appeal of this type of action for U.S. policymakers.

THE "MISSILE GAP" (1959–1961). In the late 1950s some people in the United States were concerned that the apparent Soviet lead in the "race for space" also indicated a Soviet lead in missile-based strategic weaponry. The main critics were Democratic aspirants for the 1960 presidential nomination, including Sens. John F. Kennedy and Stuart Symington. The Eisenhower administration knew, by virtue of the U.S. reconnaissance program, that the accusations were untrue, but it did not respond to the charges in order to safeguard the sources of the intelligence. When the Kennedy administration took office, it learned that the charges were indeed untrue, but the new secretary of defense, Robert McNamara, came to believe that intelligence had inflated the Soviet threat to safeguard the defense budget. This was an early example of intelligence becoming a political issue, raised primarily by the party out of power.

The way in which the missile gap is customarily portrayed in intelligence history is incorrect. According to the "legend," the intelligence community, perhaps for base and selfish motives, overestimated the number of Soviet strategic missiles. This is incorrect on several grounds. The overestimate came largely from political critics of the Eisenhower administration, not the intelligence agencies. In reality, critics overestimated the number of strategic-range Soviet missiles, and the intelligence community underestimated the number of medium- and intermediate-range missiles that the Soviets were building to cover their main theater of concern, Europe. McNamara's distrust of what he perceived as self-serving Air Force parochialism moved him to create the Defense Intelligence Agency.

THE BAY OF PIGS (1961). The abysmal failure of the attempt to overthrow Fidel Castro by CIA-trained Cuban exiles showed the limits of large-scale paramilitary operations in terms of their effectiveness and of the United States' ability to mask its role in them.

THE CUBAN MISSILE CRISIS (1962). Although now widely seen as a success, the confrontation with the Soviet Union over its planned deployment of missiles in Cuba was initially a failure in terms of intelligence. All analysts, with the notable exception of DCI John McCone (1961–1965), had argued that Soviet premier Nikita Khrushchev would not be so bold or rash as to place missiles in Cuba. The missile crisis was also a success, in that U.S. intelligence discovered the missile sites before they were completed, giving President Kennedy sufficient time to deal with the situation without resort to force. U.S. intelligence was also able to give President Kennedy firm assessments of Soviet strategic and conventional-force capabilities, which bolstered his ability to make difficult decisions. Finally, the intelligence community's performance went a long way toward rehabilitating its reputation after the Bay of Pigs.

THE VIETNAM WAR (1964–1975). The war in Vietnam had three important effects on U.S. intelligence. First, during the war concerns grew that frustrated policymakers were politicizing intelligence to be supportive of policy. The Tet offensive in 1968 is a case in point. Faced with intelligence indicating preparations for a large-scale Viet Cong offensive, President Lyndon Johnson had two unpalatable choices. He could prepare the public for the event, but then face being asked how this large scale enemy attack was possible if the United States was winning the war. Alternatively, he could attempt to ride out the attack, confident that it would be defeated. Johnson took the second choice. The Viet Cong were defeated militarily in Tet, but the attack and the scale of military operations that the United States undertook to defeat them turned a successful intelligence warning and a military victory into a major political defeat. Unfortunately, many assumed that the attack was a surprise.

Often-heated debates on the progress of the war took place between military and nonmilitary intelligence analysts. This was seen most sharply in the "order of battle" debate, which centered on how many enemy units were in the field. Third, and more long-lasting and important, the war severely undercut the cold war consensus under which intelligence operated.

THE ABM TREATY AND SALT I ACCORD (1972). These initial strategic arms control agreements between the United States and the Soviet Union explicitly recognized and legitimized the use of "national technical means" (that is, a variety of satellites and other technical collectors) by both parties to collect needed intelligence, and they prohibited overt interference with national technical means. Furthermore, these agreements created the new issue of verification—the ability to ascertain whether treaty obligations were being met. (Monitoring, or keeping track of Soviet activities, had been under way since the inception of the intelligence community, even before arms control.) U.S. intelligence inevitably was dragged into these activities, with new accusations by some people that intelligence was being politicized. Those concerned that the Soviets were cheating held that this was either being undetected or ignored. Arms control advocates argued that the Soviets were not cheating or, if they were, the cheating was minimal and therefore inconsequential, regardless of the terms of the agreements, and they maintained that some cheating was preferable to unchecked strategic competition. Either way, the intelligence community found itself to be a fundamental part of the debate.

INTELLIGENCE INVESTIGATIONS (1975–1976). In the wake of revelations that the CIA had violated its charter by spying on U.S. citizens, a series of investigations examined the entire intelligence community. A panel chaired by Vice President Nelson Rockefeller concluded that violations of law had occurred. Investigations by House and Senate special committees went deeper, discovering a much wider range of abuses.

Coming so soon after the Watergate scandal and the loss of South Vietnam, these intelligence hearings further undermined the public's faith in government institutions, in particular the intelligence community, which had been largely sacrosanct. Since these investigations, intelligence has never regained the latitude it once enjoyed and has had to learn to operate with much more openness and scrutiny. Also, Congress faced the fact of its own lax oversight. Both the Senate and the House created permanent intelligence oversight committees, which have taken on much more vigorous oversight of intelligence and are now major consumers of intelligence themselves.

IRAN (1979). In 1979 Ayatollah Ruhollah Khomeini's revolution forced the shah of Iran from his throne and into exile. U.S. intelligence, due in part to policy decisions made by several administrations that severely limited collection, was largely blind to the growing likelihood of this turn of events. Nevertheless, the intelligence community took much of the blame for the result. Some people even saw the shah's fall as the inevitable result of the 1953 coup that had restored him to power.

IRAN-CONTRA (1986–1987). The administration of Ronald Reagan botched its attempt to use proceeds from missile sales to Iran (which not only contradicted the administration's own policy of not dealing with terrorists but also violated a law) to sustain the contras in Nicaragua—despite congressional restrictions on such aid. The project provoked a constitutional crisis and congressional investigations. The affair highlighted a series of problems, including the limits of oversight in both the executive branch and Congress, the ability of executive officials to ignore Congress's intent, and the disaster that can result when two distinct and disparate covert actions become intertwined. The affair also undid much of President Reagan's efforts to rebuild and restore intelligence capabilities.

THE FALL OF THE SOVIET UNION (1989–1991). Beginning with the collapse of the Soviet satellite empire in 1989 and culminating in the dissolution of the Soviet Union itself in 1991, the United States witnessed the triumph of its long-held policy of containment. The collapse was so swift and so stunning that few can be said to have anticipated it.

Critics of the intelligence community argued that this was the ultimate intelligence failure, given the centrality of the Soviet Union as an intelligence community issue. Some people even felt that this "failure" justified radically reducing and altering the intelligence community. Defenders of U.S. intelligence argued that the community had portrayed much of the inner rot that led to the Soviet collapse.

This debate has not ended; significant questions remain not only about U.S. intelligence capabilities but also about intelligence in general and what can reasonably be expected from it. (See chap. 11 for a detailed discussion.)

THE AMES SPY SCANDAL (1994) AND THE HANSSEN SPY CASE (2001). The arrest and conviction of Aldrich Ames, a CIA employee, on charges of spying for the Soviet Union and for post-Soviet Russia for almost ten years shook U.S. intelligence. Espionage scandals had broken before; in the "year of the spy" (1985), several cases came to light—the Walker family, Ron Pelton, Larry Wu-tai Chin.

Ames's unsuspected treachery was, in many respects, more searing. Despite the end of the cold war, Russian espionage had continued. Ames's career revealed significant shortcomings in CIA personnel practices (he was a marginal officer with a well-known alcohol problem), in CIA counterespionage and counterintelligence, and in CIA–FBI liaison to deal with these issues. The affair also revealed continuing shortcomings in how the executive branch shared information bearing on intelligence matters with Congress.

The arrest in 2001 of FBI agent Robert Hanssen on charges of espionage underscored some of the concerns that first arose in the Ames case and added new ones. Hanssen and Ames apparently began their espionage activities at approximately the same time, but Hanssen was undetected for much longer. The fact that he was a counterintelligence expert gave him advantages in escaping detection. Hanssen, like Ames, spied for both the Soviet Union and post-Soviet Russia. Hanssen's espionage also meant that the "damage assessment" done after Ames was arrested would have to be revised, as both men had access to some of the same information. Finally, the Hanssen case was a severe black eye for the FBI, which had been so critical of the CIA's failure to detect Ames.

THE TERRORIST ATTACKS (2001). The terrorist attacks in the United States in September 2001 were important for several reasons. First, although Osama bin Laden's enmity and capabilities were known, the nature of these specific attacks had not been detected in advance. Although some critics called for the resignation of DCI George Tenet (1997–), President George W. Bush supported him. However, Congress began a broad investigation into the performance of the intelligence community. Second, in the immediate aftermath of the attacks there was broad political support for a range of intelligence actions to combat terrorism, including calls to lift the ban on assassinations and to increase the use of human intelligence. The major legislative response to the attacks, the U.S.A. PATRIOT Act of 2001, did allow greater latitude in some domestic intelligence/law enforcement collection and took steps to improve coordination between these two areas. Finally, in the first phase of combat operations against terrorism, there were dramatic new developments in intelligence-collection capabilities, particularly the use of UAVs (unmanned aerial vehicles, or pilotless drones) and more "real time" intelligence support for U.S. combat forces. (See chap. 5 for details.)

A FINAL NOTE

Again, this list is not exhaustive, nor is it meant to be. Indeed, such an exercise can provoke a good argument among practitioners and students of intelligence. This list delineates trends and events that have played a major role in shaping the U.S. intelligence community.

KEY TERMS

competitive analysis

monitoring

national intelligence

national technical means (NTM)

politicized intelligence

verification

FURTHER READINGS

Most histories of U.S. intelligence tend to be CIA-centric, and these readings are no exception to that generalization. Nonetheless, these readings still offer some of the best discussions of the events and issues discussed in this chapter.

Ambrose, Stephen E., with Richard H. Immerman. *Ike's Spies: Eisenhower and the Espionage Establishment.* Garden City, N.Y.: Doubleday, 1981.

Brugioni, Dino A. *Eyeball to Eyeball: The Inside Story of the Cuban Missile Crisis.* Ed. Robert F. McCort. New York: Random House, 1990.

Colby, William E., and Peter Forbath. *Honorable Men: My Life in the CIA.* New York: Simon and Schuster, 1978.

Draper, Theodore. *A Very Thin Line: The Iran-Contra Affair.* New York: Hill and Wang, 1991.

Gates, Robert M. *From the Shadows.* New York: Simon and Schuster, 1996.

Hersh, Seymour. "Huge CIA Operations Reported in U.S. Against Anti-War Forces, Other Dissidents in Nixon Years." *New York Times,* December 22, 1974.

Houston, Lawrence R. "The CIA's Legislative Base." *International Journal of Intelligence and Counterintelligence* 5 (winter 1991–1992).

Jeffreys-Jones, Rhodri. *The CIA and American Democracy.* New Haven: Yale University Press, 1989.

Lowenthal, Mark M. *U.S. Intelligence: Evolution and Anatomy.* 2d ed. Westport, Conn.: Praeger, 1992.

Montague, Ludwell Lee. *General Walter Bedell Smith as Director of Central Intelligence: October 1950–February 1953.* University Park: Pennsylvania State University Press, 1992.

Moynihan, Daniel Patrick. *Secrecy: The American Experience.* New Haven: Yale University Press, 1998.

Persico, Joseph. *Casey: From the OSS to the CIA.* New York: Viking, 1990.

Powers, Thomas. *The Man Who Kept the Secrets: Richard Helms and the CIA.* New York: Knopf, 1979.

Ranelagh, John. *The Rise and Decline of the CIA.* New York: Touchstone, 1987.

Troy, Thomas F. *Donovan and the CIA: A History of the Establishment of the Central Intelligence Agency.* Frederick, Md.: University Publications of America, 1981.

U.S. Senate. Select Committee to Study Governmental Operations with Respect to Intelligence Activities [The Church Committee]. Final Report, Book IV: *Supplementary Detailed Staff Reports on Foreign and Military Intelligence.* 94th Cong., 2d sess., 1976. [Also known as the Karalekas report, after its author, Anne Karalekas.]

Wohlstetter, Roberta. *Pearl Harbor: Warning and Decision.* Stanford: Stanford University Press, 1962.

Wyden, Peter. *Bay of Pigs: The Untold Story.* New York: Simon and Schuster, 1979.

Chapter 3

The U.S. Intelligence Community

This chapter describes the structure and functioning of the U.S. intelligence community and offers alternative ways of thinking about them. The U.S. intelligence community is generally perceived as being hierarchical and bureaucratic, emphasizing vertical lines of authority. Figure 3-1 offers such a view but also categorizes agencies by intelligence budget sectors: National Foreign Intelligence Program (NFIP), Joint Military Intelligence Program (JMIP), and Tactical Intelligence and Related Activities (TIARA).

The National Security Council (NSC) has authority over the director of central intelligence (DCI), who in turn has control over the CIA. The CIA, unlike the Bureau of Intelligence and Research (INR) at State or the Defense Intelligence Agency (DIA) in Defense, has no cabinet-level patron. The CIA's main clients are the president and the National Security Council (NSC). This relationship has both benefits and problems. On the one hand, it gives the CIA access to the ultimate decision maker. On the other hand, the president—unlike the secretaries of state and defense or the chairman of the Joint Chiefs of Staff—has other responsibilities beyond national security. Moreover, it is more difficult to engage the president in intelligence turf issues than it is to involve cabinet-level officers. The director of central intelligence (DCI) must engage other departments on his own, perhaps to his ultimate bureaucratic disadvantage.

The secretary of defense controls much more of the intelligence community on a day-to-day basis than does the DCI. The panoply of agencies that are part of the Department of Defense (DOD)—National Security Agency, Defense Intelligence Agency, National Imagery and Mapping Agency, Defense airborne reconnaissance programs, and the service intelligence units—vastly outnumber the CIA, in terms of both people and dollars. At the same time, the secretary of defense is unlikely to have the same level of interest in intelligence as the DCI does. In fact, much of the responsibility for intelligence within DOD is customarily delegated to the deputy secretary of defense.

FIGURE 3-1   The Intelligence Community: An Organizational View

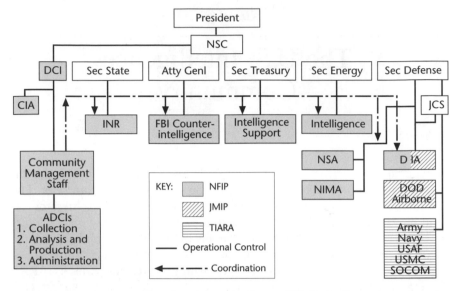

Source: U.S. House Permanent Select Committee on Intelligence, IC21: The Intelligence Community in the 21st Century. 104th Cong., 2d sess., 1996.

Figure 3-1 is somewhat deficient in that it does not describe the varied functions of the agencies, which are central to their relationships. Indeed, there are several different ways of looking at the U.S. intelligence community in order to get a better appreciation of what it does and how it works.

ALTERNATIVE WAYS OF LOOKING AT THE INTELLIGENCE COMMUNITY

Before examining further the structure of the intelligence community, it is useful to look at its basic functions.

There are, in effect, two broad functional areas: management and execution. Within each of them are many specific tasks. The first area encompasses the management of requirements, resources, collection, and production. Execution includes the development of collection systems, the actual collection and production of intelligence, and maintenance of the infrastructure support base. In Figure 3-2 a horizontal rule divides

FIGURE 3-2   Alternative Ways of Looking at the Intelligence Community:
A Functional Flow View

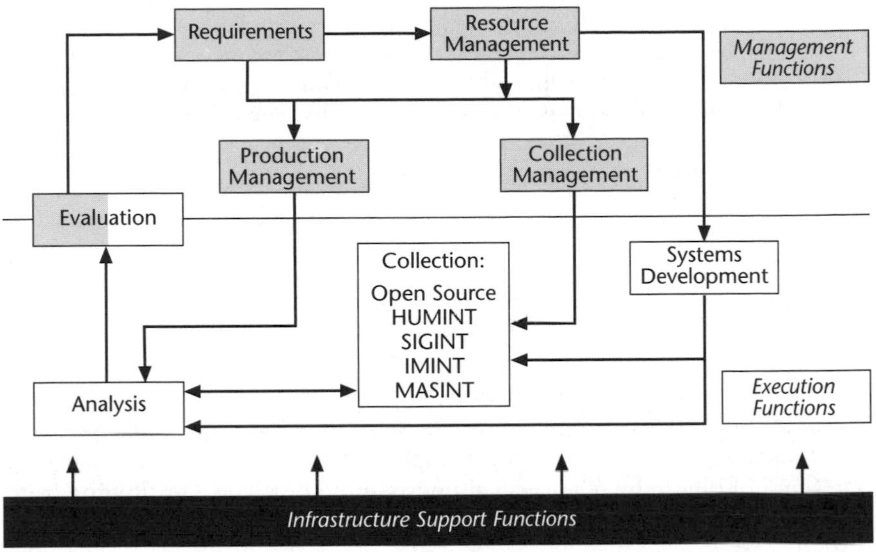

Source: U.S. House Permanent Select Committee on Intelligence, IC21: The Intelligence Community in the 21st Century. 104th Cong., 2d sess., 1996.

management and execution, but one function straddles the rule: evaluation. Evaluation is not one of the strongest functions of the intelligence community. Relating intelligence means (resources: budgets, people) to intelligence ends (outcomes: analyses, operations) is an extremely difficult task and is not undertaken with great relish. However, it is a very important task and one that could yield dividends to intelligence managers if done more systematically and broadly.

The flow suggested by Figure 3-2 is admittedly idealized, but it gives a very good idea of how the main managerial and execution concerns relate to one another. The flow is circular, going in endless loops. If one were to suggest starting at a particular point, it would be requirements. Without them, very little that happens afterward makes sense. Given their proper role, requirements should drive everything else.

The various aspects of collection—systems development and collection itself—occupy much more of the figure than does analysis. This reflects the realities of the intelligence community, whether desirable or not.

The "Simplicity" of Intelligence

In the baseball movie *Bull Durham*, a manager tries to explain to his some-what hapless players the simplicity of the game they are supposed to be playing: "You throw the ball; you hit the ball; you catch the ball."

Intelligence has a similar deceptive simplicity: you ask a question; you collect information; you answer the question.

In both cases, there are many devils in the details.

THE MANY DIFFERENT
INTELLIGENCE COMMUNITIES

Within the U.S. intelligence community are many different intelligence communities. Figure 3-3 gives a better sense of what they are by showing what each agency or subagency component does, while still preserving the sense of hierarchy. The vertical lines should be viewed as flowing from the topmost organizations through each of the agencies or components below.

At the top of the hierarchy are the individuals who are major intelligence managers, major clients, or both. The president is the major client but is not an intelligence manager. All of the cabinet secretaries are clients, and two of them—the secretaries of state and defense—control significant intelligence assets. State has INR; DOD has the entire panoply of defense intelligence organizations, which respond to a broad range of needs. DOD organizations participate in national-level intelligence processes and products, providing indications and warning of impending attack (see chap. 6) and intelligence support for military operations at all levels—from theater (broad regional commands) down to tactical (small units engaged in operations or combat). The attorney general has control over the FBI; Energy has a small intelligence office devoted to its specific concerns; and Commerce controls the commercial attachés, who are assigned to embassies and serve an overt intelligence function. The DCI is manager of the CIA and, through the Community Management Staff (CMS), coordinator of the larger national intelligence effort.

At the next level down are the builders of various types of technical collection systems. The main one is the National Reconnaissance Office (NRO), which is responsible for the design, building, and (via the Air Force or NASA) the launch of satellite collection systems. DOD also has an airborne reconnaissance responsibility for "air breathing" systems such as unmanned aerial vehicles (UAVs) or drones, which are of increasing

FIGURE 3-3   Alternative Ways of Looking at the Intelligence Community:
A Functional View

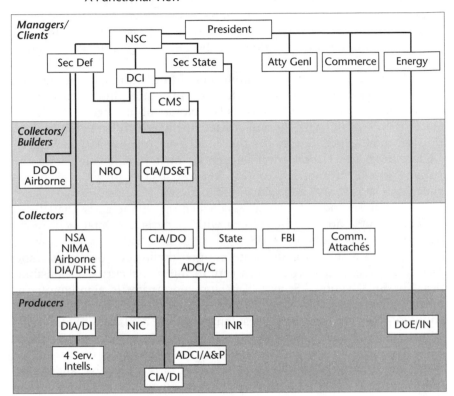

importance on the battlefield for tactical collection and, in the Afghanistan campaign, for air attack as well. Finally, the CIA's Directorate of Science and Technology (DS&T) has a role in some technical collection programs.

A variety of offices are responsible for the collection (including processing and exploitation) of intelligence. Within DOD are the National Security Agency (NSA), which collects signals intelligence (SIGINT); the National Imagery and Mapping Agency (NIMA), which processes and exploits imagery (IMINT); the Defense airborne systems; and the Defense HUMINT Service (DHS) of DIA, whose duties are reflected in its name. The CIA is responsible for espionage (human intelligence—HUMINT) collection via the Directorate of Operations (DO). State collects for itself and for others via its array of embassies and Foreign Service officers, although its activities are not "tasked intelligence"—that is, they are not undertaken in response to a specific requirement, as are the others listed here. Commerce collects via the commercial attachés. The FBI collects counterintelligence information via its National Security Division and has legal attachés posted in many U.S. embassies overseas. In 1996 Congress created the position of assistant DCI for collection, whose job is to assist the DCI in his community-wide role by helping coordinate collection activities under the CMS.

The most important of the producers of finished intelligence are the three agencies responsible for producing "all-source" intelligence: CIA's Directorate of Intelligence (DI), DIA's Directorate of Intelligence (DI), and State's INR. Within DOD, the four service intelligence offices also produce finished intelligence. Energy has the intelligence office noted above. The DCI controls the National Intelligence Council (NIC), comprising the national intelligence officers (NIOs) and responsible for national intelligence estimates (NIEs) and some other analyses. The position of assistant DCI for analysis and production was created in 1996 to assist the DCI in his community-wide role by helping with analysis and intelligence production activities under the CMS.

Figure 3-3 does not delineate counterintelligence or counterespionage functions. Each agency has certain internal security responsibilities. The FBI's National Security Division coordinates foreign counterintelligence activities in the United States. CIA/DO has its own counterintelligence and counterespionage components. In addition, the Director of NSA is also the director of the Central Security Service (CSS), with responsibility for safeguarding the communications of the United States from interception. The basic relationships, strengths, and weaknesses noted in the first figure are still evident here, but it is easier to discern functions in Figure 3-3.

INTELLIGENCE COMMUNITY
RELATIONSHIPS THAT MATTER

All "wiring" diagrams, no matter how sophisticated, are deceptive. They portray where agencies sit in relation to one another, but they cannot portray how they interact and which relationships matter and why. Moreover, although we are loath to admit it, personalities do matter. However much we like to think of government as one of laws and institutions, the personalities and relationships of the people filling these important positions also affect agency working relations.

THE DCI'S RELATIONSHIPS. The relationship between the DCI and the president is crucial for the institutional well-being of the intelligence community. The DCI is the embodiment of the intelligence community, and the president is the ultimate policy consumer. DCI Richard Helms (1966–1973) put it succinctly when he observed that the DCI's authority derives directly from the perception that he has access to the president. If this is not the case and he is not included in meetings where intelligence should be a contributor, there are several ramifications. For the DCI, the problem is personal and professional; for the intelligence community, the poor relationship means it is being left out of the process; in the perception of others who become aware of the problem, the role of the DCI is diminished. DCI John McCone (1961–1965) enjoyed good access to President John F. Kennedy and, initially, to Lyndon Johnson, but Johnson began to exclude McCone when the DCI disagreed with his incremental approach to the war in Vietnam. After a short period of frustration, McCone resigned. Similarly, DCI James Woolsey (1993–1995), after his resignation, made no secret of the fact that he had little access to President Bill Clinton.

How close should the relationship between the DCI and the president be? Some observers worry that if it is too close, the DCI may lose some of the intelligence objectivity that he should be bringing to the policy process. Policymakers must be able to rely upon the professionalism of the DCI. Still, if the intelligence community were forced to choose between the two extremes, an overly close relationship would probably be preferable to a very distant one.

One indication of the closeness of the relationship between the DCI, the president, and other senior officers is cabinet rank. By law, the members of the cabinet are the secretaries of the executive departments. Presidents have accorded cabinet rank to other top officials, such as the ambassador to the United Nations, as a courtesy and a sign of their enhanced status. The designation has little meaning, since the United States does not have government by cabinet, as does Britain. In 1981 President Reagan conferred cabinet rank on DCI William Casey (1981–1987), largely as a consolation for not having chosen him to be secretary of state. Some people criticized the move, arguing that the cabinet is a policymaking body and the DCI is not a policymaker but rather an adviser to policymakers, similar to the DCI's status on the NSC. Casey's successor, Judge William Webster (1987–1991), made it clear that he did not want this designation and would refuse it.

It has been suggested that the DCI, like the director of the FBI, be appointed to a fixed term of office—the FBI director now serves for ten years. The main argument in favor of a fixed term is that it would make the DCI a more professional and less political appointment. (Politicization was always possible but did not become a reality until 1977, when incoming President Jimmy Carter asked for the resignation of DCI George H. W. Bush.)

A second argument in favor of a fixed term is that it would allow DCIs to serve under presidents who had not appointed them, thus increasing the chances for objectivity. The main argument against it, and one that has been voiced by several former DCIs, goes back to the personal nature of the relationship between the DCI and the president. The concern is that, under a fixed DCI term that overlaps the cycle of elections, the president would inherit a DCI not of his choosing and with whom there would be no rapport, thus increasing the likelihood that the DCI's access would diminish.

Moreover, the DCI and the director of the FBI do not hold comparable positions. The DCI is responsible for the entire intelligence community, whereas the director of the FBI runs an agency within an executive department (Justice). The obviously strained relations between FBI Director Louis Freeh and both Attorney General Janet Reno and President Clinton during the latter part of the Clinton administration underscore the problems that can arise with a fixed term.

The secretary of state is the chief foreign policy officer below the president; the DCI should be an arm of foreign policy. At least two issues are important in the relationship between the secretary of state and the DCI: coordinating proposed intelligence operations with foreign policy goals and using the State Department (that is, the Foreign Service) as cover for clandestine intelligence officers overseas. Inevitably, tension arises between the bureaucracies under these two officials. Few DCIs and secretaries of state have the warm relationship that Allen Dulles and his brother John Foster Dulles enjoyed. More often, there is a slight edge to the relationship, if not outright competition.

Overseas, there has been a long tradition of tension between U.S. ambassadors and their senior CIA officers, usually called chiefs of station. The ambassador is in charge of the entire "country team"—all U.S. personnel assigned to the embassy, regardless of their parent organization. (In larger country teams there may be representatives from State, CIA, Defense, Justice, Treasury, Commerce, and Agriculture.) But chiefs of station do not always keep the ambassador—whether career Foreign Service or political appointee—apprised of their intelligence activities. Despite repeated efforts to address the problem, it still occurs.

As has been noted, on a day-to-day basis, the secretary of defense controls more of the intelligence community (NSA, DIA, NIMA, the service intelligence units) than does the DCI (CIA, NIC). The secretary of defense also represents the vast majority of the intelligence client base (some have suggested as much as 80 percent), because of the broad range of defense intelligence requirements. Moreover, the intelligence budget is hidden within the defense budget and, in many ways, is beholden to it. Therefore, the relationship between the secretary of defense and the DCI is very important. No matter how collegial the relationship may appear, it is not one of equals.

Much of the secretary of defense's authority for intelligence usually devolves to the deputy, who becomes, in effect, the chief operating officer for defense intelligence. Thus, many of the issues that arise between DOD and the DCI are worked out by the DCI and deputy secretary of defense.

The relationship between the DCI and Congress has three key components. The first is the power of the purse. Congress not only funds the intelligence community (and the rest of the government) but can, through its funding decisions, affect intelligence programs. Although it is generally believed that Congress reduces presidential budget requests, it has in many instances championed programs and funded them despite opposition from the executive.

The second component of the Congress–DCI relationship is, again, personal. DCIs have occasionally not gotten along with their overseers, to the ultimate detriment of the DCIs and the intelligence community. William Casey was fairly contemptuous of the oversight process, which cost him support, even among his political allies. James Woolsey ended up in a constant public squabble with the chairman of the Senate Intelligence Committee, Dennis DeConcini, D-Ariz. John Deutch (1995–1997) had a difficult relationship with the House Intelligence Committee. The question of the rights and wrongs in each of these cases is irrelevant. Simply put, the DCI can only lose in the end.

The third component of the relationship between Congress and the DCI is the public perception of intelligence and support for it. Because of the secrecy surrounding intelligence, citizens get a glimpse of it mainly through congressional activities. Even without knowing the details of hearings, the fact that a congressional committee is investigating an intelligence issue affects media and public perceptions. And, as is usually the case, bad news tends to get reported more often than good news. After all, if the intelligence community is doing its job, why have a hearing or investigation?

THE RELATIONSHIP BETWEEN THE DEPUTY DCI FOR COMMUNITY MANAGEMENT AND THE OFFICE OF THE SECRETARY OF DEFENSE. Congress created this second deputy DCI position in 1996 to give the DCI better support in his community-wide role. The main day-to-day interaction between intelligence and DOD occurs at the level of the deputy DCI for community management (DDCI/CM) and the Office of the Secretary of Defense (OSD). DOD tends to look at the intelligence community warily, worrying that the community managers might not be looking after DOD needs and that they might be assuming too much power over defense intelligence. The key to this relationship is the credibility of the

DDCI/CM with OSD, that is, that the DDCI has a working knowledge of defense intelligence programs and needs and of the defense budget process. Theirs is an unbalanced relationship, with OSD the stronger partner. If officials in OSD have the sense that the DDCI/CM is not paying adequate attention to DOD needs and privileges, they can stymie much that the DDCI/CM and the CMS reporting to this DDCI want to do.

OSD/C3I AND ITS RELATIONSHIP WITH CONGRESS. OSD/C3I stands for Office of the Secretary of Defense/Command, Control, Communications, and Intelligence; it is the civilian side of defense intelligence, with a deputy assistant secretary of defense acting as a full-time intelligence manager. This office is one of two main conduits through which defense intelligence issues reach Congress, the other being DIA itself. But given the principle of civilian control of the military, C3I is more powerful and more important than DIA. Indeed, C3I has jurisdiction over defense intelligence requirements, the various defense intelligence agencies (among them, NSA, DIA, NIMA), and some defense collection programs—the "air breathers." OSD/C3I deals with the House and Senate Armed Services Committees. OSD/C3I is also important vis-à-vis the DCI, as this Defense staff tends to function as a guardian of the authority of the secretary of defense over defense intelligence, watching warily for any possible encroachments.

INR AND THE SECRETARY OF STATE. State's Bureau of Intelligence and Research (INR) is the smallest of the three all-source analytical components (compared with CIA and DIA) and is often thought of as the weakest. A great deal of INR's ability to get things done, both in its own department and as a player in the intelligence community, depends on the relationship between the INR assistant secretary and the secretary of state and one or two other senior State officials, often referred to collectively as "the seventh floor." In some respects, the relationship among these State officials parallels that between the DCI and the president. If INR has access to the seventh floor, then it plays a greater role and has greater bureaucratic support when needed. But it is a highly variable relationship, depending on the preferences of the secretary and key subordinates. To cite two contrasting examples, Secretary of State George Shultz (1982–1989) met with all of his assistant secretaries regularly; Secretary of State James Baker (1989–1992) did not, preferring to meet with a few very senior subordinates, who then dealt with the rest of the department. Thus, under Shultz, INR had more opportunities to gain access; under Baker, most of INR's clients were other bureaus, but less so the vaunted seventh floor.

In recent years INR has taken a number of steps to increase its visibility in the State Department and to involve other bureaus more actively in setting intelligence requirements. The goal has been to increase the bureaus' appreciation of the role of intelligence and of INR, thus making them potential sources of support. The degree to which these steps have improved INR's position in its department remains to be seen.

CONGRESSIONAL RELATIONSHIPS. Also of great importance are the relationships of the two intelligence committees with each other and with the other House and Senate committees with which they must work. The oversight responsibilities of the House and Senate Intelligence Committees are not identical, which accounts for their differing sets of relationships. The Senate Intelligence Committee has sole jurisdiction over only the DCI, CIA, CMS, and the NIC. The Senate Armed Services Committee has always jealously guarded its oversight of all aspects of defense intelligence. The relationship between Senate Intelligence and Senate Armed Services has been standoffish at best and sometimes hostile. Antagonism has usually stemmed from the Senate Armed Services Committee's reactions to real or imagined efforts by Senate Intelligence to step beyond its carefully circumscribed turf. Senate Armed Services has usually responded with punitive actions of varying degrees (such as delaying action on the intelligence authorization bill).

House Intelligence has exclusive jurisdiction over the entire NFIP—all programs that transcend the bounds of any one agency or are nondefense—as well as shared jurisdiction over the defense intelligence programs. This arrangement has fostered a better working relationship between House Intelligence and House Armed Services than exists between their Senate counterparts. This is not to suggest that moments of friction do not arise, but the overall relationship between the House committees has not approached the hostility exhibited in the Senate.

Good relationships between the two intelligence committees and the House and Senate Defense Appropriations subcommittees are important for avoiding disjunctures between authorized programs and appropriated funds. All appropriators tend to resent (and would sometimes like to ignore) all authorizers. Once again, the relationship between intelligence authorizers and appropriators has been smoother in the House than in the Senate.

The House Foreign Affairs and Senate Foreign Relations Committees oversee State Department activities, but the relationship with their respective Intelligence Committees tends to be less fractious than the relationship between the Intelligence and Appropriations Committees. Finally, the two Judiciary Committees oversee the FBI.

The two Intelligence Committees themselves have an important relationship. As noted, the House committee's jurisdiction is broader than the Senate's. On the other hand, the Senate Intelligence Committee has the exclusive and important authority to confirm the nominations of the DCI and the two deputy DCIs. The two committees often choose to work on different issues during the course of a session of Congress, apart from their work on the intelligence authorization bills. Despite differences of style and emphasis, hostility or rancor has rarely intruded, even in the face of divergent viewpoints.

THE INTELLIGENCE BUDGET PROCESS

The love of money is not only the root of all evil; money is also the root of all government. How much gets spent and who makes those decisions are two of the most fundamental questions before the state. The intelligence budget is somewhat complex. It has three components, whose shares of the total intelligence budget are on the order suggested here, but with some year-to-year variance. These three programs offer yet another way to view the intelligence community.

FIGURE 3-4   Alternative Ways of Looking at the Intelligence Community:
A Budgetary View

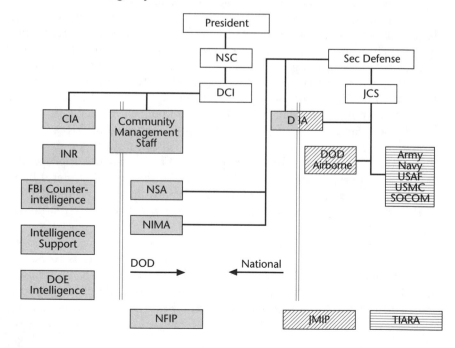

The NFIP, as its name implies, consists of programs that either transcend the bounds of an agency or are non-defense programs. The NFIP receives over half of the intelligence budget and is made up of the following:

Civilian Programs
CIA
State/INR
FBI/Counterintelligence
Treasury/Office of Intelligence
   Support
CIA Retirement and
   Disability System (CIARDS)
Defense Programs
General Defense Intelligence
   Program (GDIP)

Consolidated Cryptographic
   Program (CCP)
DOD Foreign Counter-
   intelligence Program (FCIP)
National Imagery and
   Mapping Program
National Reconnaissance
   Program (NRP)
Community-wide Program
Community Management
   Account (CMA)

JMIP is composed of programs within the Defense Department that transcend the bounds of any one military service. As the titles of some JMIP programs indicate, many of them parallel NFIP categories. The JMIP receives over a tenth of the intelligence budget and is made up of the following programs:

Defense Cryptologic Program
   (DCP)
Defense Imagery and Mapping
   Program
Defense General Intelligence
   Applications Program (DGIAP)
Defense Intelligence Tactical
   Program (DITP)

Defense Intelligence Special
   Technologies Program (DISTP)
Defense Airborne Reconnaissance
   Program (DARP)
Defense Space Reconnaissance
   Program (DSRP)
Defense Intelligence Counterdrug
   Program (DICP)

TIARA is made up of the four service intelligence programs and intelligence for the Special Operations Command. TIARA receives about one-third of the intelligence budget and is made up of the following programs:

Army intelligence
Navy intelligence
Air Force intelligence

Marine intelligence
Special Operations Command
   (SOCOM)

This budgetary view of the intelligence community indicates its complexity. Figure 3-4 arranges the various components of the intelligence

FIGURE 3-5   The Intelligence Budget: Four Phases over Three Years

It takes about three years to develop a budget and then spend the money, beginning in March of any year and continuing until September two and a half years later. The figure shows the activity for each phase and the time during which it happens.

Year 1	Mar–Sept	Oct ⌐		
Year 2		Aug	Aug ⌐	
Year 3			Sept	Oct ⌐
Year 4				Sept

Activity:	Planning	Programming	Budgeting	Execution
	Guidance:	*Request and Review:*	*Build and Submit:*	*Obligate and Spend:*
	Establishes broad guidelines of planning, programming, and budgeting.	Program resources are projected for future year requirements for dollar and manpower resources—a *multiyear* request.	Money or authority available to purchase goods and services or to hire people—for *one* or *two* years.	Committing and spending the money on authorized programs.

community by budget sectors; not all of the agencies within a budget sector are controlled by the same authority. The solid lines denote direct control. The two double vertical lines show which part of the budget and agencies are national and which are DOD. There is an overlap, as some agencies are both national and Defense, even if they fall into NFIP or JMIP. DIA straddles the line, containing both NFIP and several of the JMIP programs. Figure 3-4 also indicates the secretary of defense's preponderant control over intelligence community resources.

The intelligence budget is shaped by a process that is lengthy and complex (see Figure 3-5). The budget-building process within the executive branch takes more than a year, beginning around November when the DCI provides guidance to the intelligence program managers. The "crosswalks" between CIA and Defense—efforts at various working levels to coordinate programs and to make difficult choices between programs—are major facets of the budget process. Crosswalks can take place at the program level or below and can go as high as the DCI and the secretary or deputy secretary of defense. The executive process ends the following December, thirteen months after it began, with the DCI sending a final intelligence budget to the president for final approval.

The following February the president's budget goes to Congress, where a new, eight-month process begins. This consists of hearings in the various authorization and appropriations committees, committee markups of the bills, floor action, conference committees between the House and Senate to work out differences—both houses must pass identical bills—and final passage, after which the bill goes to the president to

Eight Simultaneous Fiscal Years

Over the course of a fiscal year (October to the end of the following September), eight concurrent fiscal years are in some state of being. This shows the situation during fiscal 2003:

FYs 2001, 2002: past fiscal years, some funds still being spent
FY 2003: current fiscal year, funds being spent
FY 2004: budget being developed by executive branch and Congress
FY 2005: program nearing completion in executive branch
FY 2006: in early development in executive branch
FYs 2007, 2008: in long-range planning in executive branch

be signed. By this time, the executive branch is already working on the next budget. It is important to highlight a major difference between the president's budget and that of Congress. The president's budget is a recommendation. It is serious and detailed but only a recommendation. Congress passes the actual budget that allocates money. Or, as the old saying goes, "The president proposes and Congress disposes."

This seemingly endless process points up another important aspect of the intelligence budget. At any given point during the year, as many as eight different fiscal-year (October 1–September 30) budgets are in some form of use or development. (*See box, "Eight Simultaneous Fiscal Years."*) Two past fiscal-year budgets are still in use, if we take into account the actual spending of funds that have been appropriated, in addition to the budget for the current year. Although funds for salaries and similar expenses are spent in a single fiscal year, other funds—such as those to build highly complex technical collection systems—are spent over the course of several years.

The budget for the following fiscal year is going through the political processes. The budget for the year after that is undergoing its year-long build in the executive branch. Finally, there are two future years in various states of somewhat imprecise planning.

A great deal of influence accrues to those individuals in both branches of government who can master the process and the details of the budget.

KEY TERMS

ADCI/A&P   Assistant director of central intelligence for analysis & production

ADCI/C   Assistant director of central intelligence for collection
CIA   Central Intelligence Agency

CMS   Community Management Staff

C3I   Command, control, communications, and intelligence

DCI   Director of central intelligence

DDCI   Deputy director of central intelligence

DDCI/CM   Deputy director of central intelligence for community management

DHS   Defense HUMINT (human intelligence) Service

DI   Directorate of Intelligence (both CIA and DIA)

DIA   Defense Intelligence Agency

DO   Directorate of Operations (CIA)

DOD   Department of Defense

DOE   Department of Energy

DS&T   Directorate of Science and Technology (CIA)

FBI   Federal Bureau of Investigation

HUMINT   Human intelligence

IMINT   Imagery intelligence

INR   Bureau of Intelligence and Research, State Dept.

JCS   Joint Chiefs of Staff

JMIP   Joint Military Intelligence Program

NFIP   National Foreign Intelligence Program

NIC   National Intelligence Council

NIE   National intelligence estimate

NIMA   National Imagery and Mapping Agency

NIO   National intelligence officer

NRO   National Reconnaissance Office

NSA   National Security Agency

NSC   National Security Council

OSD   Office of the Secretary of Defense

SIGINT   Signals intelligence

SOCOM   Special Operations Command

TIARA   Tactical intelligence and related activities

UAV   Unmanned aerial vehicles (drones)

FURTHER READINGS

The following readings provide background on the current organization and structure of the U.S. intelligence community and also include some studies of proposed changes that would enable the intelligence community to deal more effectively with the challenges it will face in the future.

Elkins, Dan. *An Intelligence Resource Manager's Guide.* Washington, D.C.: Joint Military Intelligence Training Center, Defense Intelligence Agency, 1997.

Johnson, Loch K. *Secret Agencies: U.S. Intelligence in a Hostile World.* New Haven: Yale University Press, 1996.

Lowenthal, Mark M. *U.S. Intelligence: Evolution and Anatomy.* 2d ed. Westport, Conn.: Praeger, 1992.

Richelson, Jeffrey T. *The U.S. Intelligence Community.* 4th ed. Boulder: Westview Press, 1999.

U.S. Commission on the Roles and Responsibilities of the United States Intelligence Community. *Preparing for the 21st Century: An Appraisal of U.S. Intelligence.* Washington, D.C., U.S. Government Printing Office, 1996.

U.S. House Permanent Select Committee on Intelligence. *IC21: The Intelligence Community in the 21st Century.* Staff study, 104th Cong., 2d sess., 1996.

Chapter 4

The Intelligence Process— A Macro Look: Who Does What for Whom?

The term *intelligence process* refers to the various steps or stages in intelligence, from policymakers perceiving a need for information to the community's delivery of an analytical intelligence product to them. This chapter offers an overview of the entire intelligence process and introduces some of the key issues in each phase. Succeeding chapters deal in greater detail with the major phases.

Intelligence, as practiced in the United States, is commonly thought of as having five steps, to which this book adds two more. The seven phases of the intelligence process are: identifying requirements, collection, processing and exploitation, analysis and production, dissemination, consumption, and feedback.

Identifying requirements means defining those policy issues or areas to which intelligence is expected to make a contribution. It may also mean specifying the collection of certain types of intelligence. The impulse is to say that all policy areas have intelligence requirements, which they do. However, intelligence capabilities are always limited, so priorities must be set, with some requirements getting more attention, some getting less, and some perhaps getting little or none at all. The key issues are: Who sets these requirements and priorities and then conveys them to the intelligence community? What happens, or should happen, if policymakers fail to set these requirements on their own?

Once requirements and priorities have been established, the necessary intelligence must be collected. Some requirements will be better met by specific types of collection; some may require the use of several types of collection. Making these decisions among always-constrained collection capabilities is a key issue, as is the question of how much can or should be collected to meet each requirement.

As noted in the first chapter, collection produces information, not intelligence. That information must be processed and exploited before it can be regarded as intelligence and given to analysts. In the United States, constant tension exists over the allocation of resources to collection and to processing and exploitation, with collection inevitably coming out the winner, to the point where much more is collected than can be processed or exploited.

The previous processes are meaningless unless the intelligence is given to analysts who are experts in their respective fields and can turn the intelligence into a variety of reports that will, it is hoped, respond to the needs of the policymakers. The types of products chosen, the quality of the analysis, and the continuous tension between current intelligence products and longer-range products are major issues.

The issue of moving the analysis to the policymakers stems directly from the multitude of analytical vehicles available for disseminating intelligence. Decisions must be made as to how widely intelligence should be distributed and how urgently it should be passed or flagged for the policymaker's attention.

Most discussions of the intelligence process end here, with the intelligence having reached the policymakers whose requirements first set everything in motion. However, two important phases remain: consumption and feedback.

Policymakers are not "blank slates" or automatons who are impelled to action by intelligence. Indeed, how they consume intelligence—whether in the form of written or oral briefings—and the degree to which the intelligence is used are important issues.

Although feedback does not occur nearly as often as the intelligence community might desire, a dialogue between intelligence consumers and producers should take place after the intelligence has been received. Policymakers should give the intelligence community some sense of how well their intelligence requirements are being met and discuss any adjustments that need to be made to any parts of the process. Ideally, this should happen while the issue or topic is still relevant, so that improvements and adjustments can be made. Failing that, even an *ex post facto* review can be tremendously helpful.

The following sections give a better sense of the key questions and issues that are involved in each phase of the intelligence process.

REQUIREMENTS

Each nation has a wide variety of national security and foreign policy interests. Some nations have more than others. Of these various interests, the primacy of some is self-evident: those that deal with large and known threats, those that deal with neighboring or proximate states, and those that are more severe. But the international arena is dynamic and fluid, so occasional readjustments of priorities are likely even among the agreed-upon key interests.

Given that intelligence should be an adjunct to policy and not a policymaker in its own right, intelligence priorities should reflect policy priorities. Ideally, policymakers should have well-considered and well-established views of their own priorities and convey these clearly to their intelligence apparatus. Some of the requirements may be obvious or so long-standing that no discussion is needed. The cold war concentration on the Soviet Union was one of these.

But what happens if the policymakers do not decide, find that they cannot decide, or fail to convey their priorities to the intelligence community? Who sets intelligence priorities then? The question is neither frivolous nor hypothetical. Senior policymakers often assume that their needs are known by their intelligence providers. After all, the key issues are apparent. A former secretary of defense once told the author exactly that. When asked if he ever considered giving his intelligence officers a more precise definition of his needs, he said, "No. I assumed they knew what I was working on." There is strong reason to believe that his view was not unique.

An obvious way to fill the requirements gap left by policymakers would be for the intelligence community to assume this task on its own. However, in a system like that of the United States, where a strict line divides policy and intelligence, this solution may not be possible. Intelligence officials may feel that the limits on their role preclude making the decision; policymakers may view intelligence officials who seek to fill the void as a threat to their function and may even react with hostility.

The intelligence community faces two unpalatable choices. The first is to fill the requirements vacuum, running the risk of being wrong or accused of having overstepped into the realm of policy. The second choice is to overlook the absence of defined requirements and to continue collection and the phases that follow, based on the last-known priorities and the intelligence community's sense of priorities, knowing that it may be accused of failing to meet important priorities. In short, there is no good choice when such a vacuum occurs.

Some intelligence managers might take issue with this interpretation of their choices. They would note, correctly, that one function of intelligence is to look ahead, to identify issues that are not high priority at present but may be so in the future. But, as important as this function is, it is difficult to get policymakers to focus on issues that are far off or only possibly important. They are hard-pressed to work on the issues demanding immediate attention. Thus, the requirements conundrum remains.

Conflicting or competing priorities are also an issue. Although some sense of order may be easily imposed on certain issues, others may end up claiming equal primacy. Again, ideally the policymakers should make the difficult choices. In reality, most governments are large enough to have various competing sectors of interest either between or within departments or ministries. The end result is that, once again, the intelligence community may be left to its own devices. In an intelligence community like that of the United States, parts of the community may reflect the preferences of the policymakers to whom they are most closely tied. In some cases, there may be no final adjudicating authority, leaving the intelligence community to do the best it can. The DCI should be the final adjudicator, but the director's ability to impose priorities on a day-to-day basis across the entire intelligence community remains limited. All issues tend to get shorter shrift when too many are competing for attention.

The hidden factor that drives priorities is resources. It is impossible to cover everything. The United States, for example, has long had interests in every part of the globe, although some are more significant and more central than others. For decades, the U.S. intelligence community has used a variety of processes to set priorities. The most recent, used here as an example, is Presidential Decision Directive 35 (PDD-35), signed by President Bill Clinton in 1995.

PDD-35 divides intelligence issues into "hard targets" and "global coverage." Hard targets are the so-called rogue states (Cuba, Iran, Iraq, Libya, North Korea), and the transnational issues (weapons proliferation, narcotics, international crime, terrorism). Global coverage is everything else. Although PDD-35 was conceived of as a way to parcel out resources across the board, the lion's share of collection and other assets, of necessity, goes to the hard targets.

PDD-35 also gives support to military operations (known as SMO) one of the highest priorities. Although everyone would agree that supporting the military is important, some critics have argued that the emphasis on SMO, prior to the 2001 terrorist attacks, has led to an increasing "militarization" of intelligence, to the detriment of other intelligence consumers in the civil national security agencies.

PDD-35 also divides issues into tiers, which connote the relative priority of the issues. Issues can and do move up and down in the tier system. The problem is that issues do not receive significant attention until after they have begun moving up to the higher-priority tiers, at which point they must compete with the issues already in that bracket. "Tier creep" can become a problem, as analysts or policymakers seek higher priority for certain issues. Tier creep is further exacerbated by the difficulty encountered in returning issues to lower-priority status once they have become less urgent. This underscores the problem with any intelligence requirements system. Such a system is, of necessity, static. Even if the requirements are reviewed and re-ranked periodically, they remain "snapshots" in time. Policymakers or intelligence officials must decide at some point on the requirements and resources to be applied to them. However, the nature of international relations is such that unexpected issues inevitably crop up with little or no warning. Thus, the system that preserves a modicum of flexibility or a modest reserve capability will be more responsive to the realities of intelligence requirements. In reality, policymakers have little time or inclination to conduct periodic reviews of intelligence priorities, even as often as annually. As a result, static, potentially outdated requirements and the necessity to make requirements decisions on its own remain problems for the intelligence community.

Moreover, if a requirement cannot be met with current collection systems, developing the technical systems or the human sources to meet the requirement will take time. Thus, uncertainty about requirements or lower priorities for some of them will affect the development of collection capabilities.

COLLECTION

Collection derives directly from requirements. It is also the first—and perhaps the most important—facet of intelligence where budgets and resources come into play. Technical collection is extremely expensive, and, given that different types of systems offer different benefits and capabilities, the administration and Congress must make difficult budget choices. Also, the needs of agencies vary, further complicating the choices.

How much information should be collected? Or, put another way, does more collection mean better intelligence? The answer to these questions is ambiguous. On one hand, the more information that is collected, the more likely it will include the required intelligence. On the other hand, not everything that is collected is of equal value. Some of this information may have little or no value. Analysts must wade through the material—to process and exploit it—to find the intelligence that is really needed. This is often referred to as the "wheat versus chaff" problem. In other words, increased collection also increases the task of finding the truly important intelligence.

An interesting phenomenon, found at least in the U.S. intelligence community, is that different analytical groups may prefer different types of intelligence. For example, the CIA may put greater store in clandestine human intelligence (espionage), in part because it is a product of CIA activities. Other "all-source" analysts, on the other hand, have sometimes shown less regard for clandestine human sources than has the CIA, placing greater emphasis on signals intelligence, for example.

PROCESSING AND EXPLOITATION

Intelligence collected by technical means—imagery, signals, test data, and so on—does not arrive in ready-to-use form. It must be processed from complex signals into images or intercepts, and these must then be exploit-ed—analyzed if they are images, perhaps decoded, and probably translat-ed if they are signals. Processing and exploitation are key steps in con-verting technically collected information into intelligence.

As noted above, in the United States collection always outruns pro-cessing and exploitation. We collect much more than we can ever process and exploit. Technical collection systems have always found greater favor in the executive branch and Congress. They have an appeal that is lack-ing in the systems and personnel required for processing and exploitation. One of the reasons for this appeal is emotional and is perhaps best explained by reviewing an analogous situation in the defense budget. Les Aspin, chairman of the House Armed Services Committee (1985–1993) and later the secretary of defense (1993–1994), once observed that both Congress and the executive branch favored procurement (buying new weapons) over operations and maintenance (keeping already purchased systems functioning). Buying new systems was more appealing to the decision makers in both branches and also to the more important defense contractors. Operations and maintenance, although important, are less exciting and less glamorous. Collection is akin to procurement and is much more appealing than processing and exploitation.

Collection advocates argue, usually successfully, that collection is the bedrock of intelligence, that without it the entire enterprise has little meaning. Collection also has support from the companies (prime con-tractors and their numerous subcontractors) who build the technical col-lection systems and who lobby for follow-on systems. Processing and exploitation, on the other hand, are in-house intelligence community activities. Although these "downstream activities" (that is, the steps that follow collection) are also dependent on technology, the technology is not in the same league, in terms of contractor profit, as collection systems.

The large and still growing disparity between collection and process-ing/exploitation results in a great amount of collected material never being used. It simply dies on the cutting-room floor. Advocates of pro-cessing and exploitation therefore argue that the image or signal that is not processed and not exploited is identical to the one that is not collect-ed—it has no effect at all.

There is no "proper" ratio between collection and processing/exploitation. In part, the ratio will depend on the issue, available resources, and policymakers' demands. But many who are familiar with the U.S. intelligence community believe that the relationship between these two phases is badly out of balance. Interestingly, the congressional committees that oversee intelligence have increasingly expressed concern about this imbalance, urging the intelligence community to put more money into processing and exploitation. This is often referred to as the

TPEDs problem (pronounced tee-peds). TPEDs refers to Tasking, Processing, Exploitation, and Dissemination. Tasking is the assigning of collectors to specific tasks. Of the four parts of TPEDs, tasking and dissemination are the least problematic for the intelligence community or for Congress. It is the processing and exploitation gap that is of highest concern to Congress.

ANALYSIS AND PRODUCTION

There is major, often daily, tension between current intelligence and long-term intelligence. Current intelligence focuses on issues that are at the forefront of the policymakers' agenda and are receiving their immediate attention. Long-term intelligence deals with trends and issues that may not be an immediate concern but are important and may come to the forefront, especially if they do not receive some current attention. The skills for preparing the two types of intelligence are not identical, nor are the intelligence products that can or should be used to disseminate them to policymakers. But a subtle relationship exists between current and long-term intelligence. Like collection versus process/exploitation, a proper balance—not necessarily 50–50—should be the goal.

The U.S. system of competitive analysis—that is, having the same issue addressed by several different analytical groups—entails some analytical costs. Although the goal is to bring disparate points of view to bear on an issue, intelligence community products written within this system run the risk of succumbing to "group think," with lowest-common-denominator language resulting from intellectual compromises. Alternatively, agencies can indulge in endless and—at least to the policy consumers—meaningless "footnote wars," whose only goal is to maintain a separate point of view regardless of the salience of the issue at stake.

Analysts should have a key role in helping determine collection priorities. Although the United States has instituted a series of offices and programs to improve the relationship between analysts and the collection systems on which they are dependent, the connection between the two has never been particularly strong or responsive.

The training and the mind-sets of analysts are important. Analysts must often deal with intelligence that is contradictory, both internally and when viewed in light of their strongly held professional beliefs and perhaps their own past work. The way in which analysts deal with these contradictions depends on their training and the nature of the broader analytical system, including the review process.

Finally, it is important to recognize that analysts are not intellectual ciphers. They are likely to have ambitions and will want their issues to receive a certain degree of high-level attention. This is not meant to suggest that they will resort to intellectually dishonest means to gain attention, but that possibility must be kept in mind by their superiors within the intelligence community and by policymakers.

DISSEMINATION AND CONSUMPTION

The process of moving the intelligence from the producers to the consumers is largely standardized. The intelligence community has a set "product line" to cover the types of reports and customers with which it must deal. The product line ranges from bulletins on fast-breaking and important events to studies that may take a year or more to complete.

Some of the better-known intelligence products are described below:

PRESIDENT'S DAILY BRIEFING. The PDB is delivered every morning to the president and some of the most senior presidential advisers by the PDB staff at the CIA. The PDB changes in format to suit the preferences of each president.

SENIOR EXECUTIVE INTELLIGENCE BRIEF. The SEIB—for decades known as the *National Intelligence Daily*—is an early-morning intelligence newspaper prepared by the CIA, in coordination with the other intelligence producers, for several hundred senior officials in Washington. Copies are distributed throughout the executive branch, as well as to the intelligence oversight committees in Congress.

THE SECRETARY'S MORNING SUMMARY (SMS) AND MILITARY INTELLIGENCE DIGEST (MID). Unlike the SEIB, which is theoretically a product of the entire intelligence community, the SMS is prepared by INR; the MID is prepared by DIA. Although both of these products are primarily for the policymakers within their own departments, the SMS and MID are also circulated elsewhere in the executive branch. Thus, in the sense of offering a different array of issues and perhaps different analyses, the SMS and the MID are counterparts to the SEIB. On any given day, the SEIB, SMS, and MID will cover some of the same issues, as well as issues that are of particular interest to their primary readers alone. In 2001, INR abandoned the SMS, relying on other vehicles to communicate with its major policy customers.

NATIONAL INTELLIGENCE ESTIMATES. NIEs are the responsibility of national intelligence officers (NIOs), who are members of the National Intelligence Council, which reports directly to the DCI. NIEs represent the considered opinion of the entire intelligence community and, once completed and agreed to, are signed by the DCI for presentation to the president and other senior officials. The drafting of NIEs can take anywhere from a few months to a year or more. Special NIEs, or SNIEs (pronounced "sneeze"), are written on more urgent issues and on a fast-track basis.

The PDB, SEIB, SMS, and MID are all current intelligence products, focusing on events of the past day or two at most and on issues that are being dealt with at present or will be dealt with over the next few days. NIEs are long-term intelligence products that attempt to estimate (not predict) the likely direction an issue will take in the future. Ideally, NIEs should be anticipatory, focusing on issues that are likely to be important in the near future and for which there is sufficient time to arrive at a community-wide judgment. This ideal is not always met, and some NIEs are drafted on issues that are already on policymakers' agendas. If these same issues demand current analysis, it will be distributed through other analytical vehicles or via a SNIE.

The following are among the issues that must be dealt with in dissemination:

- Among the large mass of material being collected and analyzed each day, what is important enough to report?
- To which policymakers should it be reported—the most senior or lower-ranking ones? To many or just a few?
- How quickly should it be reported? Is it urgent enough to require immediate delivery, or can it wait for one of the reports that senior policymakers receive the next morning?
- How much detail should be reported to the various intelligence consumers? How long should the report be?
- What is the best vehicle for reporting it—one of the products mentioned above, a memo, a briefing?

The intelligence community customarily makes these decisions. They entail a number of factors and occasional trade-offs between conflicting goals. Ideally, the community employs a "layered approach," using a variety of intelligence products to convey the same intelligence—in different formats and degrees of detail—to a broad array of policymakers. Its decisions should also reflect an understanding of the needs and preferences of the policymakers and should be adjusted as administrations change.

Most discussions of the intelligence process do not include the consumption phase, since the intelligence is complete and has been delivered. However, this approach ignores the key role played by the policy community throughout the entire intelligence process.

FIGURE 4-1   The Intelligence Process: A CIA View

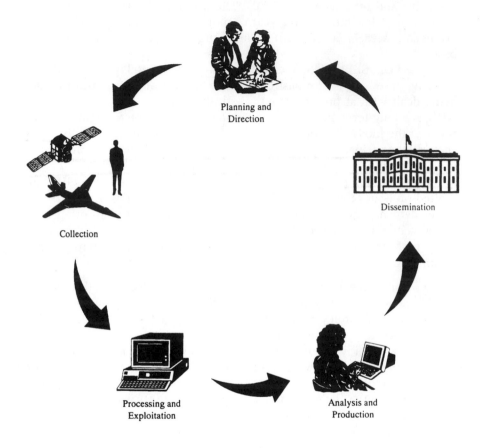

Planning and
Direction

Collection

Dissemination

Processing and
Exploitation

Analysis and
Production

Source: Central Intelligence Agency, *A Consumer's Handbook to Intelligence,* September 1993.

FEEDBACK

Communications between the policy community and the intelligence community are at best imperfect throughout the intelligence process. This is most noticeable after intelligence has been transmitted. Ideally, the policymakers would be giving continual feedback to their intelligence producers—what has been useful, what has not, which areas need continuing or increased emphasis, which can be reduced, and so on.

In reality, the community receives feedback less often than it desires, and it certainly does not receive feedback in any systematic manner, for

FIGURE 4-2   The Intelligence Process: A Schematic

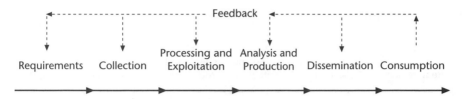

several reasons. First, few people in the policy community have the time to think about or to convey their reactions. They work from issue to issue, with little time to reflect on what went right or wrong before pushing on to the next issue. Also, few policymakers think feedback is necessary. Even when the intelligence they are receiving is not exactly what they need, they usually do not bother to inform their intelligence producers. The failure to provide feedback is analogous to the policymakers' inability or refusal to help define requirements.

THINKING ABOUT THE INTELLIGENCE PROCESS

Given the importance of the intelligence process as both a concept and an organizing principle, it is worth thinking about how the process works and how best to conceptualize it.

Figure 4-1 is published by the CIA in *A Consumer's Handbook to Intelligence*. It presents the intelligence cycle (as the guide calls it) as a perfect circle. Beginning at the top, policymakers provide planning and direction, and the intelligence community collects intelligence, which is then processed and exploited, analyzed and produced, and disseminated to the policymakers.

Although meant to be little more than a quick schematic presentation, the CIA diagram misrepresents some aspects and misses many others. First, it is overly simple. It has an end-to-end completeness that misses many of the vagaries in the process, as noted above. It is also oddly unidimensional. A policymaker asks questions and, after a few steps, gets an answer. There is no feedback, nor does the diagram convey that the process might not be completed in one cycle.

A more realistic diagram would show that at any stage in the process it is possible—and sometimes necessary—to go back to an earlier step. Initial collection may prove unsatisfactory and may lead policymakers to change the requirements; processing and exploitation or analysis may reveal gaps, resulting in new collection requirements; consumers may

FIGURE 4-3   The Intelligence Process: Multilayered

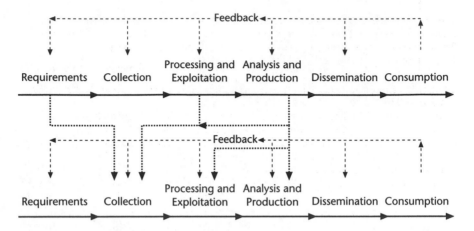

change their needs or ask for more intelligence. And, on occasion, intelligence officers may receive feedback.

This admittedly imperfect process can be portrayed as in Figure 4-2. This diagram, although better than the CIA's, remains somewhat unidimensional. A still better portrayal would capture the more than occasional need to go back to an earlier part of the process in order to meet unfulfilled or changing requirements, collection needs, and so on.

Figure 4-3 shows how in any one intelligence process issues will likely arise (the need for more collection, uncertainties in processing, results of analysis, changing requirements) that will cause a second or even third intelligence process to take place. Ultimately, one could repeat the process lines over and over to portray continuing changes in any of the various parts of the process and the fact that policy issues are rarely resolved in a single neat cycle. This diagram is a bit more complex, but it also gives a much better sense of how the intelligence process operates in reality, being linear, circular, and open-ended all at the same time.

KEY TERMS

analysis and production
collection
consumption
dissemination
downstream activities
feedback
footnote wars

processing and exploitation
requirements
support to military operations
   (SMO)
tier creep
TPEDs

FURTHER READINGS

The intelligence process in the United States has become so routinized in its basic steps and forms that it is not often written about analytically as an organic whole. These readings are among the few that attempt to examine the process on some broader basis.

Central Intelligence Agency. *A Consumer's Handbook to Intelligence*. Langley, Va.: CIA, 1993.

Johnson, Loch. "Decision Costs in the Intelligence Cycle." In *Intelligence: Policy and Process*. Ed. Alfred C. Maurer et al. Boulder: Westview Press, 1985.

————. "Making the Intelligence 'Cycle' Work." *International Journal of Intelligence and Counterintelligence* 1 (winter 1986–1987).

Krizan, Liza. *Intelligence Essentials for Everyone*. Joint Military Intelligence College, Occasional Paper No. 6. Washington, D.C.: Government Printing Office, 1999.

Chapter 5

Collection and the Collection Disciplines

Collection is the bedrock of intelligence. Indeed, intelligence collection has been written about since the biblical references to spies in the Book of Joshua. Without collection, intelligence is little more than guesswork—perhaps educated guesswork, but guesswork nonetheless. The United States and several other nations use multiple means of collecting the intelligence they require. The means are driven by two factors: the nature of the intelligence being sought and the ability to acquire it in various ways. In the United States the various means of collecting intelligence are sometimes referred to as "collection disciplines" or "INTs." This chapter discusses the overarching themes that affect all means of collection, then addresses what the various INTs provide as well as their strengths and weaknesses.

OVERARCHING THEMES

Several themes or issues cut across the various collection disciplines and tend to drive many of the debates and decisions on intelligence collection. These themes are important because they point out that collection involves more than the questions of "What can we collect?" or "Should we collect this?" Collection is a highly complex government activity that is subject to numerous decisions and stress points.

BUDGET. Technical collection systems, many of which are based on satellites, are very expensive. These systems and programs are a major expenditure within the U.S. intelligence budget. Thus, costs will always constrain the ability to operate a large number of collection systems at the same time. Moreover, since different types of satellites are employed for different types of collection (imagery versus signals), policymakers have to make difficult trade-offs. Significant costs are also associated with launching satellites. The larger the satellite, the larger the rocket required to put it into orbit. Finally, the costs of processing and exploitation (P&E), without which collection is meaningless, should be factored into the total expense. Builders of collection systems often ignore the latter as part of their estimates for collection.

During the cold war, cost issues for technical collection rarely surfaced. The sense of threat, coupled with the fact that there was no better way to collect intelligence on the Soviet Union, tended to support the high costs of the systems. Also, decision makers placed greater emphasis on collection systems than on the processing and exploitation needed to deal with the intelligence collected. In the post–cold war period, given the absence of any large and potentially overwhelming threat, these collection costs have become more vulnerable politically. The terrorist attacks in 2001 raised further questions about the utility of these systems, as terrorist targets are less susceptible to collection via technical means and may require greater use of human intelligence.

The budget is also important because it is a major means by which Congress influences and even controls intelligence activities. As noted, Congress tended to be supportive of collection requirements throughout the cold war, but it was also inclined to support the disparity between collection and the less-favored processing and exploitation. Some changes began to appear in the mid-1990s. The House Intelligence Committee, for example, advocated the use of some smaller imagery satellites, both for greater flexibility and to save on building and launching costs. This committee also tried to redress the collection/P&E balance, emphasizing the importance of TPEDs.

COLLECTION SYNERGY. One of the major advantages of having multiple means of collection is that one system or discipline can provide tips or clues that can be further collected against by other systems. For major requirements, more than one type of collection is used; the collectors are designed to be cooperative when the system is working correctly. The goal of the U.S. intelligence community is to produce all-source intelligence, or fusion intelligence, that is, intelligence based on as many collection sources as possible in order to compensate for the shortcomings of each and to profit from their combined strength. All-source intelligence reflects collection in depth. At the same time, the diverse array also allows collection managers to increase collection in breadth, that is, to increase the number of issues being covered, albeit with less depth for a particular issue.

An excellent example of collection synergy is the Cuban missile crisis of 1962. Although analysts were slow to understand that Soviet premier Nikita Khrushchev was willing to make such a risky move as deploying medium- and intermediate-range missiles in Cuba, the intelligence community brought a variety of collection means to bear. Anti-Castro Cubans still on the island provided some of the first reliable evidence that missiles were being deployed. A human source provided the data that targeted the U-2 flights over a trapezoid bounded by four towns in western Cuba. Imagery then provided crucial intelligence about the status of the missile sites and the approximate time before completion, as did Soviet technical manuals turned over to the United States by Col. Oleg Penkovsky, a spy in the employ of the United States and Britain. Imagery and naval units gave the locations of Soviet ships bringing the missiles to the almost-completed sites. Finally, Penkovsky also provided the United States with excellent authoritative information on the state of Soviet strategic forces, which indicated overwhelming U.S. superiority.

THE VACUUM CLEANER PROBLEM. Those familiar with U.S. technical collection systems often note that they are vacuum cleaners, not microscopes. These collectors sweep up a great deal of information, within which *may* be the intelligence actually being sought. As previously noted, this problem is sometimes referred to as "wheat versus chaff." Roberta Wohlstetter, in her classic study *Pearl Harbor: Warning and Decision,* refers to this problem as "noise versus signals," noting that the signals one wishes to receive and to know are often embedded in a great deal of surrounding noise.

No matter which metaphor one uses, the issue remains the same: collection is less than precise. Indeed, this problem underscores the importance of processing and exploitation.

The issue then becomes how to extract the desired intelligence from the mountain of information. One answer would be to increase the number of analysts who deal with the incoming intelligence, but that raises further demands on the budget. Another possible response, even less palatable, would be to collect less. But, even then, there would be no assurance that the "wheat" remained in the smaller volume still being collected.

COMPETING COLLECTION PRIORITIES. Since the number of collection platforms, or spies, is limited, policymakers must make choices among competing collection requirements. As noted above, they use various systems to set priorities, but some issues inevitably get shorter shrift, or may be ignored altogether, in favor of those that are seen as more pressing.

Both policymakers and the intelligence officers acting on their behalf request increased collection on certain issues. However, their requests are made within a system that is inelastic in terms of both technical and human collectors. Every collection request that is fulfilled means another collection issue or request goes wanting; it is a zero-sum game. That is

India's Nuclear Test, 1998

In May 1998 the newly elected government of India resumed testing nuclear weapons, as it had promised in its election campaign. The U.S. intelligence community did not detect the test preparations.

As a result, the DCI asked retired Adm. David Jeremiah to review the intelligence community's performance on this "hard target" issue—preventing the proliferation of nuclear weapons.

Jeremiah reported several findings, including the fact that—given the Indian government's avowed intention to test, which required no clandestine collection at all—intelligence performance could have been better. But he also noted that collection assets that might have picked up indications of the impending test were focused on the Korean demilitarized zone (DMZ), at the request of the commander of U.S. forces in Korea.

No one will deny the importance of the Korean DMZ. As one director of the National Security Agency put it, the Korean DMZ was the only place in the world in the late 1990s where someone else could decide if the United States would go to war. (This was before the terrorist attacks in 2001.) The Korean DMZ is a constant concern. It could be argued that, for a brief period in May 1998, Indian test activities should have been accorded a higher priority.

why a priority system is necessary in the first place. Moreover, the system has little or no "surge" capacity; few collection systems (airplanes, drones, and ship-based systems) or spies are waiting in reserve for an emergency. Even if additional satellites have already been built, launching them requires a ready rocket of the appropriate size, an available launch pad, and other resources. (The Soviet Union used a different collection model. Soviet satellites lacked the life spans of their U.S. counterparts. During crises, the Soviets supplemented current collection assets with additional-usually short-lived satellites, which were kept on hand with launch vehicles ready.) Similarly, one does not simply tap a spy and send him or her off to a new assignment. Cover stories need to be created, along with the inevitable paraphernalia; training may be necessary; and a host of other preparations must be made. Inelasticity of resources makes the priorities system difficult at best.

If an emergency arises, collection resources will be shifted away from lower-priority issues, which can result in difficult—and sometimes mistaken—choices. (*See box, "India's Nuclear Test, 1998."*)

Why Classify?

Numerous critics of the U.S. classification system have argued—not incorrectly—that classification is used too freely and sometimes for the sake of denying information to others who have a legitimate need for it.

However, there is a rationale and some sense to the way in which classification is intended to be used. Classification derives from the damage that would be done if the information were revealed. Thus, classification related to intelligence collection underscores both the importance of the information and the fragility of its source—something that would be very difficult to replace if revealed.

The most common classification is SECRET (CONFIDENTIAL is rarely used any longer), followed by TOP SECRET. Within TOP SECRET are numerous TOP SECRET/CODEWORD compartments—meaning specific bodies of intelligence based on their sources. Admission to any level of classification or compartment is driven by an individual's certified "need to know" that specific type of information.

Each classification level is defined; current definitions are found in Executive Order 12958 of April 17, 1995 (italics added):

- CONFIDENTIAL: information whose unauthorized disclosure "could be expected to cause *damage* to the national security."
- SECRET: information whose unauthorized disclosure "could be expected to cause *serious damage* to the national security."
- TOP SECRET: information whose unauthorized disclosure "could be expected to cause *exceptionally grave damage* to the national security."

Higher levels of access are useful bureaucratic levers for those who have them in contrast to those who do not.

PROTECTING SOURCES AND METHODS.   The details of collection capabilities—and even the existence of some capabilities—are among the most highly classified secrets of any state. In U.S. parlance, classification is referred to as the protection of sources and methods. It is one of the primary concerns of the entire intelligence community and a task specifically assigned by law to the director of central intelligence.

Several levels of classification are in use, reflecting the sensitivity of the intelligence or intelligence means. (*See box, "Why Classify?"*) The security classifications are driven by concerns that the disclosure of capabilities will allow those nations that are collection targets to take steps to prevent collection, thus effectively negating the collection systems.

However, the levels of classification also impose costs, some of which are financial. The physical costs of security—guards, safes, and special means of transmitting intelligence—are high. Added to these is the expense of security checks for individuals who are to be entrusted with classified information (see chap. 7 for details).

Some people argue that the classifications impose still other costs. Critics maintain that the classification system is used inappropriately and even promiscuously, classifying material either too highly or in some cases classifying material that does not deserve this designation. Critics are also concerned that the system can be abused to allow the intelligence community to hide mistakes, failures, or even crimes.

Beyond the costs of the classification system and its potential abuse, the need to conceal sources and methods limits the use of intelligence as a policy tool. For example, in the late 1950s Khrushchev broke a nuclear-test moratorium and blustered about the Soviet Union's growing strategic nuclear forces. President Dwight Eisenhower, bolstered by the first U.S. images of the Soviet Union, knew that the United States enjoyed a strong strategic superiority. But, in order to protect sources and methods, Eisenhower did not reply to Khrushchev's false boasts. What might have been the results if the United States had released some imagery to counter the Soviet claims? Would the release have spurred the Soviets to greater weapons-building efforts? Would it have severely undercut Soviet foreign policy? Would it have affected U.S. intelligence capabilities, even though the Soviets already knew they were being overflown by satellites and U-2s? These questions are not answerable, but they give a good feel for the nature of the problem.

More recently, the U.S. intelligence community has grown concerned about protecting intelligence sources and methods during post–cold war military operations that involve cooperation with nations that are not U.S. allies. Even among allies the United States employs gradations of intelligence sharing, having the deepest such relationship with Britain, followed closely by Australia and Canada. Intelligence relations with other NATO allies are close, albeit less so than with the "English-speaking cousins." But some recent operations, such as in Bosnia, have involved military operations with nations that are viewed with lingering suspicion, such as Russia or Ukraine. In these cases the need to protect intelligence sources and methods must be balanced against the need to share intelligence—not only for the sake of the operation but also to ensure that military partners in the operation are not put in a position where their actions or inactions prove to be dangerous to U.S. troops.

LIMITATIONS OF SATELLITES. All satellites are limited by the laws of physics. Most orbiting systems can spend only a limited time over any target. On each successive orbit the satellites will shift to a slightly different coverage pattern. (Satellites correspond to the motion of the Earth, as they are trapped within the Earth's gravitational pull. Thus, satellites' orbits move from west to east with each pass.) Moreover, satellites travel in predictable orbits. Potential targets of a satellite can derive the orbit from basic knowledge about its launch and initial orbit. Unfortunately, for a variety of reasons, some individuals and organizations attempt to make this information available. It enables nations to take steps to avoid collection—in part by engaging in activities they wish to keep secret only when satellites are not overhead.

Satellites that are in geosynchronous orbit stay over the same spot on Earth at all times. But to do this they must be 22,000 miles above Earth. The great distance between the collectors and their targets raises the problem of transmitting collected information back to Earth. Collection can be precise only up to a point, thus explaining the "vacuum cleaner" problem noted above. Satellites can also be flown in sun-synchronous orbits, that is, moving in harmony with the Earth's rotation so as to always remain where there is daylight, but this produces a very easily tracked orbit. This orbit is better for commercial satellites than for national imagery satellites.

THE "STOVEPIPES" PROBLEM. Intelligence practitioners often refer to collection "stovepipes." This term refers to two characteristics of intelligence collection. First, all of the technical collection disciplines—imagery (IMINT), signals intelligence (SIGINT), and measurement and signatures intelligence (MASINT)—and the nontechnical human intelligence, or espionage (HUMINT), have end-to-end processes, from collection through dissemination. (Open-source intelligence—OSINT—does not.) Thus, there is a "pipeline" from beginning to end. Second, the collection disciplines are separate from one another, and are often competitors. The various INTs sometimes vie with one another to respond to requests for intelligence—largely as a means of assuring continuing funding levels—regardless of which INT is best suited to provide the required intelligence. Often, several of the INTs respond, regardless of their applicability to the problem. Within the U.S. intelligence system there are a variety of positions and fora designed to coordinate the various INTs, but no single individual exercises ultimate control over all of them. The "stovepipes" are therefore complete but quite individual and separate processes.

Intelligence officers also sometimes talk about the "stovepipes within the stovepipes." Within specific collection disciplines there are likely to be separate programs and processes that work somewhat independently of one another and do not have insights into one another's operations, but have an aggregate competitive effect that influences a particular INT. This is, in part, the natural result of the compartmentation of various programs for the sake of security, but it further exacerbates the stovepipes issue.

THE OPACITY OF INTELLIGENCE. One of the stated goals or ideals of the U.S. intelligence process is to have "analysis-driven collection." This is a shorthand way of recognizing that collection priorities should reflect the intelligence needs of those crafting the analysis. It further reflects the expectation, occasionally misplaced, that analysts have received a sense of the priorities from policymakers. In reality, however, the collection and analytical communities do not operate as closely as this ideal would imply. One of the most striking aspects of this separation is the view held by many analysts, including veteran ones, that the collection system is a "black box" into which they have little insight. Analysts will express the view that they have no real sense of how collection tasking decisions are made, what gets collected for which reasons, or how they receive their intelligence. To many analysts, the collection process is something of a mystery. This could simply be dismissed as the failure of one professional group to understand the methods of another group. But the divide goes to the heart of collection, often leaving analysts with the view that they have absolutely no influence on collection, and that whatever sources they do get are somewhat random and fortuitous. This view is also significant in that the intelligence community spends a substantial amount of time educating analysts about collection, with little apparent return on the investment. This perceived opacity of collection also undercuts the goal of having analysis drive collection.

RECONNAISSANCE GAMES—DENIAL AND DECEPTION. In an obverse of the problem noted above—in which a target uses knowledge about the collection capabilities of an opponent to avoid collection (known as "denial")—the target can use the same knowledge to transmit information to a collector. This information can be either true or false (if the latter, it is called "deception"). For example, a nation can display an array of weapons as a means of deterring attack. Such a display may reveal actual capabilities or may be staged in order to present a false image of strength. A classic example was the Soviet Union's sending its limited number of strategic bombers in large loops around Moscow during parades so they could be repeatedly counted by U.S. personnel in attendance, thus inflating Soviet air strength. The use of decoys or dummies to fool imagery, or false communications to fool SIGINT, also falls into this category. The Allies exploited these techniques prior to D-Day to raise German concerns about an invasion in the Pas de Calais rather than Normandy. The Allies created a nonexistent invasion force, replete with inflatable dummy tanks and streams of false radio traffic, all under the supposed command of Gen. George S. Patton.

The intelligence community has devoted ever-increasing resources to the issue of "denial and deception," also known as D&D. Intelligence officials seek to know which nations are practicing D&D, how they may have obtained the intelligence that made D&D possible, and then seek to design countermeasures to circumvent D&D. As more and more information about U.S. intelligence sources and methods becomes publicly available, D&D becomes an increasing constraint on collection.

RECONNAISSANCE IN THE POST–COLD WAR WORLD. The U.S. collection array was largely built to respond to the difficulties of penetrating the Soviet target—a closed society with a vast land mass, frequent bad weather, and a long-standing tradition of secrecy and deception. At the same time, our primary targets of interest—military capabilities—existed in extensive and well-defined bases with a large supporting infrastructure and exercised with great regularity, thus alleviating the problem to some extent.

Does the United States require the same extensive array of collection systems to deal with post–cold war intelligence issues? On the one hand, the threat to the United States has lessened. On the other hand, intelligence targets are more diffuse and more geographically disparate than before. Also, some of the leading intelligence issues—the so-called transnational issues such as narcotics, terrorism, and crime—may be less susceptible to the technical collection capabilities built to deal with the Soviet Union or other "classic" political-military intelligence problems. Many of the current collection targets are "nonstate" actors with no fixed geographic location and no vast infrastructure that offers collection opportunities. These transnational issues may require greater human intelligence, albeit in geographic regions where the United States has fewer capabilities.

Overhead imagery capabilities have gone commercial. IKONOS, LANDSAT, SPOT, and other satellites have ended the U.S. and Russian monopoly on overhead imagery. Any nation—or transnational group—can order imagery from commercial vendors. They may even do so through false fronts to mask their identity. This commercial capability remains so new that its implications have not been completely thought out by those building the commercial systems and by intelligence agencies. On the positive side, commercial imagery offers opportunities, freeing classified collection systems for the truly hard targets. On the negative side, it may offer hostile states or terrorists access to useful imagery via false fronts—buyers who serve to mask the ultimate users of the imagery. "Shutter control"—who controls what the satellites will photograph—is already an issue between those in the U.S. government who seek to limit photography of Israel and those who own the satellites. As will be discussed below, dramatic changes occurred in the U.S. use of commercial imagery during the Afghanistan campaign, affecting each of these issues and perhaps suggesting a new relationship between the intelligence community and these commercial providers.

Finally, open-source information (OSINT) is growing rapidly. The collapse of a number of closed, Soviet-dominated societies drastically reduced the "denied targets" area. One intelligence veteran observed that during the cold war 80 percent of the information about the Soviet Union was secret and 20 percent was open, but in the post–cold war period the ratio had more than reversed for Russia. Theoretically, the greater availability of open-source intelligence should make the intelligence community's job easier. However, this community was created to collect secrets; collecting open-source information is not a wholly analogous activity. The intelligence community has had difficulties assimilating open-source information into its collection stream. Moreover, the intelligence community harbors some institutional prejudice against open-source intelligence, as it seems to run counter to the very purposes for which the intelligence community was created. (It is worth noting that the OSS had an overt branch—Research and Analysis—but it apparently had little influence on the operations of the postwar intelligence community.)

THE COLLECTION DISCIPLINES: STRENGTHS AND WEAKNESSES

Each of the collection disciplines has strengths and weaknesses. But when evaluating them—especially the weaknesses—it is important to remember that the goal is to involve as many collection disciplines as possible on the major issues. This should allow the collectors to gain advantages from mutual reinforcement and from individual capabilities that can compensate for shortcomings in the others.

IMAGERY. IMINT is also referred to as PHOTINT (photo intelligence). It is a direct descendant of the brief practice of sending soldiers up in balloons during the U.S. Civil War. In World Wars 1 and II both sides used airplanes to obtain photos. Airplanes are still employed, but several nations now utilize imagery satellites. In the United States, the National Reconnaissance Office (NRO) develops these satellites. The National Imagery and Mapping Agency (NIMA) is responsible for processing and exploiting imagery. Some imagery also comes via the Defense Department's airborne systems, such as unmanned aerial vehicles (UAVs), or drones.

The term *imagery* is somewhat misleading in that it is generally considered to be a picture produced by an optical system akin to a camera. Some imagery is produced by optical systems, usually referred to as electro-optical (EO) systems. Early satellites contained film that was jettisoned in capsules and recovered. Modern satellites transmit their images as signals, or data streams, that are received and reconstructed as images.

Infrared imagery (IR) produces an image based on the heat reflected by the surfaces being recorded. IR provides the ability to detect "warm" objects (for example, engines on tanks or planes inside hangars). Imagery can also be produced by radar, which has the ability to "see" through cloud cover. Some systems, referred to as multispectral or hyperspectral imagery (MSI and HSI), derive "images" from spectral analysis. These images are not photographic per se but are built by reflections from several bands across the spectrum of light, some visible, some invisible. They are usually referred to as measurement and signals intelligence (MASINT).

The level of detail provided by imagery is called "resolution." Resolution refers to the smallest object that can be distinguished in an image, expressed in size—1 meter, 10 meters, and so on. Designers of imagery systems must make a trade-off between the resolution and the size of the scene being imaged. The better the resolution, the smaller the scene. (See box, "How Much Resolution Is Enough?") Several press accounts say that U.S. satellites now have resolutions of 10 inches. Commercial imagery is now available at a resolution of 0.5 meter (or just under 20 inches), meaning that an object half a meter in size can be distinguished in an image. (By agreement with the U.S. government, commercial vendors are subject to a twenty-four-hour delay from the time of collection before they can release any imagery with resolution better than 0.82 meter, or just over 32 inches.)

During the cold war it was often popular to refer to the ability to "read the license plates in the Kremlin parking lot"—a wholly irrelevant parameter. Different collection needs have different resolution requirements. For example, keeping track of large-scale troop deployments requires much less detail than tracking the shipment of military weapons. Indeed, the U.S. intelligence community developed the science of "crateology," by which analysts were able to track Soviet arms shipments based on the size and shape of crates being loaded or unloaded from Soviet-bloc cargo vessels. (This analytical practice was subject to deception simply by using purposely missized crates to mask the nature of the shipments.)

Imagery offers a number of advantages over other collection means. First, it is sometimes graphic and compelling. When shown to policymakers, an easily interpreted image is often worth a thousand words. Second, imagery is easily understood much of the time by policymakers. Even though few of them, if any, are trained imagery analysts, all are quite accustomed to seeing and interpreting images. From family photos to newspapers, magazines, and news broadcasts, we all spend part of our day not only looking at images but also interpreting them. Imagery is also easy to use with policymakers in that little or no interpretation is necessary as to how it was acquired. Although the method by which images are taken

How Much Resolution Is Enough?

The degree of resolution that analysts desire depends on the nature of the target and the type of intelligence that is being sought. For example, one-meter resolution will allow fairly detailed analysis of man-made objects or subtle changes to terrain. Ten-meter resolution will lose some detail but will allow the identification of buildings by type or the surveillance of large installations and associated activity. Twenty- to thirty-meter resolution will cover a much larger area but will allow the identification of large complexes such as airports, factories, and bases.

Thus, the degree of resolution has to be appropriate to the analyst's need. Sometimes high resolution is the correct choice; sometimes it is not.

from space, transmitted to earth, and processed is more complex than using a 35mm camera, policy clients are sufficiently informed to trust it and take it for granted.

Another advantage of imagery is that many of the targets make themselves available. Military exercises in most nations are conducted on regular cycles and at predictable locations, making them highly susceptible to IMINT. Finally, an image of a certain site will often provide information not just about one activity but some ancillary ones as well. Here a distinction must again be made between these military targets, which are quite familiar to the intelligence community, and the challenges posed by terrorism. In brief, terrorism presents a smaller imagery target. Although there may be training camps, as was the case of al Qaeda in Afghanistan, terrorist cells or networks are far smaller, less elaborate, and have less visible infrastructure than do the traditional political-military targets.

Imagery suffers a number of disadvantages as well. The very graphic quality that is an advantage is also a disadvantage. An image can be too compelling, leading to hasty or ill-formed decisions or to the exclusion of other, more subtle intelligence that may be contradictory. Also, the intelligence on an image may not be self-evident; it may require interpretation by trained photo interpreters who can "see" things that the untrained person cannot. At times, the policymakers must take on faith that the skilled analysts are correct. (See box, "The Need for Photo Interpreters—Two Cases in Point.")

Another disadvantage of imagery is that it is, quite literally, a snapshot, a picture of a particular place at a particular time. This is sometimes referred to as the "where and when" phenomenon. Imagery is a static piece of intelligence, telling you something about where and when it was taken

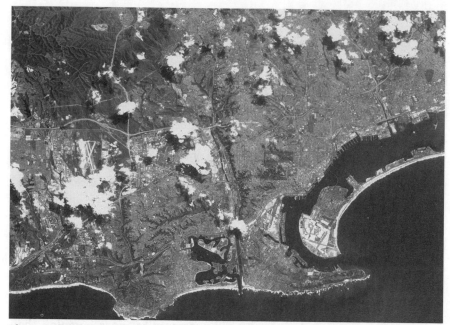

These satellite photos of San Diego, California, illustrate differences in resolution. (Resolution numbers indicate the size of the smallest identifiable object.) They also show recent advances in commercial satellite imagery. The top photo has 25-meter (75 feet) resolution; major landforms—the hills and Mission Bay—are identifiable at lower center. Larger man-made objects—piers, highways, runways at North Island U.S. Naval Air Station—can be seen on the peninsula to the right.

At 5-meter (15 feet) resolution, clarity improves dramatically. North Island and San Diego International Airport are visible, as are rows of boats in the marinas and wakes of boats in the bay. Taller buildings in downtown San Diego can be seen at upper center. Shadows indicate this image was taken in mid- to late morning.

At 4-meter resolution (12 feet), individual buildings and streets can be seen, along with each boat in the marinas. At the bottom, a cruise ship is docked at the terminal. Individual cars can be seen in the parking lot above the piers.

At 1-meter (39 inch) resolution, each building stands out. Individual cars are seen in parking lots and streets. Railroad tracks are visible on a diagonal at the top right, as are paths and small groups of trees in the Embarcadero Marine Park, just below the marina at the upper right. Photos courtesy of Space Imaging, Inc.

The Need for Photo Interpreters—
Two Cases in Point

Two incidents underscore the difficulty of interpreting even not-so-subtle images.

One of the signs of planned Soviet missile deployments in Cuba in 1962 was an image of a peculiar road pattern called "the Star of David" because of its resemblance to that symbol. To the untrained eye it would look like an odd road interchange, but trained U.S. photo interpreters recognized it as a pattern they had seen before—in Soviet missile fields. But to run into a senior policymaker's office exulting about a Star of David road pattern without explaining it, and perhaps bringing along samples from imagery of the Soviet Union, might lead to ridicule. Interpreters also found soccer fields—a sign of non-Cuban activity.

In the late 1970s and early 1980s, when Cuba was sending expeditionary forces to various parts of the Third World, one of the signs of their arrival was newly constructed baseball fields. Cuban troops play baseball for recreation. Again, to inform an official that the Cubans must be in Angola or Ethiopia because baseball fields have been spotted is almost ludicrous. Some supporting analysis is required, perhaps including a note that only the United States, Cuba, Mexico, Canada, Japan, and Nicaragua take baseball this seriously, and all of the others can be eliminated as unlikely to have large troop concentrations in these regions.

but nothing about what happened before or after that was done. Analysts can perform a "negation search," looking at past imagery to determine when an activity commenced. This can be done by computers comparing images, in a process called "automatic change extraction." The site can be revisited to watch for further activity. But a single image will not reveal everything.

Because details about U.S. imagery capabilities have become better known, states can take steps to deceive collection—through the use of camouflage or dummies—or to preclude collection by conducting certain activities at times when they are unlikely or less likely to be observed.

The war against terrorism led to two major developments in the use of imagery. First, the government greatly expanded its use of commercial imagery. In October 2001, the National Imagery and Mapping Agency (NIMA) bought exclusive and perpetual rights to all imagery of Afghanistan taken by the IKONOS satellite, operated by the Space Imaging Company. As noted above, this satellite has a resolution of 0.8 meter. This expanded the overall collection capability of the United States and allowed it to reserve more sophisticated imagery capabilities for those

The famous "Star of David" photo of a Soviet air defense site in Cuba, 1962. The unique road pattern, previously seen only in the USSR, helped alert U.S. analysts to the pending Soviet missile deployment. Photo courtesy of the Central Intelligence Agency.

areas where they were most needed, while IKONOS took up other collection tasks. The use of this commercial imagery also makes it easier for the United States to share imagery with other nations or the public without revealing classified capabilities. At the same time, foreign governments that may be hostile to the United States or may see the Afghanistan campaign as a means of gauging U.S. military capabilities were denied access to imagery. This purchase also denied the use of this commercial imagery to news media, which might be eager to use it as a means of reporting on and assessing the conduct and success of the war.

An interesting ancillary effect of this purchase of commercial imagery was to circumvent the "shutter control" issue. As noted above, the United States can impose shutter control over commercial satellites operated by U.S. companies for reasons of national security. There were concerns that civil-liberties groups or the news media would mount a legal challenge to an assertion of shutter control, the outcome of which was uncertain. By simply purchasing the imagery, NIMA avoided the entire issue. (The French Ministry of Defense banned the sale of SPOT images of the Afghan war zone. SPOT has a 10-meter resolution.)

A second major imagery development has been the expanded use of UAVs (unmanned aerial vehicles). The use of pilotless drones for imagery is not new, but their role and capability have expanded greatly. UAVs offer two obvious advantages over satellites and manned aircraft. First, unlike satellites, they can fly closer to areas of interest and "loiter" over them rather than making a high-altitude orbital pass. Second, unlike manned aircraft, UAVs do not put lives at risk, particularly from surface-to-air missiles (SAMs). Not only are UAVs unmanned; the operators can be safely located great distances (even thousands of miles) from the area of operation, linked to the UAV by satellite. A third advantage is that the UAVs produce "real time" images—they carry high-definition television and infrared cameras—that is, video images that are immediately available for use rather than having to be processed and exploited first.

The United States currently relies on two UAVs, the Predator and the Global Hawk. Predator operates at up to 25,000 feet, flying at the relatively slow speeds of 84 to 140 miles per hour. It can be based as far as 450 miles from a target and still operate over the target for sixteen to twenty-four hours. Predator not only provides real-time imagery but has now been mated with air-to-ground missiles, allowing immediate attacks on identified targets rather than having to relay the information to nearby air or ground units. Global Hawk operates at up to 65,000 feet at a speed of up to 400 miles per hour. It can be based 3,000 miles from the target and can operate over the target for twenty-four hours. Global Hawk is designed to conduct both broad area and continuous spot coverage.

Finally, it is important to note the proliferation of space-based imagery capabilities. Once the exclusive preserve of the United States and the Soviet Union, this field has expanded rapidly. France and Israel have independent imagery satellites. India has a nascent capability; China is rapidly developing one; and Germany has decided to create such a capability. There is also increased cooperation among current and would-be imagery satellite powers. Israel is reported to have cooperative imagery relationships with Taiwan, India, and Turkey. Perhaps more significant, France is working with several European partners—Spain, Italy, and Belgium—on its next generation of imagery satellites. This independent capability within NATO could prove troublesome, as the United States may have to deal with allies having their own imagery and different interpretations of events. This apparently happened in 1996, when France refused to support a U.S. cruise missile attack on Iraq because the French maintained that their imagery did not show significant Iraqi troop movements into Kurdish areas.

Imagery proliferation also has a commercial aspect. A British firm, Surrey Satellite Technology, has pioneered a range of imagery satellites, including "nano" and "microsatellites" weighing as little as 6.5 kilograms, or just over 14 pounds. These satellites do not approach resolutions of the best national systems, but they are certainly sufficient for many nations' needs. Among this firm's clients are Britain, Thailand, Nigeria, Algeria, and China. These satellites also have the ability to get close to other satellites and image them, which is of concern to the United States because of their potential to be used as anti-satellite (ASAT) weapons. Several nations, including Australia, South Korea, and Malaysia, as well as some current Surrey customers, are also looking at small satellite demonstration projects.

SIGNALS INTELLIGENCE. SIGINT is a twentieth-century phenomenon. British intelligence pioneered the field during World War I, successfully intercepting German communications by tapping underwater cables. The most famous product of this work was the Zimmermann Telegram, a German offer to Mexico of an anti-U.S. alliance that Britain made available to the United States without revealing how it was obtained. With the advent of radio communications, cable taps were augmented by the ability to "pluck" signals from the air. The United States also developed a successful signals intercept capability that survived World War I. Prior to World War II the United States broke Japan's Purple code; Britain, via ULTRA, read German codes.

Today signals intelligence can be gathered by Earth-based collectors—ships, planes, ground sites or satellites. Again, U.S. SIGINT satellites are built by the NRO. The National Security Agency (NSA) is responsible for both carrying out U.S. signals intelligence activities and protecting the United States against hostile SIGINT.

SIGINT actually consists of several different types of intercepts. The term is often used to refer to the interception of communications between two parties, which is also known as communications intelligence (COMINT). SIGINT can also refer to the pickup of data relayed by weapons during tests, which is sometimes called telemetry intelligence (TELINT). Finally, SIGINT can refer to the pickup of electronic emissions from modern weapons and tracking systems (military and civil), which are useful means of gauging their capabilities, such as range and frequencies on which systems operate. This is sometimes referred to as electronic intelligence (ELINT).

The ability to intercept communications is highly important, since it gives insight into what is being said, planned, and even considered. This is as close as one can come, from a distance, to reading the other side's mind, a goal that cannot be achieved by imagery. Reading the actual messages and analyzing what they mean is called "content analysis." Tracking communications also gives a good "indication and warning." As with imagery, COMINT relies to some degree on the regular behavior of those being watched, especially among military units. Messages may be sent at regular hours or regular intervals, using known frequencies. Changes in those

---

SIGINT versus IMINT

A director of the National Security Agency once made the following distinction between imagery and signals intelligence: "IMINT tells you what has happened; SIGINT tells you what will happen."

It is a bit of an exaggeration—and was said tongue in cheek—but it captures an important difference between the two INTs.

---

patterns—either increases or decreases—may be indicative of a larger change in activity. Monitoring changes in communications is known as "traffic analysis," which has more to do with the volume and pattern of communications than it does with the content. (*See box, "SIGINT versus IMINT."*)

COMINT also has some weaknesses. First and foremost, it depends on the presence of communications that can be intercepted. If the target goes silent or opts to communicate via secure landlines rather than through the air, then the ability to undertake COMINT ceases to exist. It might be possible to tap the landlines, but this is obviously a more difficult task than remote interception from a ground site or satellite. The target also can begin to encrypt—or code—its communications. Within the offensive/defensive struggle over SIGINT is a second struggle, that between encoders and codebreakers, or cryptographers. "Crypies," as they are known, like to boast that any code that can be constructed can also be solved. But we are far removed from the Elizabethan age of relatively simple ciphers. Computers greatly increase the ability to construct complex, one-time use codes. At the same time, computers also make it more possible to attack these codes. Finally, the target can use false transmissions as a means of creating less compromising patterns or of subsuming important communications amid a flood of meaningless ones—in effect, increasing the ratio of noise to signals.

Another issue is the vast quantity of communications now available: telephones of all sorts, faxes, e-mails. Even a focused collection plan will collect more COMINT than can be processed and exploited. One means of coping with this is the "key-word search," in which the collected data are fed into computers that look out for specific words or phrases. These are used as indicators of the likely value of an intercept. It is not a perfect system but provides a necessary filter to deal with the flood of collected intelligence. TELINT and ELINT offer valuable information on weapons capabilities that would otherwise be unknown or would require far more risky human intelligence operations. However, as the United States learned from its efforts to monitor Soviet arms, the weapons tester can employ many techniques to maintain secrecy. Like communications, test data can be encrypted. It can also be encapsulated—that is, recorded within the weapon being tested and released in a self-contained capsule that will be recovered—so that the data are never transmitted as a signal that would be susceptible to interception. If the data are transmitted, they can be sent in a single "burst" rather than throughout the test, greatly increasing the difficulty of intercepting and reading the data. Or the data can be transmitted via a "spread spectrum," that is, using a series of frequencies through which the data will move at irregular intervals. The testing nation's receivers can be programmed to match the frequency changes, but this will greatly increase the difficulty of intercepting the full data stream.

The war against terrorism has underscored a growing concern for SIGINT. As with the other collection disciplines, SIGINT was developed to collect intelligence on the Soviet Union and other nations. Terrorist cells offer much smaller signatures, which may not be susceptible to interception by remote SIGINT sensors. Therefore, a growing view is that future SIGINT will have to rely on sensors that have been physically placed close to the target by humans. In effect, HUMINT will become the enabler for SIGINT. There are also signs that terrorist groups have increasing knowledge about U.S. SIGINT capabilities and therefore take steps to evade SIGINT detection by such means as using cell phones only once or avoiding cell phones and faxes.

MEASUREMENT AND SIGNATURES INTELLIGENCE. TELINT and ELINT are both major contributors to a little-understood branch of intelligence known as measurement and signatures intelligence (MASINT). This type of intelligence refers to weapons capabilities and industrial activities. Multispectral and hyperspectral imagery (MSI and HSI), discussed above, also contribute to MASINT.

An arcane debate rages between those who see MASINT as a separate collection discipline and those who see it as simply a product, or even a by-product, of SIGINT and other collection capabilities. For our purposes, it is sufficient to understand that MASINT exists and that, in a world increasingly concerned about such issues as proliferation of weapons of mass destruction, it is of growing importance. For example, MASINT can help identify the types of gases or waste leaving a factory, which can be extremely important in chemical-weapons identification. It can also help identify other specific characteristics (composition, material content) of weapons systems.

MASINT has suffered as a collection discipline because of its relative novelty and its dependence on the other technical INTs for its products. Often analysts or policymakers look at a MASINT product without knowing it. MASINT is a potentially important INT still struggling for recognition. It is also more arcane and requires analysts with more technical training to be able to use it fully. At present, policymakers are less familiar with it—and probably less comfortable—than they are with IMINT or SIGINT. MASINT is controlled by an office within DIA, the Central MASINT Office (CMO), rather than being a separate agency. Some of its advocates believe that MASINT will never make a full contribution until it has more bureaucratic clout. Others, even some sympathetic to MASINT, do not believe this INT needs the panoply of a full agency.

HUMAN INTELLIGENCE. HUMINT is espionage—spying—and is sometimes referred to as the world's second-oldest profession. It is as old as the Bible. Joshua sent two spies into Canaan before leading the Jewish people across the Jordan River. Spying is what most people think about when they hear the word "intelligence," whether they conjure up famous spies from history such as Nathan Hale or Mata Hari (both failures) or the many fictional spies such as James Bond. In the United States HUMINT is largely the responsibility of the CIA, through its Directorate of Operations (DO). DIA also has a HUMINT capability with the Defense HUMINT Service (DHS).

HUMINT largely involves sending agents to foreign countries, where they attempt to recruit foreign nationals to spy. Agents must identify individuals who have access to the information that we may desire; gain their confidence and assess their weaknesses and susceptibility to being recruited; and make a "pitch" to them, suggesting a relationship. Sources may accept a pitch for a variety of reasons: money, disaffection with their own government, blackmail, or thrills. Once the pitch has been accepted, the agent must meet with his or her sources regularly to receive information, holding meetings in a manner and in places that will reduce the risk of being caught and then transmitting the information back home.

Diplomatic reporting is a type of HUMINT, although it tends to receive less credibility in some circles because of its overt nature. After all, the foreign government official knows, when speaking to a diplomat, that his or her remarks are going to be cabled to that diplomat's capital. As will be discussed below, an espionage source is likely to be thinking the same thing. Nonetheless, some people prefer more traditional HUMINT, even if the source's reliability remains uncertain, rather than diplomatic reporting.

In addition to gaining the skills required for this activity, agents have to maintain their "cover stories"—the overt lives that give them a plausible reason for being in that foreign nation. There are two types of "cover": official and nonofficial. Agents with official cover hold another government job, usually posted out of the embassy. Official cover makes it easier for the agent to maintain contact with his or her superiors but raises the risk of being suspected as an agent. Nonofficial cover (called NOC—pronounced "knock") avoids any overt connection between the agent and his or her government but can make it more difficult to keep in contact. NOCs need a full-time job that explains their presence; they cannot make contact with superiors or colleagues overtly. For the CIA, at least, there are some limits on the jobs that NOCs can hold. Clergy and Peace Corps volunteers are both off limits. Journalism is an ideal cover for a NOC, as journalists have a plausible reason for being in a foreign country, for seeking out officials and asking questions. However, professional journalists have long protested any such use of cover, arguing that if one spy posing as a journalist were to be unmasked, then all journalists would be suspect and perhaps in danger. Proponents counter that journalism is a profession like any other and should be available for use. All told, the use of NOCs is more complex than is official cover for spies.

Some HUMINT sources volunteer. They are called "walk-ins." Colonel Oleg Penkvosky, Aldrich Ames, and Robert Hanssen were all walk-ins. Walk-ins raise a host of other issues: Why have they volunteered? Do they really have access to valuable intelligence? Are they real volunteers or a means of entrapment—called "dangles." Dangles can be used for a variety of purposes, including identifying hostile intelligence personnel or gaining insights into the intelligence requirements or methods of a hostile service. According to press accounts reporting on the post-Hanssen investigation led by former Director of the FBI and DCI Judge William Webster, the Soviet Union suspected that Hanssen was a dangle and protested to the United States about this provocation, which the United States denied but, unfortunately, did not follow up.

In addition to recruiting foreign nationals, HUMINT agents may undertake more direct spying, such as stealing documents or planting sensors. Some of their information may come through direct observation of activity. Thus, HUMINT involves more than just espionage.

An important adjunct to one's own HUMINT capabilities are those of allied or friendly services. Known as foreign liaison relationships, they offer several important advantages. First, the friendly service will have greater familiarity with its own region. Second, its government may maintain a different pattern of relations with other states, more friendly in some cases or even having diplomatic relations where one's own government does not. These HUMINT-to-HUMINT relationships are somewhat formal in nature and tend to be symbiotic. They also entail risks, as one can never be entirely sure of the liaison partner's security procedures. Thus, there will be different degrees of liaison, depending on past experience, shared needs, the sense of security engendered, the depth and value of the intelligence being shared, and so forth. It is also important to remember that some liaison relationships may be with intelligence services that do not have the same standards in terms of operational limits, acceptable activities, and other criteria. A choice will therefore have to be made between the value of the information being sought or exchanged and the larger question of the propriety of a relationship with this service. Nevertheless, liaison is a very important means of increasing the breadth and depth of available HUMINT.

It is worth noting that foreign intelligence liaison is carried out on an agency-by-agency basis rather than by the intelligence community as a whole. CIA, DIA, and NSA, for example, create and conduct their own liaison relationships, which does raise questions about the possible need for better coordination to avoid duplication. Thus, the stovepipes problem carries over into foreign liaison.

In the war against terrorism, several nations have apparently offered intelligence support to the United States, including some whose services may also be considered occasionally hostile. These types of liaison relationships call for extra caution regarding intelligence sharing, and there may be lingering questions about the depth and detail of the intelligence received. On the other hand, exchanging useful intelligence is also a good way for nations to build confidence in one another.

Espionage provides a very small part of the intelligence that is collected. IMINT and SIGINT produce a greater volume of intelligence. But HUMINT, like SIGINT, has the major advantage of affording access to what is being said, planned, and thought. Moreover, clandestine human access to another government also may offer opportunities to influence that government by feeding it false or deceptive information. For intelligence targets where the technical infrastructure may be irrelevant as a fruitful target—such as terrorism, narcotics, or international crime, where the "signature" of activities is rather small—HUMINT may be the only available source.

HUMINT also has disadvantages. First, it cannot be done remotely, as is the case with various types of technical collection. It requires proximity and access and therefore must contend with the counterintelligence capabilities of the other side. It is also far riskier, as it jeopardizes individuals, and, if they are caught, could have political ramifications that are less likely to occur with technical collectors.

HUMINT is far less expensive than the various technical collectors, although it still involves costs for training, special equipment, and the accoutrements spies need to build successful cover stories.

Like all the other collection INTs, HUMINT is susceptible to deception. Some critics argue that it is the most susceptible to deception. The "bona fides" of human sources will always be subject to question initially and, in some cases, may never be wholly resolved. Many questions will arise and linger. Why is this person offering to pass information—ideology, money, vengeance? Of course, he or she will claim to have good access to valuable information, but how good is it? Is it consistent, or is this a single event? How good is the information? Is this person a "dangle," offered as a means of passing information that the other side wants to have passed—either because it is false or because it will have a specific effect? Is this person a double agent who will be collecting information on your HUMINT techniques and capabilities even as he or she passes information to you?

HUMINT agents must walk a fine line between prudent caution and the possibility that too much caution will lead them to deter or reject a promising HUMINT source. For example, the United States initially rejected the services of Col. Oleg Penkovsky, who then turned to the British, who accepted him. Only later did the United States take on this valuable spy. Deception is particularly difficult to deal with, because people naturally are reluctant to accept the fact that they are being deceived. On the other hand, people might slip into a position where they trust no one, which can result in turning away sources who might have been very valuable.

HUMINT's unique sources and methods raise another issue. These sources are considered to be extremely fragile, since good human penetrations take so long to develop and risk the lives of the case officers, their sources, and perhaps even the sources' families. Therefore, the intelligence analysts who receive HUMINT reports may not be told the details of the source or sources. Analysts are not informed, for example, that "this report comes from a first secretary in the Fredonian Foreign Ministry." Instead, the report will include information on the access of the source, the past reliability of the source, or variations on this concept. Sometimes several sources may be blended together in a single report. Although the masking of HUMINT sources promotes their preservation, it may have the unintended effect of devaluing the reports for analysts, who may not fully appreciate the value of the source and the information.

HUMINT also puts one in contact—and perhaps into relationships— with unsavory individuals such as terrorists and narco traffickers. If one is going to penetrate such groups or develop other types of relationships with them, some may become recipients of money or other forms of payment. As will be discussed in chap. 13, these types of relationships raise moral and ethical issues for some people. In the aftermath of the September 2001 attacks, special attention was given to the so-called Deutch rules about HUMINT recruitment. In 1995, DCI John Deutch (1995–1997) ordered a "scrub" of all HUMINT assets, with a particular focus on persons who in the past had been involved in serious criminal activity or human-rights violations. This scrub was the result of revelations that some past CIA assets in Guatemala had violated human rights, including those of some Americans resident in that country. New rules were promulgated, requiring headquarters approval of any such recruitments in the future. After the terrorist attacks, these rules were widely criticized, with many people asserting that they had limited the CIA's ability to penetrate terrorist groups. CIA officials maintained that no valuable relationship was ever turned down because of the Deutch rules. Critics countered, however, that the very existence of the rules bred timidity in the DO, as officers would be more cautious about whom they recruited, running the risk of losing useful sources, rather than have these recruitments be scrutinized on the basis of changing standards. By the end of 2001, the Deutch rules were no longer considered an operational factor.

Writing in the aftermath of the September 2001 attacks, Deutch defended his rules, arguing that they allowed DO officers to recruit with clear guidelines and focused on acquiring high-quality agents.

In the United States, constant tension exists between HUMINT and the other collection disciplines. The dominance of technical collection periodically gives rise to calls for a greater emphasis on HUMINT. So-called intelligence failures, such as the fall of the shah of Iran in 1979, the unexpected Indian nuclear tests in 1998, and the 2001 terrorist attacks have led to demands for more HUMINT.

Again, there is no "right balance" between HUMINT and the other collection disciplines. Indeed, such an idea runs counter to the concept of an all-source intelligence process that seeks to apply as many collection disciplines as possible to a given intelligence need. But not every collection INT will make an equal or even similar contribution to every issue. Clearly, it is better to have a collection system that is strong and flexible and can be modulated to the intelligence requirement at hand than to have one that swings between apparently opposed fashions of technical and human collection.

As with all other INTs, it is difficult, if not impossible, to put an ultimate value on HUMINT. Interestingly, it is one of the two most democratic INTs (along with OSINT), as any nation or group can conduct HUMINT. Clearly, it would be preferable to have good HUMINT access for key issues. But cases like Ames and Hanssen raise questions about HUMINT's value. These two spies provided the Soviet Union and Russia with invaluable information, largely about U.S. spy penetrations in that country but also, in the case of Hanssen, about technical collection operations and capabilities. When their activities are added to other espionage revelations—such as Kampiles (IMINT), the Walkers (SIGINT), and Pelton (SIGINT)—the Soviet Union/Russia gained substantial knowledge about U.S. collection capabilities. Yet the Soviet Union lost the cold war and ceased to exist as a state. One could argue, on the one hand, that all of this HUMINT ultimately proved to be of no value, thus raising questions about HUMINT's utility. On the other hand, one could argue that no amount of HUMINT—or any other INT—can save a state that has profound internal problems.

One of the major concerns in HUMINT is the possibility that a spy will be caught and unmasked, with attendant personal risk for the spy and political embarrassment for the state that sent him. Interestingly, even a successful long-term espionage penetration can prove costly. The case of Gunter Guillaume is illustrative. Guillaume was an East German spy who was able to penetrate the West German government, rising to a senior position in the office of Chancellor Willy Brandt. When Guillaume's espionage was uncovered in 1974, Brandt was forced to resign. Many people believed that the political cost of the operation exceeded any gains in intelligence. Brandt's *Ostpolitik*—or favorable policy toward East Germany—was never resumed by his successors, at great cost to East Germany, perhaps even greater than any intelligence that Guillaume produced over the years. Similarly, the fate of Jonathan Pollard (see chap. 15 for more details), who passed classified intelligence to Israel, became a constant irritant in U.S.-Israeli relations, again outweighing the value of the intelligence that Pollard provided.

For the United States, at least, it remains important to view HUMINT as part of a larger collection strategy rather than as the single INT that will meet our most important intelligence needs. Indeed, to place that sort of expectation on any one INT is bound to set it up for disappointment at best and perhaps even failure.

OPEN-SOURCE INTELLIGENCE. To some, OSINT may seem like a contradiction in terms. How can information that is openly available be considered intelligence? This question reflects the misconception discussed in chapter 1 that intelligence must inevitably be about secrets. Much of it is, but not to the exclusion of openly available information. As noted above, even during the height of the cold war, according to one senior intelligence official, at least 20 percent of the intelligence about the Soviet Union came from open sources.

OSINT includes a wide variety of information and sources:

- Media: newspapers, magazines, radio, television, and computer-based information
- Public data: government reports, official data such as budgets and demographics, hearings, legislative debates, press conferences, speeches
- Professional and academic: conferences, symposia, professional associations, academic papers, and experts

One of the hallmarks of the post–cold war world is the increased availability of OSINT. The ratio of open source to classified intelligence on Russia has more than reversed from its 20:80 ratio during the cold war. The number of closed societies and "denied areas" has decreased dramatically. Some of the former Warsaw Pact states are now NATO allies. This does not mean that classified collection disciplines are no longer needed, but that the areas in which OSINT is available have expanded.

The major advantage of OSINT is its accessibility, although it still requires collection. OSINT needs less processing and exploitation than the technical INTs or HUMINT, but it still requires some P&E. Given the diversity of OSINT, it may be more difficult to manipulate for the purpose of deception than are other INTs. OSINT is also useful for helping put the secret information into a wider context, which can be extremely valuable.

The main disadvantage of OSINT is its volume. In many ways, it represents the worst "wheat and chaff" problem. Some argue that the so-called information revolution has made OSINT more difficult without a corresponding increase in usable intelligence. Computers have increased the ability to manipulate information; however, the amount of derived intelligence has not increased apace.

One interesting OSINT phenomenon is "echo." This is the effect of a single media story being picked up and repeated by other media sources until the story takes on a much larger life of its own, appearing more important than it actually is. Echo is difficult to deal with unless one is aware of the original story and can therefore knowingly discount its effect.

Popular misconceptions about OSINT persist, even within the intelligence community. OSINT is not free. Buying print media costs the intelligence community money, as do various other services that are useful— if not essential—in helping analysts manage, sort, and sift large amounts of data more efficiently. Another misconception is that the Internet is the main fount of OSINT. Experienced intelligence practitioners have discovered that the Internet—meaning searches among various sites—yields no more than 3 to 5 percent of the total OSINT "take."

Despite the fact that OSINT has always been used, it remains undervalued by significant segments of the intelligence community. This attitude derives from the fact that the intelligence community was created to discover secrets. If OSINT could largely meet the United States' national security needs, the intelligence community would look very different. Some intelligence professionals have mistakenly equated the degree of difficulty involved in obtaining information with its ultimate value to analysts and policymakers. Contributing to this pervasive bias is the fact that OSINT has always been handled differently by the intelligence community. All of the other INTs have dedicated collectors, processors, and exploiters.

PIZZINT: Some Intelligence Humor

In addition to IMINT, SIGINT, HUMINT, OSINT, and MASINT, intelligence officers, in their lighter moments, speak of some other INTs. One of the most famous is PIZZINT—pizza intelligence. This refers to the belief that Soviet officials based in Washington would keep watch for large numbers of pizza delivery trucks going late in the evening to the CIA, the White House, the Defense Department, and the State Department as an indication that a crisis was brewing somewhere. The notion was that after seeing many trucks making deliveries, they would hurry back to the Soviet embassy to alert Moscow that something must be going on somewhere.

Some other INTs that intelligence officers talk about with tongue firmly in cheek are:

LAVINT: I heard it in the men's room (lavatory intelligence).

RUMINT: rumor.

REVINT: revelation intelligence.

DIVINT: divine intelligence.

With the exception of the Foreign Broadcast Information Service (FBIS), which monitors foreign media broadcasts, OSINT does not have dedicated collectors, processors, and exploiters. Instead, analysts are largely expected to act as their own OSINT collectors, a concept that other INTs would consider ludicrous. This is unfortunate, since OSINT is the perfect place to start any intelligence collection. By first determining what material is available from open sources, intelligence managers could focus their clandestine collectors on those issues where such means were really needed. Properly used, OSINT could be a very good intelligence collection resource manager.

The Kosovo air war produced a new and interesting OSINT stream. Individuals in Serbia who said they were opposed to the Milosevic government sent e-mails to intelligence firms in the United States, giving reports on the relative success of NATO air strikes, the mood in Belgrade, and related matters. Dealing with such reports is problematic as there is no assured means of authenticating them. The most reliable reports would come from known and trusted sources, probably based on past reporting. Establishing an independent capability to accomplish this may not be possible during hostilities. Some sources may prove to be reliable over time. But one has to be on guard for the possibility, if not the likelihood, of at least some level of disinformation from the targeted regime. In the case of Kosovo, at least some of the sources apparently proved to be reliable, thus establishing a new OSINT stream.

TABLE 5-1 A Comparison of the Collection Disciplines

INT	Advantages	Disadvantages
IMINT	Graphic and compelling	Perhaps overly graphic and compelling
	Use seems familiar to policy-makers	Still requires interpretation
	Ready availability of some targets—particularly military exercises	Literally a "snapshot" of a moment in time; very static
	Can be done remotely	Subject to problems of weather, spoofing
		Expensive
SIGINT	Offers insights into plans, intentions	Signals may be encrypted or encoded—requiring them to be "broken"
	Voluminous material	Voluminous material
	Military targets tend to communicate in regular patterns	May encounter communications silence, use of secure lines, spoofing via phony traffic
	Can be done remotely	Expensive
HUMINT	Offers insights into plans, intentions	Riskier in terms of lives, political fallout
	Relatively inexpensive	Requires more time to acquire and validate sources
		Problems of dangles, false feeds, double agents
MASINT	Extremely useful for issues such as proliferation	Expensive
	Can be done remotely	Little understood by most users
		Requires a great deal of processing and exploitation
OSINT	More readily available	Voluminous
	Extremely useful as a place to start all collection	Less likely to offer insights available from clandestine INTs

COLLECTION—CONCLUSION

Each collection discipline offers unique advantages that are well-suited to some types of intelligence requirements but brings with it certain disadvantages as well (see Table 5-1). By deploying a broad and varied array of collection techniques, the United States derives two advantages: it is able to exploit the advantages of each type of INT, which, ideally, will compensate for the shortcomings of the others; it is able to apply more than one collection INT to an issue, which enhances the likelihood of meeting the collection requirements for that issue. However, the intelligence community cannot provide answers to every question that is asked, nor does it have the capability to meet all possible requirements at any given time. The collection system is simultaneously powerful and limited.

The cost of collection was rarely an issue during the cold war because of the broad political agreement on the need to stay informed about the Soviet threat. In the post–cold war world, prior to the September 2001 attacks, the absence of any overwhelming strategic threat made the cost of collection systems more difficult to justify; this led some people to question whether there was a need for the level of collection capability that the United States maintained during the cold war. Prior to the terrorist attacks, the United States experienced greatly diminished threats to its national security, but faced ongoing concerns that are more diverse and diffuse than was the largely unitary Soviet problem, raising new collection challenges. It is important to keep in mind the fact that, as horrific as the September 2001 attacks were, terrorism still does not pose the same potentially overwhelming threat to the existence of the United States as did a hostile nuclear-armed Soviet missile force. Ultimately, there is no yardstick for measuring national security problems against a collection array in order to determine how much collection is enough. It is likely that, for the foreseeable future, collection requirements will continue to outrun collection capabilities.

KEY TERMS

all-source intelligence
anti-satellite weapon (ASAT)
automatic change extraction
collection disciplines
communications intelligence
    (COMINT)
content analysis
cryptographers
dangle

deception
denial
denied areas
denied targets
echo
electronic intelligence (ELINT)
encryption
espionage
geosynchronous orbit

human intelligence (HUMINT)
imagery intelligence (IMINT)
indications and warning
INTs
key-word search
measurement and signatures
   intelligence (MASINT)
negation search
noise versus signals
nonofficial cover (NOC)
official cover
open-source intelligence (OSINT)
photo intelligence (PHOTINT)

pitch
resolution
shutter control
signals intelligence (SIGINT)
sources and methods
spies
sun-synchronous orbit
telemetry intelligence (TELINT)
traffic analysis
UAVs (unmanned aerial vehicles)
walk-in
wheat versus chaff

FURTHER READINGS

For ease of use, these readings are grouped by activity. Although there are numerous books by spies and about spying, very few of them have good discussions of the craft of espionage and the role it plays, as opposed to its supposed derring-do aspects.

General Sources on Collection

Burrows, William. *Deep Black: Space Espionage and National Security.* New York: Random House, 1986.
Wohlstetter, Roberta. *Pearl Harbor: Warning and Decision.* Stanford: Stanford University Press, 1962.

Espionage

Burgstaller, Eugen F. "Human Collection Requirements in the 1980's." In *Intelligence Requirements for the 1980's: Clandestine Collection.* Ed. Roy F. Godson. Washington, D.C.: National Strategy Information Center, 1982.
Hitz, Frederick P. "The Future of American Espionage." *International Journal of Intelligence and Counterintelligence* 13 (spring 2000): 1–20.
Hulnick, Arthur S. "Intelligence Cooperation in the Post–Cold War Era: A New Game Plan?" *International Journal of Intelligence and Counterintelligence* 5 (winter 1991–1992): 455–465.
Phillips, David Atlee. *Careers in Secret Operations: How to Be a Federal Intelligence Officer.* Frederick, Md.: Stone Trail Press, 1984.
Wirtz, James J. "Constraints on Intelligence Collaboration: The Domestic Dimension." *International Journal of Intelligence and Counterintelligence* 6 (spring 1993): 85–89.

Imagery

Baker, John C., Kevin O'Connell, and Ray A. Williamson, eds. *Commercial Observation Satellites: At the Leading Edge of Transparency.* Washington, D.C.: Rand Corporation, 2001.
Brugioni, Dino A. "The Art and Science of Photo Reconnaissance." *Scientific American* (March 1996): 78–85.
———. *Eyeball to Eyeball: The Inside Story of the Cuban Missile Crisis.* Ed. Robert F. McCort. New York: Random House, 1990.

————. *From Balloons to Blackbirds: Reconnaissance, Surveillance, and Imagery Intelligence—How It Evolved.* McLean, Va.: Association of Former Intelligence Officers, 1993.

Best, Richard A., Jr. *Airborne Intelligence, Surveillance, and Reconnaissance (ISR): The U-2 Aircraft and Global Hawk UAV Programs.* Washington, D.C.: Congressional Research Service, Library of Congress, 2000.

Central Intelligence Agency. *CORONA: America's First Satellite Program.* Ed. Kevin C. Ruffner. Washington, D.C.: CIA, 1995.

Day, Dwayne A., et al., eds. *Eye in the Sky: The Story of the Corona Spy Satellites.* Washington, D.C.: Smithsonian Institution Press, 1998.

Lindgren, David T. *Imagery Analysis in the Cold War.* Annapolis: U. S. Naval Institute Press, 2000.

Peebles, Christopher. *The Corona Project: America's First Spy Satellite.* Annapolis: U.S. Naval Institute Press, 1997.

Richelson, Jeffrey T. *America's Secret Eyes in Space: The U.S. Keyhole Spy Satellite Program.* New York: Harper and Row, 1990.

————. "High Flyin' Spies." *Bulletin of the Atomic Scientists* 52 (September–October 1996): 48–54.

Shulman, Seth. "Code Name CORONA." *Technology Review* 99 (October 1996): 23–25, 28–32.

SPOT Image Corporation. "Satellite Imagery: An Objective Guide." Reston, Va.: SPOT, 1998.

Open-Source Intelligence

Lowenthal, Mark M. "Open Source Intelligence: New Myths, New Realities." *Defense Daily News,* November 1998. [http://www.defensedaily.com/reports; http://www.defensedaily.com/reports/osintmyths.htm]

————. "OSINT: The State of the Art, the Artless State." *Studies in Intelligence* (fall 2001): 61–66.

Satellites

Klass, Philip. *Secret Sentries in Space.* New York: Random House, 1971.

U.S. National Commission for the Review of the National Reconnaissance Office. *Report: The National Commission for the Review of the National Reconnaissance Office.* Washington, D.C.: Government Printing Office, November 14, 2000. (Also available at http://www.nrocommission.com)

Secrecy

Moynihan, Daniel Patrick. *Secrecy: The American Experience.* New Haven: Yale University Press, 1998.

Secrecy. Report of the Commission on Protecting and Reducing Government Secrecy, Washington, D.C., 1997.

Signals Intelligence

Aid, Matthew M., and Cees Wiebes. *Secrets of Signals Intelligence During the Cold War and Beyond.* Portland, Ore: Frank Cass, 2001.

Bamford, James. *Body of Secret: Anatomy of the Ultra-Secret National Security Agency—From the Cold War Through the Dawn of a New Century.* New York: Doubleday, 2001.

————. *The Puzzle Palace: A Report on America's Most Secret Agency.* Boston: Viking, 1982.

Brownell, George A. *The Origin and Development of the National Security Agency.* Laguna Hills, Calif.: Aegean Park Press, 1981.

Kahn, David. *The Codebreakers.* Rev. ed. New York: Scribner, 1996.

National Security Agency and Central Intelligence Agency. *VENONA: Soviet Espionage and the American Response, 1939–1957.* Ed. Robert Louis Benson and Michael Warner. Washington, D.C.: NSA and CIA, 1996.

Warner, Michael, and Robert Louis Benson. "Venona and Beyond: Thoughts on Work Undone." *Intelligence and National Security* 12 (July 1996): 1–13.

Chapter 6

Analysis

Despite all the attention lavished on the operational side of intelligence (collection and covert action), analysis is the mainstay of the process, providing civil and military policymakers with information directly related to the issues they face and the decisions they have to make. As the discussion of dissemination in chapter 4 indicated, intelligence products do not arrive once or twice a day, but in a steady stream throughout the day. Certain documents, particularly the daily intelligence products, are received first thing in the morning, but other intelligence reports can be delivered when they are ready or may be held for delivery at a specific time.

Although not all intelligence practitioners will agree, the ongoing production and delivery of intelligence can have a numbing effect on policymakers. Intelligence analysis can become part of the daily flood of information—intelligence products, commercially provided news, reports from policy offices embassies, and military commands, and so on. One of the challenges for intelligence is to make itself stand out from this steady stream.

This goal can be achieved in two ways. One is to emphasize the unique nature of the intelligence sources. But this is not the preferred choice of intelligence officials, who believe that they are much more than just conduits for their sources and that their analysis adds value to the intelligence they collect. The other way for intelligence to achieve prominence is to produce analysis that stands out on its own merits by adding value. The value added includes the timeliness of intelligence products, the ability of the community to tailor products to specific policymakers' needs, and the objectivity of the analysis. But the fact that value-added intelligence is discussed as often as it is within the intelligence community suggests that this goal is not achieved as often as desired.

MAJOR THEMES

It is very difficult to prescribe how to produce value-added intelligence—or to measure the frequency with which it is produced—because intelligence officers and their policy clients do not agree on what adds value. Indeed, for policy clients, value added is a very idiosyncratic and personal attribute. Therefore, this chapter discusses several issues that have been problems for intelligence analysis for many years. Analysis is much more than sitting down with the collected material, sifting and sorting it, and coming up with a brilliant piece of prose that makes sense of it all. The themes addressed here reflect major decisions that have to be made in the analytical process and areas of controversy that have proved to be resilient or recurrent.

FORMAL REQUIREMENTS—DO THEY MATTER? In the ideal intelligence-process model, policymakers give some thought to their main requirements and then communicate them to the intelligence managers. This formal process often does not happen, leaving these managers to make educated guesses, many of which are either obvious or well grounded.

Some people argue that this less formal process is, in reality, much better than the ideal one, since most of the requirements are fairly well known and do not need to be defined through a formal process. For example, most people, if asked to name the main U.S. intelligence priorities during the cold war, would have mentioned a number of Soviet-related issues. Even in the less clear post–cold war period prior to the September 2001 attacks, a similar exercise would have yielded such obvious answers as narcotics, terrorism, proliferation, Russia's reform and stability, and the various regional trouble spots of the moment, such as the Balkans, the Middle East, and North Korea. Interestingly, this list parallels the U.S. intelligence priorities as stated in the Clinton administration's Presidential Decision Directive 35. After September 2001, terrorism became the primary but not the sole issue.

The real importance of the requirements process may lie in giving the intelligence community some sense of priority among the requirements rather than defining the issues that need coverage. Assigning priorities is especially important and difficult in the absence of a single overwhelming issue, as was the case from roughly 1991 (the end of the Soviet Union) until 2001. The real problem is that when several issues are considered to be of roughly equal importance, no single one of them truly has priority.

CURRENT VERSUS LONG-TERM INTELLIGENCE. This is one of the perennial analytical issues. Current intelligence—reports and analysis on issues that may not extend more than a week or two into the future—is the mainstay of the intelligence community, the product most often requested and seen by policymakers. In many respects, current intelligence "pays the rent" for the intelligence community.

But many intelligence analysts are frustrated by the emphasis on current intelligence. Having developed expertise in an area and analytical skills, they wish to write longer-range analyses that look beyond current demands. However, few policymakers are likely to read papers with longer horizons—not owing to lack of interest but rather to lack of time and the inability to pull away, even briefly, from the current pressing issues. Thus, a conflict arises between what the policymakers need to read and what many analysts wish to produce.

A middle ground exists by virtue of the fact that the intelligence community does not make a stark choice between one type of product and another. In the course of any given day, a range of analysis is produced. But the fact remains that the current intelligence products predominate in terms of resources and the way policymakers perceive the intelligence community.

CRISES VERSUS THE NORM. One of the ways in which requirements are set is in response to crises. Crisis-driven requirements also represent the ultimate victory of current over long-range intelligence needs.

Given the limited nature of collection and analytical resources, certain issues inevitably receive short shrift or even no attention at all. And just as inevitably, annual requirements planning regularly fails to predict which of the seemingly less important issues will erupt into a crisis at some point during the year. Thus, the planning exercises are to some degree self-fulfilling—or self-denying—prophecies.

Analytical managers must find a way to create or preserve some minimal amount of expertise against the moment when a less important issue erupts and suddenly moves to the top of policymakers' concerns. The intelligence community has only a small collection reserve, no analytical reserve, and a limited capacity to move assets to previously uncovered but now important topics. Assets therefore move from hot topic to hot topic, with other topics receiving little or no coverage.

Despite the problem of defining requirements and the vagaries of international relations, the intelligence community is on the spot when it "misses" an issue—fails to be alert to its eventuality or is unprepared to deal with it when it occurs. In part, the high expectations are deserved, since one of the functions of intelligence is strategic warning. But strategic warning is usually taken to mean advance notice on issues that would pose a threat to national security, not regional crises that might require some level of involvement. Such crises strain the image of the intelligence community as well as its resources, since policymakers in both branches and the media tend to be harsh—sometimes fairly, sometimes not—in their view of "misses."

THE WHEAT VERSUS CHAFF PROBLEM. This problem, already discussed as part of collection, ultimately becomes an analytical issue. Although much that is collected does not get processed and exploited, the amount that does is still formidable. Even in the age of computers, few technical shortcuts have been found to help analysts deal with this problem. The intelligence community has adopted some analytical tools (that is, various software programs to assist in some part of analysis, such as text mining and data mining) and has examined many others, but no major breakthroughs have been made. Thus, to a very large degree, the analysts' daily task of sifting through the incoming intelligence germane to their portfolio remains a grind, whether done electronically or on paper. Sifting is not just a matter of getting through the accumulated imagery, signals, open-source reporting, and other data. It is also the much more important matter of seeing this mass of material in its entirety, of being able to perceive patterns from day to day and reports that are anomalous. To repeat, there are no shortcuts. Sifting requires training and experience. Although some intelligence practitioners think of analysts as the "human in the loop," the analysts' expertise should be an integral part of collection sorting as well.

ANALYST TRAINING. Until very recently, the intelligence community did not spend a significant amount of time on analyst training. This training is most useful in giving incoming analysts a sense of how the larger community works, what is expected of them, and the ethos and rules of the community. No amount of training, however, can obviate the fact that much of what an analyst learns comes through on-the-job training. Analysts arrive with certain skills learned in college or at the graduate level and then are assimilated into their specific intelligence agency or unit. They learn basic processes and requirements, the daily work schedule, and preferred means of expression, all of which vary from agency to agency. They become familiar with the types of intelligence with which they will be working.

The minimum skills for all analysts are knowledge of one or more specific fields, appropriate language skills, and a very basic ability to express themselves in writing. (See box, "Choosing Good Analysts.") But these are basic skills, a foundation upon which better skills must be built. Some of the new skills to be mastered are parochial. Each intelligence agency has its own corporate style that must be learned. More important, analysts must learn to cope with the wheat versus chaff problem and to write as succinctly as possible. These two skills reflect the demands of current intelligence and

---

Choosing Good Analysts

Napoleon reportedly asked new officers on his staff one question: "Are you lucky?" Napoleon understood that luck in battle, although intangible, was a useful attribute.

A senior intelligence official used to ask his subordinates two questions about new analysts they wished to hire: "Do they think interesting thoughts? Do they write well?" This official believed that, with these two talents in hand, all else would follow with training and experience.

---

the fact that policymakers are busy and prefer economies of style. The bureaucratic truism remains that shorter papers will usually best longer papers in the competition for policymakers' attention.

Another important skill that analysts must learn is objectivity. Although intelligence analysts can and often do have strong personal views about the issues they are covering, these have no place in their intelligence products. Analysts will be listened to because of their accumulated expertise, not the forcefulness of their views. Indeed, presenting personal views would cross the line between intelligence and policy. Still, analysts need training to learn how to filter out their views, especially when these run counter to the intelligence at hand or the policies being considered.

A more subtle and very difficult skill to master is cultivating the intelligence consumer without politicizing the intelligence as a means of currying favor.

Finally, there is the question of how far training (or experience) can take a given analyst. Any reasonably intelligent individual with the right skills and education can be taught to be an effective analyst. But the truly gifted analyst—like the truly gifted athlete, musician, or scientist—is inherently better at his or her job by virtue of inborn talents. In all fields, such individuals are rare. They must be nurtured. But the benefits they derive from training are different from those that less gifted analysts derive.

MANAGING ANALYSTS. Managing intelligence analysts presents a number of unique problems. A major concern is developing career tracks. Analysts need time to develop true expertise in their fields, but intellectual stagnation can set in if an analyst is left to cover the same issue for too long. Rotating analysts among assignments quickly helps them avoid stagnation and allows them to learn more than one area. But this career pattern raises the possibility that analysts will never gain real expertise in any one area, becoming instead "generalists." Ideally, managers seek to create some middle ground—providing analysts with assignments that are long enough for them to gain expertise and substantive knowledge while also providing sufficient opportunities to shift assignments and maintain intellectual freshness. Nor is there any specific time frame for assignments; the length depends on the individual analyst, the relative intensity of the current assignment, and on the demands generated by intelligence requirements at the time. More intense jobs tend to argue for somewhat shorter tours to avoid burnout. But these issues also tend to have higher priority, demanding greater expertise and consistency of staffing. Thus, there are again competing needs.

The criteria for promotion are another management issue. As government employees, intelligence analysts are generally assured of promotions up to a level that can be described as "high middle." The criteria for promotion through these grades are not overly rigorous. Ideally, promotions should come as a result of merit, not time served. But what criteria should a manager consider in evaluating an intelligence analyst for merit promotion: accuracy of analysis over the past year, writing skills, increased competence in foreign languages and foreign area knowledge, participation in a specific number of major studies? And how should a manager weigh the various criteria?

The competition is stronger for more senior assignments than for those at the lower level, and the criteria for selection are different. The qualities that first merit promotion—keen analytical abilities—are the ticket to management positions, where responsibilities and pay are greater. Ironically, or perhaps sadly, analytical skills have little to do with, and are little indication of, the ability to carry out managerial duties. But, with few exceptions, management positions have been the only route to senior promotion. The CIA has created a Senior Analytical Service, which allows analysts to reach senior ranks solely on the basis of their analytical capabilities.

ANALYSTS' MIND-SETS. Analysts, as a group, exhibit a set of behaviors that can affect their work. Obviously, not all analysts exhibit each of these characteristics all of the time, and some analysts may never display any of them. Still, many of these traits are common among this population.

One of the most frequent flaws of analysts is mirror imaging, which assumes that other leaders, states, and groups share motivations or goals similar to those most familiar to the analyst. (See box, "Mirror Imaging: Political Analysis.") "They're just like us" is the quintessential expression of this view. The prevalence of mirror imaging is not difficult to understand. We learn, from an early age, to expect certain behavior of others.

Mirror Imaging: Political Analysis

Here are two examples of how mirror imaging can affect analysis. During the cold war, some Kremlinologists and Sovietologists would talk about Soviet "hawks" and "doves" or try to assess which Soviet leaders belonged to which group. No empirical evidence existed to suggest that there were Soviet hawks and doves. Instead, the fact that the U.S. political spectrum included hawks and doves led to the facile assumption that the Soviet system must have them as well.

Second, during the late 1980s some analysts working on Iran spoke of Iranian "extremists" and "moderates." When pressed by skeptical peers as to their evidence for the existence of "moderates," the analysts argued: if there are extremists, there must be moderates. Again, they were reflecting other political systems they knew, as well as making a faulty assumption. Some of their colleagues argued that Iranian politics might comprise "extremists" and "ultra extremists."

The golden rule is based on this concept of reciprocal motives and behavior. Unfortunately, as an analytical tool, mirror imaging fails to take into account such matters as differences of motivation, perception, or action based on national differences, subtle differences of circumstance, different rationales, and the absence of any rationale.

As noted previously, a classic example of mirror imaging was the U.S. analysis of Japan's likely actions in 1941. Although many U.S. analysts and policymakers expected Japan to attack somewhere, they ruled out a direct attack on the United States largely because, if put in a similar position, they would not have attacked a nation so much more powerful in terms of war-making potential. But in Tokyo the steady decline in the Japanese potential dictated a different answer—a direct attack on the most formidable foe.

To avoid mirror imaging, managers must train analysts to recognize it when it intrudes in their work and must establish a higher-level review process that is alert to this tendency.

Clientism is a flaw that occurs when analysts become so immersed in their subjects—usually after working on an issue for too long—that they lose their ability to view issues with the necessary criticality. (In the State Department this phenomenon is usually called "clientitis," which can be defined as "an inflammation of the client," although it is used when referring to someone who has "gone native" in his or her thinking.) Analysts can spend time apologizing for the actions of the nations they cover rather than analyzing them. The same safeguards that analysts and their managers put in place to avoid mirror imaging are required to avoid clientism.

"ON THE GROUND KNOWLEDGE." Analysts have varying degrees of direct knowledge about the nations on which they write. During the cold war, U.S. analysts had difficulty spending significant amounts of time in the Soviet Union or its satellites, nor were they able to travel widely in those nations. Similarly, intelligence analysts may have less contact with the senior foreign officials about whom they write than do the U.S. officials who must deal with these foreigners. Their distance from the subjects being analyzed can occasionally be costly to analysts, in terms of how their policy consumers view the intelligence they receive. Indeed, some policy clients may have more "in-country" experience or direct contact with foreign leaders than do the intelligence analysts.

This problem can be compounded when dealing with terrorists, with whom there are few opportunities for direct or prolonged contact and perhaps little shared basis of rationality by which to gauge their motives or likely next actions.

Analysts, like everyone else, are proud of their accomplishments. Once they have mastered a body of knowledge, they may look for opportunities—no matter how inappropriate—to display that knowledge in detail. Analysts can have difficulty limiting their writing to those facts and analyses that may be necessary for a specific consumer need. The analyst may want the consumer to have a greater appreciation for where the issues being discussed fit in some wider pattern; the analyst may want to share (or show off) some larger part of his or her knowledge. Unfortunately—and perhaps too frequently—the policy client wants to know "only about the miracles, and not the lives of all the saints who made them happen." Analysts require training, maturity, and supervision to cure this behavior. Some analysts get the message sooner than others; some never get it at all and produce analysis that requires greater editing to pare it down to the essential message, which can cause resentment on the part of the edited analyst. On the other hand, the intelligence provider may lose the attention of the policy client if he or she gives too much material, large portions of which do not seem entirely relevant to the policymaker's immediate needs.

Just as analysts want to show the depth of their knowledge, so, too, they want to be perceived as experienced—perhaps far beyond what is true. Again, this is a common human failing. Professionals in almost any field, when surrounded by peers and facing a situation that is new to them but not to the others, will be tempted to assert their familiarity, whether genuine or not. Given the choice between appearing jaded ("been there, done that") and naïve ("Wow! I've never seen that before!"),

Jaded versus Naïve—A Cautionary Example

In April 1986 the operators of the Chernobyl nuclear reactor in the Soviet Union caused an explosion by running an unauthorized experiment on a Sunday evening. On Monday afternoon, Sweden reported, with some concern, higher than normal radioactive traces in their air monitors, which they had placed in many cities.

In the United States an intelligence manager asked one of his senior analysts what he made of the Swedish complaints. The analyst downplayed them, saying the Swedes were always concerned about their air and often made such complaints for the smallest amounts of radiation. The issue was forgotten and everyone went home at a decent hour. The next day the truth became known, and analysts spent a frantic day catching up with the facts at Chernobyl.

How could this have been handled differently? At a minimum, inquiries could have been made in Sweden regarding the types of radiation. The answer would have identified the source as a reactor rather than a weapon. The prevailing winds over Sweden could have been surveyed to identify the source. But the jaded approach precluded all of this.

Some years later the intelligence manager had an opportunity to meet with some of his Swedish counterparts. They had analyzed the radiation and checked the winds and concluded, initially, that a reactor at nearby Ignalina, across the Baltic Sea in Soviet territory, was leaking. They could not know, initially, that the leak was from a reactor much farther away, but they were much closer to the truth than were U.S. intelligence officials.

analysts usually choose the former. (*See box, "Jaded versus Naïve—A Cautionary Example."*) The risk of being caught seems small enough, and it is preferable to being put down by someone else who displays greater experience ("The same thing happened in Bessarabia in 1958. I thought you knew that.").

Unfortunately, the jaded approach carries costs. First, it represents intellectual dishonesty, something all analysts should avoid. Second, it proceeds from the false assumption that each incident is much like others, which may be true at some superficial level but may be false at very fundamental levels. Finally, being jaded closes the analyst's thinking, regardless of his or her level of experience, to the possibility that an incident or issue may be entirely new, requiring wholly new types of analysis.

Credibility is one of the most highly prized possessions of analysts. Although they recognize that it is not possible to be correct all of the time, they are concerned that policymakers are holding them accountable to some perhaps impossible standard. Their concern about credibility—which is largely faith and trust in the integrity of the intelligence process and in the ability of the analysts whose product is at hand—can lead them to downplay or perhaps mask sudden shifts in analyses or conclusions. For example, let us say that intelligence analysis has long shown a production rate of fifteen missiles a year in a hostile state. One year, because of improved collection and new methodologies, the estimated production rate (which is still just an estimate) goes to forty-five missiles per year. Policymakers may view this increase—on the order of 300 percent—with alarm. Rather than present the new number with an explanation as to how it was derived, an analyst might be tempted to soften the blow. Perhaps a brief memo could be issued, suggesting changes in production. Then a second memo, saying that the rate is more likely twenty to twenty-five missiles per year, and so on, until the policymaker sees a more acceptable analytical progression to the new number rather than a sudden spike upward. Of course, this will take time and it is intellectually dishonest.

Intelligence products that are written on a recurring basis—such as certain types of national intelligence estimates—may be more susceptible than other products to this type of behavior, since they establish benchmarks that can be reviewed more easily than, say, a memo that is not likely to be remembered unless the issue is extremely important and the shift is dramatic.

Although policymakers have taken retribution on analysts for sudden shifts in estimates, more often than not the fear in the minds of analysts is greater than the likelihood of a loss of credibility. Much will depend on the prior nature of the relationship between the analyst and the policymaker, the latter's appreciation for the nature of the intelligence problem, and the intelligence community's past record. If several revisions have been made in the recent past, there is reason to suspect a problem. If revision is an isolated phenomenon, it is less problematic. The nature of the issue, and its importance to the policymaker and the nation, will also matter. (See box, "Soviet Defense Spending.")

Very few intelligence products are written by just one analyst and then sent along to the policy client. Most have peer reviews and managerial reviews and probably the input of analysts from other offices or agencies. This is especially true for the intelligence product that several Western agencies call "estimates." The participation of these other analysts and agencies adds a further dimension to the analytical process—bureaucratics, which brings with it various types of behaviors and strategies.

More likely than not, several agencies will have strongly held and diametrically opposed views on key issues within an estimate. How should these be dealt with? The U.S. system in both intelligence and policymaking is consensual. No votes are taken; no lone wolves are cast out or beaten to the ground. Everyone must find some way to agree. But if

---

Soviet Defense Spending

The level of Soviet defense spending—usually expressed as a percentage of gross national product (GNP)—was a key intelligence issue during the cold war.

At the end of the Ford administration (1974–1977), intelligence estimates of the percentage of Soviet GNP going to defense rose from a range of 6–7 percent to 13–14 percent, largely because of new data, new modeling techniques, and other factors unrelated to Soviet output. This revision was discomforting to the incoming Carter administration. In his inaugural address, President Carter signaled that he did not want to be constantly concerned with the Soviet issue, that he had other foreign policy issues to pursue. A more heavily armed Soviet Union was not good news.

Carter prided himself on his analytical capabilities. When faced with the revised estimates, he reportedly chided the intelligence community, noting that they had just admitted to a 100 percent error in past estimates. That being the case, why should he believe them now?

---

intellectual arguments fail, consensus can be reached in many other ways, few of which have anything to do with analysis:

- Backscratching and logrolling. Although these two behaviors are usually thought of in legislative terms, they also can come into play in intelligence analysis. Basically, they involve a trade-off of concerns: "You accept my view on p. 15 and I'll accept yours on p. 38." Obviously, substance is not a major concern here.
- False hostages. Agency A is opposed to a position being taken by Agency B but is afraid its own views will not prevail. Agency A can stake out a false position on another issue that it will defend very strongly, not for the sake of the issue itself, but so that it has something to trade in the backscratching and logrolling.
- Lowest-common-denominator language. One agency believes that the chance of something happening is high; another thinks it is low. Unless these views are strongly held, the agencies may compromise—"a moderate chance"—as a means of resolving the issue. This example is a bit extreme, but it captures the essence of the behavior—an attempt to paper over differences, almost literally, with different words that everyone can accept.
- Footnote wars. Sometimes none of the other techniques will work. In the U.S. estimative process, an agency can always add a footnote in which it expresses "alternative views." Or more than one agency

might add a footnote, or agencies may take sides on an issue. This can lead to vigorous debates as to whose view will appear in the main text and whose in the footnote.

ANALYTICAL STOVEPIPES. As noted earlier, it is common to speak of the collection stovepipes—the fact that the separate INTs are managed independently and often are rivals to one another. Within the U.S. all-source community there are also analytical stovepipes. Again, the three all-source analytical groups—CIA/DI, DIA/DI, and State/INR—each exist to serve specific policymakers. They also come together on a variety of community analyses, most often the NIEs. Efforts to manage—or, even more minimally—to oversee and coordinate their activities reveal a "stovepipe mentality" not unlike that exhibited by the collection agencies. The three all-source agencies tend to have a wary view of efforts by officials with community-wide responsibilities to deal with them as linked parts of a greater analytical whole. The analytical agencies manifest this behavior less overtly than do the collectors, so it is more difficult to recognize. It may also be surprising to some people, perhaps more so than when collectors exhibit this behavior. After all, each of the collectors operates in a unique field, with a series of methodologies that are also unique. The analytical agencies, however, are all in the same line of work, often concerned with the exact same issues. But bureaucratic imperatives and a clear preference for their responsibilities in direct support of their particular policy clients, as opposed to interagency projects, contribute to these analytical stovepipes.

All of these behaviors can leave the impression that the estimative process—or any large-group analytical efforts—is false intellectually. That is not so. However, it is also not a purely academic exercise. Other behaviors intrude, and more than just analytical truths are at stake. There will be winners and losers in the estimative process, and careers may rise and fall as a result.

ANALYTICAL ISSUES

In addition to the mind-set and behavioral characteristics of analysts noted above, several issues within analysis itself need to be addressed.

COMPETITIVE VERSUS COOPERATIVE ANALYSIS. As important as the concept of competitive analysis is to U.S. intelligence, concern has also been expressed about the need to bring together analysts of various agencies or disciplines to work on major ongoing issues, in addition to the collaborative process of national intelligence estimates (NIEs). This led DCI

Robert Gates (1991–1993) to create "centers." Most of them have focused on transnational issues:

- Counternarcotics Center (CNC)
- Counterterrorism Center (CTC)
- Non-proliferation Center (NPC)
- Counterintelligence Center (CIC)

In addition to these and some other centers, the intelligence community has formed task forces to deal with certain issues; among these was the Balkans task force, which has operated since the 1990s, monitoring the range of issues related to the breakup of Yugoslavia.

There has been a bureaucratic debate on the nature of the centers. Although their goal is to bring the various intelligence components into a single place, most of the centers have been located in and dominated by the CIA. Some people argue that this undercuts the centers' basic goal, to reach across agencies. Defenders of the system argue that housing the centers in the CIA gives them access to many resources not available elsewhere and also protects their budgets and staffing. A 1996 review by the staff of the House Intelligence Committee validated the concept of the centers but urged that they be less CIA-centric. Given the location of the centers, however, other agencies are sometimes loath to assign analysts to them, fearing that they will be essentially "lost" resources during their center service. (A similar problem used to occur on the Joint staff, which supports the Joint Chiefs of Staff. The military services—Army, Navy, Air Force, Marines—naturally preferred to keep their best officers in duties directly related to their service. This ended when Congress passed the Goldwater-Nichols Act, in 1986, which mandated a joint service tour as a prerequisite for promotion to general or admiral.)

Another issue for the centers is their duration. One of the interesting phenomena of government—in all sectors—is how ostensibly temporary bodies have a way of becoming permanent, even when the reasons for their creation have long since ended. A certain bureaucratic inertia sets in. Some people wish to see the body continue, as it is a source of power; others fear that by being the first to suggest terminating it they will look like shirkers. There is a comic aspect to this, but also a serious one, as these temporary groups absorb substantial amounts of resources and energy.

Thus, the issue for the centers—or any other groups—is determining when they are no longer needed. Clearly, the transnational issues noted above are all ongoing, but even they may change or diminish over time. One former Deputy DCI suggested a five-year "sunset provision" for all centers, meaning that every five years each center would be subject to a hard-nosed review of its functions and the requirement for its continuation.

Finally, some critics question the focus of these centers, arguing that they are very tactically focused on operational aspects of specific issues rather than on the longer-term trends. Center proponents note the presence of analysts and the working relationship between the centers and the national intelligence officers (NIOs), who can keep apprised of the centers' work and offer advice and are also responsible for the production of NIEs.

DEALING WITH LIMITED INFORMATION. Analysts rarely have the luxury of knowing everything they wish to know about a topic. In some cases, very little may be known. How does an analyst deal with this problem?

One option is to flag the problem so that the policy client is aware of it. Often, telling policy consumers what you don't know is as important as telling them what you do know. But admitting ignorance may be unattractive, out of concern that it will be interpreted as a failing on the part of the intelligence apparatus. Alternatively, analysts can try to work around the problem, utilizing their own experience and skill to fill in the blanks as best they can. This may be more satisfying intellectually and professionally, but it runs the risk of giving the client a false sense of the basis of the analysis or of the analysis being very wrong.

Another option is to arrange for more collection if time will allow it. Yet another is to widen the circle of analysts working on the problem in order to get the benefit of their views and experience.

A reverse formulation of this same problem has arisen in recent years. The question is the degree to which analysis should be tied to available intelligence. Should intelligence analyze only what is known, or should analysts delve into issues or areas that may be currently active, but for which no intelligence is available? Proponents of such a step argue that the absence of intelligence does not mean that an activity is not happening, only that the intelligence is denied to us. Opponents argue that this sort of analysis puts intelligence out on a limb, where there is no support and the likely outcome is highly speculative worst-case analysis. It is important to remember that intelligence analysis is not a legal process in which findings must be based on evidence. On the other hand, analysis written largely on supposition is not likely to be convincing to many and may be more susceptible to politicization.

CONVEYING UNCERTAINTY. Just as everything may not be known, so, too, the likely outcome may not be clear. Conveying uncertainty can be difficult. Analysts shy away from the simple but stark "We don't know." After all, they are being paid, in part, for making some intellectual leaps beyond what they know. Too often, analysts rely on "weasel words" to convey uncertainty: on the one hand, on the other hand, maybe, perhaps, and so on. These words may convey analytical pusillanimity rather than uncertainty. (Conveying uncertainty seems to be a particular problem in English, which is a Germanic language and makes less use of the subjunctive than do the Romance languages.)

Some years ago a senior analytical manager crafted a system for conveying potential outcomes by using both words and numbers—that is, a 1-in-10 chance, a 7-in-10 chance. Such numerical formulations may be more satisfying than words, but they run the risk of conveying to the policy client a degree of precision that does not exist. What is the difference between a 6-in-10 chance and a 7-in-10 chance, beyond greater conviction? In reality, the analyst is back to relying on "gut feeling." (One chairman of the National Intelligence Council did become incensed when he read an analysis that assessed "a small but significant chance" of something happening. He correctly saw this as a case of analytical pusillanimity.)

INDICATIONS AND WARNING. I&W, as it is known among intelligence professionals, is one of the most important roles of intelligence—giving policymakers advance warning of important, usually military, events. The emphasis placed on I&W in the United States reflects the cold war legacy of a long-term military rivalry and the older roots of the U.S. intelligence community in Pearl Harbor, the classic I&W failure.

I&W is primarily a military intelligence function, with an emphasis on surprise attack. It relies, to a large extent, on the fact that all militaries operate according to certain regular schedules, forms, and behaviors, which provide a base line against which to measure activity that may raise I&W concerns. In other words, analysts are looking for anything that is out of the ordinary, any new or unexpected activity that may presage an attack: calling up reserves, putting forces on a higher level of alert, dropping or increasing communications activity, imposing sudden communications silence, or sending more naval units than usual to sea. But none of these can be viewed in isolation; they have to be seen within the wider context of overall behavior.

During the cold war, for example, U.S. and NATO analysts worried about how much warning they would receive of a Warsaw Pact attack against Western Europe. Some analysts believed that they could provide policymakers, minimally, several days' warning, as stocks were positioned, additional units were brought forward, and so on. Others believed that the Warsaw Pact had sufficient forces and supplies in place to attack from "a standing start." Fortunately, the issue was never put to the test.

For analysts, I&W can be a trap rather than an opportunity. Their main fear is failing to pick up on indicators and give adequate warning, a fear that in part reflects the harsh view of intelligence when it "misses" an important event. In reaction, analysts may lower the threshold and issue warnings about everything, in effect "crying wolf." Although this may reduce the analyst's exposure to criticism, it has a lulling effect on the policymaker and can cheapen the function of I&W.

Terrorism presents an entirely new and more difficult I&W problem. As noted, terrorists do not operate from elaborate infrastructures, nor do they need to mobilize large numbers of people for their operations. Indeed, one of the attractions of terrorism as a political tool is the ability to have a large effect with minimal forces. Thus, we need an entirely new I&W concept to fight terrorism, one more likely to catch the much smaller signs of impending activity.

Policymakers may want something in addition to warning, for example, "opportunity," as one secretary of state explained to his intelligence officers; he was referring to instances where he could advance his agenda, as opposed to reacting to the actions of others. His was an interesting, challenging, and demanding request, and one dependent on having the policymaker share his goals with his intelligence officers.

ESTIMATES. As noted, the United States—as well as Britain and Australia—creates and uses analytical products called estimates. These serve two major purposes: to see where a major issue or trend will go over the next several years and to present the considered view of the entire intelligence community, not just of one agency. In the United States their community-wide origin is signified by the fact that the director of central intelligence signs completed estimates.

It is important to understand the intellectual basis of estimates. They are not predictions of the future but rather considered judgments as to the likely course of events regarding an issue of importance to the nation. Sometimes, more than one possible outcome may be included in a single estimate. The difference between "estimate" and "prediction" is crucial but often misunderstood, especially by policymakers. "Prediction" foretells the future—or attempts to. Estimates are more vague, assessing the relative likelihood of one or more outcomes. If an event or outcome were predictable—that is, capable of being foretold—one would not need intelligence agencies to estimate its likelihood. It is the uncertainty or unknowability that is key. As American baseball icon Yogi Berra said: "It is very difficult to make predictions, especially about the future."

The bureaucratics of estimates are important to their outcome. In the United States, national intelligence officers (NIOs) are responsible for preparing estimates. They circulate the terms of reference (TOR) among colleagues and other agencies at the outset of an estimate. The TOR may be the subject of prolonged discussion and negotiation, as various agencies may believe that the basic questions or lines of analysis are not being framed properly. The actual drafting is not done by the NIOs, but by someone from the NIO's office, or the NIO may recruit a drafter from one of the intelligence agencies. Once drafted, the estimate is coordinated with other agencies, that is, the other agencies read it and give comments, not all of which will be accepted, since they may be at variance with the drafter's views. Numerous meetings will be held to resolve disputes, but the meetings may end with two or more views on some aspects that cannot be reconciled. The DCI chairs a final meeting, which is attended by senior officials from various agencies. After the DCI signs the estimate, signifying he is satisfied with it, the estimate becomes "his." DCIs have been known to change the views expressed in estimates with which they disagree. This usually displeases the drafter but is within the DCI's authority.

In addition to the bureaucratic game-playing that may be involved in drafting estimates, issues of process also influence outcomes. Not every issue is of interest to every intelligence agency. But each agency understands the necessity of taking part in the estimative process, not only for its intrinsic intelligence value but also as a means of keeping watch on the other agencies.

Some issues are the subjects of repeated estimates. For example, during the cold war, the intelligence community produced an annual estimate (three volumes) on Soviet strategic forces, NIE 11-3-8. For issues of long-term importance, such as Soviet strategic forces, regular estimates are a useful way of keeping track of an issue, of watching it closely and looking for changes in perceived patterns. However, as noted, a regularly produced estimate can also be an intellectual trap, as it establishes several benchmarks that analysts will be loath to tinker with in the event of possible changes. Having produced a long-standing record on certain key issues, the estimative community will find it difficult to admit that major changes are under way that, in effect, undercut their past analysis.

Some people question the utility of estimates. Both producers and consumers have had concerns about the length of estimates and their sometimes plodding style. Critics also have voiced concerns about timeliness, in that some estimates take more than a year to complete. One of the worst examples of poor timing came in 1979. An estimate on the future political stability of Iran was being written—including the observation that Iran was "not in a prerevolutionary state"—even as the shah's regime was unraveling daily. This incongruity led the House Intelligence Committee to observe that estimates "are not worth fighting over."

COMPETITIVE ANALYSIS. The U.S. intelligence community believes in the concept of competitive analysis—having different agencies with different points of view work on the same issue. Because the United States has several intelligence agencies—including three major all-source analytical agencies (CIA, Defense Intelligence Agency, and State's Bureau of Intelligence and Research)—every relevant actor understands that the agencies will have different analytical strengths and, likely, different points of view on a given issue. By having each of them—and other agencies as well on some issues—analyze an issue, it is believed that the analysis will be stronger and more likely to give policymakers accurate intelligence.

Beyond the day-to-day competition that takes place among the various intelligence publications of each agency, the intelligence community fosters competition in other ways. Intelligence agencies occasionally form "red teams," which take on the role of the analysts of another nation or group as a means of gaining insights into their thinking. A now-famous competitive exercise was the 1976 formation of Teams A and B to review intelligence on Soviet strategic forces and doctrine. Team A consisted of intelligence community analysts, and Team B consisted of outside experts, but with a decidedly hawkish viewpoint. The teams disagreed little on the strategic systems the Soviets had built; the key issue was Soviet nuclear doctrine and strategic intentions. Predictably, Team B believed that the intelligence supported a more threatening view of Soviet intentions. However, the lack of balance on Team B largely vitiated the exercise, which could have been very useful not only for gaining insight into Soviet intentions but also for validating the utility of competitive intelligence exercises.

Dissent channels—bureaucratic mechanisms by which analysts can challenge the views of their superiors without risk to their careers—are helpful but not widely used. Such channels have long existed for Foreign Service officers in the State Department. Although less effective than competitive analysis for articulating alternative viewpoints, they offer a means by which alternative views can survive a bureaucratic process that tends to emphasize mutual consent.

A broader issue is the extent to which competitive intelligence can or should be institutionalized. To some degree, in the U.S. system it already is. But the competition among the three all-source agencies is not often pointed. They often work on the same issue, but with different perspectives that are well understood, thus muting some of the differences that may be seen.

Although the intelligence community believes in competitive analysis, not all policymakers are receptive to the idea. Some of them see no reason why agencies cannot agree on issues, perhaps assuming that there is a single answer to an issue that should be knowable. Indeed, one of the main reasons that President Harry S. Truman created the Central Intelligence Group (CIG) and its successor, the CIA, was his annoyance over receiving intelligence reports that did not agree. He wanted an agency to coordinate the reports so that he could work his way through the contradictory views.

Truman was smart enough to realize that agencies might not agree, but he was not comfortable receiving disparate reports without some coordination that attempted to make sense of the areas of disagreement. Other policymakers lack Truman's subtlety and simply cannot abide having agencies disagree, thus vitiating the concept of competitive analysis.

Finally, those who are not familiar with the idea of competitive analysis, and even some who are, may regard the planned redundancy as more wasteful than intellectually productive.

POLITICIZED INTELLIGENCE. This issue arises from the line separating policy and intelligence. As noted above, this line is best thought of as a semipermeable membrane; policymakers are free to offer assessments that run counter to intelligence analyses, but intelligence officers are not allowed to make policy recommendations based on their intelligence. For example, in the State Department in the late 1980s, the assistant secretary responsible for the Western Hemisphere, Elliot Abrams, often disagreed with pessimistic INR assessments as to the likelihood that the contras would be victorious in Nicaragua. Abrams would often write more positive assessments on his own that he would forward to Secretary of State George Shultz.

Policymakers and intelligence officers have different institutional and personal investments in the issues on which they work. The policymakers are creating policy and hope to accrue other benefits (career advancement, reelection) from a successful policy. Intelligence officers are not responsible for creating policy or for its success, yet they understand that the outcomes may affect their own status, both institutional and personal.

The issue of politicization arises primarily from concerns that intelligence officers may intentionally alter intelligence, which is supposed to be objective, in order to support the options or outcomes preferred by policymakers. These actions may have a variety of motives: a loss of objectivity regarding the issue at hand and a preference for specific options or outcomes, an effort to be more supportive, career interests, or outright pandering.

Intentionally altering intelligence is a subtle issue because it does not involve crossing the line from analysis to policy. Rather, the analyst is tampering with his or her own product so that it will be received more favorably. The issue is also made more complex by the fact that at the most senior levels of the intelligence community, the line separating intelligence from policy begins to blur. Policymakers will ask senior intelligence officials for their personal views on an issue or policy, which they may give. It is difficult to conceive of a DCI always abstaining when the president or the secretary of state asks such a question.

Political Winners and Losers

Although we would prefer to view intelligence analysis and policymaking as largely objective exercises, they inevitably get caught up in partisan politics, as two cases illustrate.

In the late 1940s and early 1950s many of the State Department's experts on China (the "China hands") had their careers sidetracked or were forced from office over allegations that they had "lost" China to the communists. Many scholars and officials customarily interpreted their treatment as a gross injustice. But, as Professor Ernest R. May of Harvard University has pointed out, the U.S. public in the elections of the early 1950s largely repudiated the anti-Chiang Kai-shek views of the China hands by returning the pro-Chiang Republicans to power. So the China hands not only had ideological foes within the government, they also had no political basis upon which to pursue their preferred policies.

Similarly, the careers of many intelligence officers and Foreign Service officers involved in crafting and promoting the SALT II treaty during the Carter administration also failed to prosper with the advent of the Reagan administration. Reagan appointees were opposed to that treaty and held these career officers responsible. Again, their careers suffered only because of an electoral victory.

One can argue that these punishments were not what the electorate had in mind, but they underscore the fact that the government and the underlying policy processes are essentially political in nature.

The size or persistence of the politicization problem is difficult to determine. Some of those who raise accusations about politicized intelligence are "losers" in the bureaucratic battles—intelligence officers whose views have not prevailed or policymakers (in the executive branch or Congress, either loyal to the current administration or in opposition) who are dissatisfied with current policy directions. Thus, their accusations may be no more objective than the intelligence that concerns them. Those unfamiliar with the process are often surprised to hear intelligence practitioners talk about "winners" and "losers." But these debates—within the policy or the intelligence community—are not abstract academic discussions. Their outcomes have real results that can be significant and even dangerous. And careers can rise and fall as well. Indeed, just as intelligence officers serve policymakers, career officers—both intelligence and policy—serve political appointees, who are less interested in the objectivity of analysis. (See box, "Political Winners and Losers.")

Politicization by intelligence officers may also be a question of perception. A consensus could probably be reached on what politicized intel-

Potential Politicization

According to press accounts in November 1998, Vice President Al Gore's staff rejected CIA reports about the personal corruption of Russian premier Viktor Chernomyrdin.

Members of the vice president's staff argued that the administration had to deal with Chernomyrdin, corrupt or not, and that the intelligence was inconclusive. Intelligence analysts countered that the administration set the standard for proof so high that it was unlikely to be met by intelligence. The analysts found that they were censoring their reports in order to avoid further disputes with the White House.

Both policy and intelligence officers denied these allegations.

ligence looked like, but there would be much less agreement on whether a specific analysis fit the definition.

Thus, politicized intelligence remains a concern, albeit a somewhat vague one. This may, in fact, make the issue all the more difficult and important. Many of these issues came out in the hearings surrounding Robert Gates's second nomination as DCI. (Gates asked President Ronald Reagan to withdraw his first nomination during the Iran-contra affair. He was subsequently renominated by President George H. W. Bush and confirmed in 1991.)

There is a second type of politicized intelligence, caused by policymakers who may react strongly to intelligence, depending on whether it confirms or refutes their preferences for policy outcomes. (See box, "Potential Politicization.") They may also use intelligence issues for partisan purposes. Two interesting examples of the partisan use of intelligence in the United States were the missile gap (1959–1961) and the "window of vulnerability" (1979–1981). In both cases, the party that was out of power (the Democrats in the first case, the Republicans in the second) argued that the Soviet Union had gained a strategic nuclear advantage over the United States, which was being ignored or not reported. In both cases, the accusing party won the election (not because of their charges) and learned that the actual intelligence did not support their accusations—which they simply claimed had been resolved!

INTELLIGENCE ANALYSIS: AN ASSESSMENT

Sherman Kent, one of the intellectual founders of the U.S. intelligence community and especially of its estimative process, once wrote that every intelligence analyst has three wishes: to know everything, to be believed, and to influence policy for the good (as he understands it). Kent's three wishes offer a yardstick by which to measure analysis. Clearly, an analyst can never know everything in a given field. Indeed, if everything were known, the need for intelligence would not exist—there would be nothing left to discover. But what Kent is getting at in his first wish is the desire of the analyst to know as much as possible about a given issue before being asked to write about it. The amount of intelligence available will vary from issue to issue and from time to time. Analysts must therefore be trained to develop some inner, deeper knowledge that will enable them to read between the lines, to make educated guesses or intuitive choices when the intelligence is insufficient.

Kent's second wish—to be believed—goes to the heart of the relationship between intelligence and policy. Policymakers pay no price for ignoring intelligence—barring highly infrequent strategic disasters such as Josef Stalin's refusal to accept the signs of an imminent German attack in 1941. Intelligence officers see themselves as honest and objective messengers who add value to the process, who provide not just sources but analysis. Their reward, at the end of the process, is to be listened to, which varies greatly from one policymaker to another.

Finally, and derived from his second wish, Kent notes that intelligence officers want to have a positive effect on policy, to help avert disaster and to help produce positive outcomes in terms of the nation's interests. But analysts really want to be more than a Cassandra, constantly warning of doom and disaster. Their wish to have a positive influence also indicates the desire to be kept informed about what policymakers are doing to enable the intelligence officers to play a meaningful role.

What, then, constitutes "good intelligence"? This is no small question, and one is reminded of Justice Byron White's response when he was asked to define pornography: "I can't define it," White said, "but I know it when I see it." Good intelligence has something of the same indistinct quality. At least four qualities come to mind. Good intelligence is:

- Timely. Getting the intelligence to the policymaker on time is more important than waiting for every last shred of collection to come in or for the paper to be pristine, clean, and in the right format. The timeliness criterion runs counter to the first of Kent's three wishes: to know everything. (*See box, "Talleyrand on Timeliness."*)
- Tailored. Good intelligence focuses on the specific information needs of the policymaker, to whatever depth and breadth are required, but without extraneous material. This must be done in a way that does not result in losing objectivity or politicizing the intelligence. Indeed, "tailored" intelligence products (those respond-

---

Talleyrand on Timeliness

Napoleon died on St. Helena in May 1821; news of his death did not reach Paris until July. Charles Maurice de Talleyrand, once Napoleon's foreign minister and later one of his foes, was dining at a friend's house when they heard of Napoleon's death. The hostess exclaimed, "What an event!"

Talleyrand corrected her. "It is no longer an event, Madam, it is news."

---

ing to a specific need or request) are among the most highly prized by policymakers.

- Digestible. Good intelligence has to be in a form and of a length that will allow policymakers to grasp what they need to know as easily as possible. This requirement tends to argue in favor of shorter intelligence products, but it is primarily meant to stress the importance of presenting the message clearly so that it can be readily understood. This does not mean that the message cannot be complex, or even incomplete. But whatever the main message is, the policymaker must be able to understand it with a minimum of effort. This is an important skill for analysts to learn. Writing a good two-page memo is much more difficult than writing a five-page memo on the same subject. As Samuel Clemens (Mark Twain) observed in a letter to a friend, "I am writing you a long letter because I don't have time to write a short one."

- Clear regarding the known and the unknown. Good intelligence must convey to the reader what is known, what is unknown, and what has been filled in by analysis, as well as the degree of confidence in all of the material. The degree of confidence is important because the policymaker must have some sense of the relative firmness of the intelligence. All intelligence involves risk by the very nature of the information being dealt with. The risk should not be assumed by the analysts alone, but should be shared with their clients.

Note that objectivity was not one of the major factors defining good intelligence. Its omission was not an oversight. The need for objectivity is so great and so pervasive that it is taken here as a given. If the intelligence is not objective, then none of the other attributes—timeliness, digestibility, clarity—matter at all.

Also note that accuracy is not a criterion. Accuracy is a more difficult standard for assessing intelligence than might be imagined. Clearly, no one wants to be wrong, but everyone recognizes the impossibility of infallibility. Given these limits, what accuracy standard should we use? One hundred percent is too high and 0 percent is too low. Splitting the difference at 50 percent accuracy is still unsatisfactory. Thus, we are left playing a numbers game—something more than 50 percent and less than 100 percent accurate.

As unsatisfactory as this standard is, other metrics are not much better. For example, we could construct a batting average over time—for an issue, for an office, for an agency, for a product line. But these, too, are all inadequate. Or we could assess the quality of intelligence on the basis of the number of products produced—estimates, analyses, images exploited. These suggestions are not meant to be as frivolous as they seem. They are meant to give a feel for the difficulty of assessing what is "good intelligence."

This is not to suggest that producing good intelligence is some sort of holy grail that is rarely achieved. Good intelligence is often achieved. But one must distinguish between the steady stream of intelligence that is produced on a daily basis and the small amount within that daily production that stands out for some reason—its timeliness, the quality of its writing, its effect on policy. The view here—and it is one that has been debated with the highest intelligence officials—is that effort is required to produce acceptable, useful intelligence on a daily basis, but that producing exceptional intelligence is much more difficult and less frequently achieved. We face a conflict between the goal of consistency and the desire to be exceptional. An entire intelligence community cannot be exceptional all the time, but it does hope to be consistently helpful to policy. Consistent intelligence and exceptional intelligence are not one and the same. (One is reminded of the cynical observation "Only the mediocre are at their best all the time.") Consistency is not a bad goal, but it allows analysis to fall into a pattern that lulls both the producer and the consumer. Thus, for all that we know about the distinctive characteristics of good intelligence, it remains somewhat elusive in reality, at least as a widely seen daily phenomenon. But, for analysts, that is one of the positive challenges of their profession.

KEY TERMS

analytical stovepipes
clientism
competitive analysis
current intelligence
estimates
long-term intelligence

lowest-common-denominator
  language
mirror imaging
national intelligence officers
  (NIOs)
politicized intelligence

FURTHER READINGS

The literature on analysis is rich. These readings discuss both broad general issues and some specific areas of intelligence analysis that have been particularly important. The CIA has declassified many of its estimates on the Soviet Union and related issues. These are listed at the end of chap. 11.

Adams, Sam. "Vietnam Cover-Up: Playing with Numbers; a CIA Conspiracy Against Its Own Numbers." *Harper's* (May 1975).

Caldwell, George. *Policy Analysis for Intelligence.* Center for the Study of Intelligence, Central Intelligence Agency. Washington, D.C.: CIA, 1992.

Clark, Robert M. *Intelligence Analysis: Estimation and Prediction.* Baltimore: American Literary Press, 1996.

Davis, Jack. *The Challenge of Opportunity Analysis.* Center for the Study of Intelligence, Central Intelligence Agency. Washington, D.C.: CIA, 1992.

Ford, Harold P. *Estimative Intelligence.* McLean, Va.: Association of Former Intelligence Officers, 1993.

———. *Estimative Intelligence: The Purposes and Problems of National Intelligence Estimating.* Washington, D.C.: Defense Intelligence College, 1989.

Gates, Robert M. "The CIA and American Foreign Policy." *Foreign Affairs* 66 (winter 1987–1988).

Gazit, Shlomo. "Estimates and Fortune-Telling in Intelligence Work." *International Security* 4 (spring 1980): 36–56.

———. "Intelligence Estimates and the Decision-Maker." *International Security* 3 (July 1988): 261–287.

Heuer, Richards J., Jr. *Psychology of Analysis.* Washington. D.C.: Central Intelligence Agency, History Staff, 1999.

Johnson, Loch K. "Analysis for a New Age." *Intelligence and National Security* 11 (October 1996): 657–671.

Lockwood, Jonathan S. "Sources of Error in Indications and Warning." *Defense Intelligence Journal* 3 (spring 1994): 75–88.

Lowenthal, Mark M. "The Burdensome Concept of Failure." In *Intelligence: Policy and Process.* Ed. Alfred C. Maurer et al. Boulder: Westview Press, 1985.

MacEachin, Douglas J. *The Tradecraft of Analysis: Challenge and Change in the CIA.* Washington, D.C.: Consortium for the Study of Intelligence, 1994.

Nye, Joseph S. *Estimating the Future.* Washington, D.C.: Consortium for the Study of Intelligence, 1994.

Pipes, Richard. "Team B: The Reality Behind the Myth." *Commentary* 82 (October 1986).

Price, Victoria. *The DCI's Role in Producing Strategic Intelligence Estimates.* Newport: U.S. Naval War College, 1980.

Reich, Robert C. "Re-examining the Team A–Team B Exercise." *International Journal of Intelligence and Counterintelligence* 3 (fall 1989).

Stack, Kevin P. "A Negative View of Comparative Analysis." *International Journal of Intelligence and Counterintelligence* 10 (winter 1998): 456–464.

Steury, Donald P., ed. *Sherman Kent and the Board of National Estimates.* Washington, D.C.: History Staff, Center for the Study of Intelligence, Central Intelligence Agency, 1994.

Turner, Michael A. "Setting Analytical Priorities in U.S. Intelligence." *International Journal of Intelligence and Counterintelligence* 9 (fall 1996): 313–336.

U.S. House Permanent Select Committee on Intelligence. *Intelligence Support to Arms Control.* 100th Cong., 1st sess., 1987.

————. *Iran: Evaluation of U.S. Intelligence Performance Prior to November 1978.* 96th Cong., 1st sess., 1979.

U.S. Senate Select Committee on Intelligence. *The National Intelligence Estimates A–B Team Episode Concerning Soviet Strategic Capability and Objectives.* 95th Cong., 2d sess., 1978.

————. *Nomination of Robert M. Gates.* Hearings. 3 vol. 102d Cong., 1st sess., 1991.

————. *Nomination of Robert M. Gates to be Director of Central Intelligence.* Report. 102d Cong., 1st sess., 1991.

Wirtz, James J. "Miscalculation, Surprise and American Intelligence after the Cold War." *International Journal of Intelligence and Counterintelligence* 5 (spring 1991): 1–16.

————. *The Tet Offensive: Intelligence Failure in War.* Ithaca: Cornell University Press, 1991.

Chapter 7

Counterintelligence

Counterintelligence refers to efforts taken to protect one's own intelligence operations from penetration and disruption by hostile nations or their intelligence services. It is both analytical and operational. Counterintelligence (sometimes referred to as CI) is not a separate step in the intelligence process but is an important function throughout the process. CI does not fit neatly with human intelligence, although CI is, in part, a collection issue. Nor does it fit with covert action. CI is one of the most difficult intelligence topics to discuss.

Counterintelligence proceeds from the fact that most nations have intelligence enterprises of some sort. By their very existence these agencies are extremely valuable intelligence targets for other nations. It is always useful to know what the other side knows and does not know and how it goes about its work. It is also extremely useful to know if the other side is undertaking similar efforts against you.

However, counterintelligence is more than a defensive activity. There are at least three types of CI:

- Collection: gaining information about an opponent's intelligence collection capabilities that may be aimed at you
- Defensive: thwarting efforts by hostile intelligence services to penetrate your service
- Offensive: having identified an opponent's efforts against your system, trying to manipulate these attacks either by "turning" the opponent's agents into double agents or by feeding them false information that they will report home

The world of spy and counterspy is murky at best. Like espionage, counterintelligence is one of the staples of intelligence fiction. But, like all other aspects of intelligence, it has less glamour than it does grinding, painstaking work.

Who Spies on Whom?

Some people assume that "friendly" spy agencies do not spy on one another. But what constitutes "friendly"? The United States and its "English-speaking cousins"—Britain, Australia, and Canada—enjoy a close intelligence partnership and do not spy on one another. Beyond that, all bets are off.

The United States allegedly spied on France for economic intelligence. Israel willingly used Jonathan Pollard, a U.S. Navy intelligence employee who passed sensitive U.S. intelligence that he believed Israel needed to know. Some people were surprised—if not outraged—that post–Soviet Russia would continue using Aldrich Ames to spy against the United States. (Subsequent revelations about the contemporary espionage of Robert Hanssen stirred less surprise—perhaps a sign of increased maturity gained through painful experience.) More recently, a House committee found that China stole nuclear secrets from the United States at a time when the two nations were strategic partners against the Soviet Union.

In the 1970s a "senior U.S. government official" (probably Henry Kissinger) observed, "There is no such thing as 'friendly' intelligence agencies. There are only the intelligence agencies of friendly powers."

INTERNAL SAFEGUARDS

All intelligence agencies establish a series of internal processes and checks, the main purposes of which are to weed out applicants who may be unsuitable and to identify current employees whose loyalty is questionable. The vetting process for applicants includes extensive background checks, interviews with the applicants and close associates, and, in the United States at least, the use of the polygraph for most agencies. It is important to note that the "ideal" candidate is not someone whose past record is spotless. It is understood that most applicants will have engaged in some level of experimentation— either sexual or drugs, or both. Some may have committed minor criminal offenses. It is crucial that an applicant be forthcoming about his or her past and be able to prove that there are no ongoing behaviors that are criminal, dangerous, or susceptible to blackmail.

The polygraph, sometimes mistakenly referred to as a lie detector, is a machine that monitors physical responses (such as pulse and breathing rate) to a series of questions. Changes in these physical signs may indicate falsehoods or deceptions. The use of the polygraph by U.S. intelligence remains controversial. Everyone acknowledges that the polygraph is imperfect and can be deceived. At least two spies, Larry Wu-tai Chin and Aldrich Ames, passed polygraph tests while they were involved in espionage against the United States. Advocates of the polygraph are quick to assert that the machine is only a tool that can point to problem areas, some of which may be resolved without prejudice. However, an individual's inability or failure to resolve such issues can lead to termination. In addition to new employees, current employees are polygraphed again at intervals of several years; contractors are also subject to polygraphs, and these machines are used with defectors as well. It is also important to note that polygraphs are not used consistently throughout the national security structure. CIA, DIA, the NRO, and NSA all use polygraphs; the State Department and Congress do not. The FBI began using polygraphs in the aftermath of the Robert Hanssen espionage case, which revealed that polygraphs had not been in use at the FBI previously. This is not to suggest that some agencies are more rigorous or more lax than others. But it does underscore a range of standards in terms of personnel security.

Beyond taking a polygraph (known as "being put on the box"), employees and prospective employees are also evaluated for other possible indicators of disloyalty. Changes in personal behavior or lifestyle—marital problems, increased use of alcohol, suspected use of drugs, increased personal spending that seems to exceed known resources, running up large debts—may be indicators that an individual is spying or susceptible to being recruited to spy. Any of these personal difficulties may befall an individual who would never consider becoming a spy, but past espionage cases indicate some reason for concern. (See box, "Why Spy?") The response of counterintelligence agents to the discovery of such problems would depend on the suspect's larger patterns of behavior, how long the problem persisted, and evidence of potentially hostile activity. In the aftermath of the Ames case—where marginal performance, alcohol abuse, and a sudden increase in fairly ostentatious personal spending should have been taken as indicators of a problem—U.S. intelligence increased the amount of personal financial information that intelligence personnel must report on a regular basis. These financial-reporting forms assume, however, that ill-gotten gains will show up in some way that is detectable with or without the cooperation of the recipient—cash, stocks, or new homes, cars, and so forth bought with cash received. However, as we have learned from both the Ames and the Hanssen cases, the country supporting the espionage may be putting some or all of the money in escrow accounts that will not be detected—or even accessed—until years after the espionage is completed. Again, the cases of Ames and Hanssen are instructive. Ames's lifestyle clearly changed—new house, new car, better clothes, cosmetic dental work—although this was before the financial-reporting forms. Outwardly, however, Hanssen's life showed virtually no signs of increased wealth.

Why Spy?

U.S. counterintelligence emphasizes personal financial issues in assessing security risks. Many of the people involved in the worst espionage cases suffered by the United States—Aldrich Ames, Robert Hanssen, the Walker spy ring, Ronald Pelton—were motivated largely by greed rather than ideology. Some exceptions to this generalization would be Julius Rosenberg, Alger Hiss, and Larry Wu-tai Chin.

By contrast, many of the people involved in the worst espionage cases in Britain—Kim Philby and his associates or George Blake, for example— spied because of ideological devotion to the Soviet Union.

Although espionage cases of either type (greed or ideology) can arise in either country, some observers have been struck by the difference noted above. Some have attempted to explain the difference, in part, by the fact that Britain has had (and still has) a class system that makes ideology a more likely reason for betrayal, although the most serious British spies have come from the upper class. In the United States, however, the main competition has always been based on economic status rather than social class.

As noted in the discussion of HUMINT, spies may also be motivated by vengeance toward superiors or agencies, by blackmail against themselves or family members, by thrills, or by involvement with a foreign national. Still, most of the spies suffered by the United States have been motivated primarily by money.

Another internal means of thwarting espionage attacks is the classification system. In U.S. intelligence parlance, the system is "compartmented." In other words, an employee being accorded the privilege of a clearance does not automatically get access to all of the intelligence information available. Admission to various compartments is based on a "need to know." Thus, someone working on a new imagery system will likely have different clearances than someone involved in running HUMINT. There are also compartments within compartments. For example, a clearance involving HUMINT may include only specific cases or types of HUMINT—for example, proliferation or narcotics.

The clearance system limits access and therefore reduces the damage that can be caused by any one source of leaks. The system is not without costs. It may become an obstacle to analysis, either wittingly or inadvertently, by excluding some analysts from a compartment crucial to their work. Administering such a system has direct costs: devising a system, tracking documents, running security checks on employees, and so forth. Indirect costs include safes, couriers, security officers to check officers' clearances, and color-coded or numerically tagged papers, to name a few. This list gives some sense of what is involved in a thorough classification scheme. And, if such a scheme is not thorough, it is nothing more than annoying and wasteful.

Other safeguards include the certified destruction of discarded material; the use of "secure" phones, which cannot be easily tapped, for classified conversations; and restricted access to buildings or to parts of buildings where sensitive material is used. These are called sensitive compartmented information facilities (SCIFs).

EXTERNAL INDICATORS AND COUNTERESPIONAGE

The discussion thus far has focused on internal measures to prevent or to identify CI problems. Counterintelligence agents also look for external indicators of problems. These may be more obvious, such as the sudden loss of a spy network overseas, a change in military exercise patterns that corresponds to satellite tracks, or a penetration of the other service's apparatus that reveals the possibility of your having been penetrated as well. (This apparently is how Robert Hanssen was detected.) The indicators may be more subtle—the odd botched operation or failed espionage meeting or a negotiation in which the other side seems to be anticipating your bottom line. These are all murkier indicators of a leak or penetration—what some have described as a "wilderness of mirrors."

In 1995 the CIA and NSA published SIGINT intercepts (code-named VENONA) that had been used to detect Soviet espionage in the United States. From 1943 to 1957 VENONA products helped identify Alger Hiss, Julius Rosenberg, Klaus Fuchs, and others working for Soviet intelligence. As VENONA showed, SIGINT can offer indications of ongoing espionage, although the references to spying may be oblique and are unlikely to identify the spy outright. The VENONA intercepts used code names for the spies but often gave enough additional information to help narrow the search.

The serious problems resulting from having been penetrated by a hostile service also highlight the gains to be made by carrying out your own successful penetration of the hostile service. Among the intelligence that may be gathered are:

- An opponent's HUMINT capabilities and targets, strengths, and weaknesses
- An opponent's main areas of intelligence interest and current shortfalls
- Possible penetrations of your service or other services

- Possible intelligence "alliances" (for example, the Soviet-era KGB used Polish émigrés in the United States for some defense-industry espionage and Bulgarian operatives for "wet affairs"—assassinations)
- Sudden changes in an opponent's HUMINT operations—new needs, new taskings, changed focuses, a recall of agents from a specific region—each of which can have a host of meanings

Discovering the presence of foreign agents may not lead automatically to their arrest. The agents also present opportunities, as they are conduits to their own intelligence services. At a minimum, you may try to curtail some of their access without their becoming aware of it and then begin feeding them false information to send home. Alternatively, counterintelligence officers may try a more aggressive approach, attempting to turn them into double agents who, although apparently continuing their activities, are now actually working for your side—providing you with information on their erstwhile employer and knowingly passing back erroneous information. But just as there are double agents, so there are triple agents—agents who have been "turned" once, discovered, and then "turned" again by their own side. The effect, again, is a wilderness of mirrors.

PROBLEMS IN COUNTERINTELLIGENCE

Several problems arise in assessing counterintelligence operations. First, by its very nature, any counterintelligence penetration is going to be covert. Counterintelligence officers are unlikely to come across initially compelling evidence about a successful hostile penetration.

Second, the basic tendency within any intelligence organization (or any organization, for that matter) is to trust your own people, who have been vetted and cleared. They work with one another every day. All of this familiarity can lead to lowering your guard or being unwilling to believe that your own people may have gone bad. This appears to have been one of the problems in uncovering the espionage of Ames; the CIA was slow to look inward for the cause of severe losses of assets in Moscow. Similarly, the FBI first concentrated on another CIA officer when hunting for the spy who was actually one of their own, Robert Hanssen.

But the alternative behavior—unwarranted suspicion—can be just as debilitating as having a spy in your midst. James Angleton, who was in charge of the CIA's counterintelligence from 1954 to 1974, became convinced that a Soviet mole—a deeply hidden spy—had penetrated the CIA. Some believed that Angleton was reacting to the fact that one of his closest

British associates, Kim Philby, had turned out to be a Soviet agent. Angleton was unable to find the mole, and some believe that he tied the CIA in knots by placing virtually anyone under suspicion. It was even suggested that Angleton himself was the mole and that he created a furor to divert attention from himself. Angleton remains a figure of extreme controversy, but his activities give some indication of the intellectual issues that can be involved in spying and counterintelligence.

For many years counterintelligence was a major source of friction between the CIA and the FBI. Some of the friction was a legacy of long-time FBI director J. Edgar Hoover's resentment toward the CIA and that agency's reciprocation of Hoover's feelings. The friction also stemmed from differing views of the problem. As noted, a discovered spy is a problem as well as a counterespionage opportunity that the CIA may wish to exploit. However, for the FBI, spying is a prelude to prosecution. As late as the Ames case of the early 1990s, the CIA and FBI were not coordinating their counterintelligence efforts, which probably prolonged Ames's activities. As a result of his arrest and the subsequent investigation, the CIA and FBI created a jointly staffed counterintelligence office to correct the mistakes of the past.

Like so much else in intelligence, it may not be possible to prove suspicions of espionage. The case of Wen Ho Lee, the scientist at Los Alamos National Laboratory, is instructive but complex. In brief, this case came up hard on the heels of the Cox Committee's report, which investigated a series of allegations about Chinese spying that largely targeted high-end technology, including U.S. nuclear weapons designs. Given the issues involved, the Department of Energy (DOE) and the national laboratories were likely places to look. (There was also a series of nasty public arguments between current and former DOE intelligence and counterintelligence officers, as well as between some of them and the FBI, over the issue of responsibility.) Lee, who was born in Taiwan, had been under investigation since 1994, but the investigation was fitful and inconclusive. He had downloaded some 400,000 pages of classified nuclear data unrelated to his own work at Los Alamos. In 2000 Lee was arrested, charged with fifty-nine counts and held in jail for more than nine months, mostly in solitary confinement. However, the government was unable to discover evidence of espionage, that is, passing the material to a foreign power. A Justice Department report castigated the FBI's handling of the investigation, concluding that if Lee was a spy, the FBI let him get away, and if he was not a spy, the bureau failed to consider other lines of investigation. Lee was eventually released and agreed to plead guilty to one felony count of illegally downloading sensitive nuclear data. The case remains, at best, inconclusive. It calls to mind Scottish law, which gives a jury the option to return a verdict of "not proven," rather than either guilty or innocent.

There are also what might be called intermediate cases—officers who come under suspicion for reasons other than espionage but who still pose risks. A good example is Edward Howard, a CIA/DO officer who was slated to be posted to Moscow in the 1980s. It was discovered that Howard had ongoing drug and criminal problems that made it impossible to consider posting him to Moscow. He was suspected of being a counterintelligence problem, but handling the situation was difficult. If sending him to Moscow was not an option, he would have to be reassigned or fired. If he were reassigned but remained a security risk because of his personal behavior, he would still be in a position to see classified material. Moreover, he would most likely feel aggrieved because of the cancellation of his overseas posting, further making him a risk. Alternatively, to fire him was risky, as he had thorough knowledge of DO tradecraft plus information about operations in Moscow. Once fired, it would be difficult, if not impossible, to keep watch on him. Ultimately, it was decided to fire Howard but keep him under FBI surveillance. He eluded this surveillance and fled to Moscow, claiming that he had not been a spy but had been driven away by the CIA. David Wise, a veteran intelligence author and certainly not above criticizing U.S. intelligence, interviewed Howard in Moscow and came away convinced that Howard's disloyalty predated his flight. The Howard case illuminates yet another problem in dealing with counterintelligence cases.

Once a spy has been identified and arrested, the intelligence community conducts a damage assessment, trying to determine exactly what intelligence has been compromised. Obviously, it is extremely useful to have the cooperation of the captured spy. In the United States, this cooperation often becomes a major negotiating point between government prosecutors and the spy's attorney: cooperation in exchange for a specific sentence or for consideration for the spy's family. As with everything else in counterintelligence, however, there are always lingering questions. The most obvious is the degree to which the spy is being honest and forthcoming. Those conducting the damage assessment must also avoid the temptation to use the fact of a discovered spy to explain intelligence losses that are unrelated to that person's espionage. One must stay firmly focused on the intelligence to which the spy had access. It may also turn out that more than one spy was operating at the same time, with access to the same intelligence. This appears to have been the case with Ames and Hanssen, whose espionage was contemporaneous and who had access to some of the same intelligence. Thus, the Hanssen damage assessment will likely require a reexamination of the Ames damage assessment, perhaps without any definitive conclusions. It is also possible that the Soviets/Russians used one set of information to confirm the other, thus having Ames and Hanssen ironically confirming each other's bona fides as useful spies.

In 1999, as part of a government-wide response to revelations about Chinese espionage, the FBI proposed splitting its National Security division into two separate units, one to deal with counterespionage and the other with terrorism. It also proposed broadening the National Security Threat List, on which it assesses counterespionage threats, to include corporations and international criminal organizations as well as foreign governments.

In addition to the FBI, which has the primary CI responsibility in the United States, and the CIA, the Defense Investigative Service and the counterintelligence units of virtually all intelligence agencies or offices share some CI responsibility. The diffusion of the CI effort reflects the organization of the community and also highlights why coordination on CI cases has been problematic.

Double agents raise a host of concerns about loyalty. Have they really been turned, or are they playing a role while remaining loyal to their own service? Investigations of U.S. citizens suspected of spying raise legal issues because of constitutional safeguards on civil liberties. Domestic phones can be tapped, but only after intelligence agents have obtained a warrant from a special federal court (the Foreign Intelligence Surveillance Court), which was set up by the Foreign Intelligence Surveillance Act of 1978 (FISA, pronounced "fy-za") to review such applications. The FISA court has apparently never refused a requested warrant. Agents also use other intrusive techniques, such as listening devices in the suspect's home or office; searches of home or office when the suspect is absent, including making copies of computer files; or going through garbage.

Prosecuting intelligence officers for spying was a major concern for the intelligence agencies, which feared that accused spies would threaten to reveal classified information in open court as a means of avoiding prosecution. This is known as "graymail" (as opposed to blackmail). To preclude this possibility, Congress in 1980 passed the Classified Intelligence Procedures Act (also known as the Graymail Law), which allows judges to review classified material in secret, so that the prosecution can proceed without fear of publicly disclosing sensitive intelligence.

As VENONA confirms, the espionage threat during the cold war was pointed and obvious, even though some cases of Soviet espionage— such as those of Rosenberg and Hiss—still remain controversial to some people. But, as the Ames and Hanssen cases indicated, Russian espionage did not end with the cold war. Indeed, neither did U.S. activities against Russia, given the various Russians arrested by dint of Ames's spying or the apparent source who led to Hanssen. In 1999 the Cox Committee, created by the House of Representatives, found that China had stolen U.S. nuclear weapons designs, apparently during the 1980s, when the two states were tacit allies against the Soviet Union. Assessing the nature and scope of the espionage threat to the United States may be more difficult in the post–cold war world than it had been before the demise of the Soviet Union, not only because the ideological conflict is over but because the sources and goals of penetrations may have changed. But it would be naïve to believe that the need for rigorous counterintelligence and counterespionage ceased with the end of the cold war.

KEY TERMS

CI
compartmented
counterespionage
counterintelligence
damage assessment

double agents
graymail
mole
need to know
polygraph

FURTHER READINGS

Reliable and comprehensible discussions of counterintelligence—apart from mere "spy stories"—are rare.

Benson, Robert Louis, and Michael Warner, eds. *VENONA: Soviet Espionage and the American Response, 1939–1957.* Washington, D.C.: National Security Agency and Central Intelligence Agency, 1996.

Godson, Roy S. *Dirty Tricks or Trump Cards: U.S. Covert Action and Counterintelligence.* Washington, D.C.: Brassey's, 1995.

Hitz, Frederick P. "Counterintelligence: The Broken Triad." *International Journal of Intelligence and Counterintelligence* 13 (fall 2000): 265–300.

Hood, William, James Nolan, and Samuel Halpern. "Myths Surrounding James Angleton: Lessons for American Counterintelligence." Washington, D.C.: Working Group on Intelligence Reform, Consortium for the Study of Intelligence, 1994.

Johnson, William R. *Thwarting Enemies at Home and Abroad: How to Be a Counterintelligence Officer.* Bethesda, Md.: Stone Trail Press, 1987.

Perkins, David D. "Counterintelligence and Human Intelligence Operations." *American Intelligence Journal* 18 (1988).

Shulsky, Abram N., and Gary J. Schmitt. *Silent Warfare: Understanding the World of Intelligence.* 2d rev. ed. Washington, D.C.: Brassey's, 1983.

U.S. House Permanent Select Committee on Intelligence. *Report of Investigation: The Aldrich Ames Espionage Case.* Report, 103d Cong., 2d sess., 1994.

———. *United States Counterintelligence and Security Concerns—1986.* Report, 100th Cong., 1st sess., 1987.

U.S. House Select Committee on U.S. National Security and Military/Commercial Concerns with the People's Republic of China (Cox Committee). Report, 106th Cong., 1st sess., 1999.

Zuehlke, Arthur A. "What Is Counterintelligence?" In *Intelligence Requirements for the 1980s: Counterintelligence*. Ed. Roy S. Godson. Washington, D.C.: National Strategy Information Center, 1980.

Chapter 8

Covert Action

Covert action, along with spying, is a mainstay of popular conceptions of intelligence. Like spying, covert action is fraught with myths and misconceptions. Even when understood, it remains one of the most controversial intelligence topics.

Covert action is defined in the National Security Act, Sec. 503 (e), as "An activity or activities of the United States Government to influence political, economic or military conditions abroad, where it is intended that the role of the United States Government will not be apparent or acknowledged publicly."

Some intelligence specialists have objected to the phrase "covert action," believing that the word "covert" emphasizes secrecy over policy. (The British had earlier referred to this activity as "special political action"— SPA.) This is an important distinction, because even though these activities are, indeed, secret, the most important point is that they are undertaken as one means to advance policy goals. This cannot be stressed enough. Proper covert actions are undertaken because policymakers have determined that these are the best way to achieve a desired end. These operations are not— or should not be—undertaken on the initiative of the intelligence agencies.

During the Carter administration (1977–1981)—which exhibited some qualms about force as a foreign policy tool—the innocuous and somewhat comical phrase "special activity" was crafted to replace covert action. The administration replaced a euphemism with a euphemism. But when the Reagan administration came into office, with very different views on intelligence policy, it continued to use the phrase "special activity" in its executive order governing intelligence.

Ultimately, what these activities are called should not matter that much. The fact that the United States has made these various changes in appellation is interesting in that they reveal a degree of official discomfort with the tool.

The classic rationale behind covert action is that policymakers need a "third option" (yet another euphemism) between doing nothing (the first option) in a situation where vital interests may be threatened and sending in military force (the second option), which raises a host of difficult political issues. Not everyone would agree with this rationale, including those who would properly note that diplomatic activity is more than "doing nothing" without resorting to force.

As with counterintelligence, it is pertinent to ask whether covert action was a product of the cold war and whether it remains relevant today. As noted in chap. 2, covert action became—under the leadership of DCI Allen Dulles during the Eisenhower administration (1953–1961)—an increasingly attractive option. It had both successes and failures but was seen as a useful tool in a broad-based struggle with the Soviet Union. In the post–cold war period one could conceive of situations—against terrorists or narcotics traffickers—where some sort of covert action might be the preferred means of action.

THE DECISION-MAKING PROCESS

To repeat, covert action makes sense—and should be undertaken—only when tasked by duly authorized policymakers in pursuit of specific policy goals that cannot be achieved by any other means. Covert action cannot substitute or compensate for a poorly conceived policy. The structure that follows, therefore, presumes that policymakers have formulated legitimate policy goals and that covert action is not only a viable means but also the best means of achieving them. The planning process for covert action must begin with policymakers justifying the policy and defining clearly the national security interests and goals that are at stake.

Maintaining a capability for covert action entails expenses, not only for the operation itself but also for the infrastructure involved in mounting the action. Even though covert actions are not planned and executed overnight, a certain level of preparedness—such as equipment, transportation, false documents, and trained personnel, including foreign assets—must be kept on hand at all times. Forming and maintaining this standby capability takes time and costs money. But the key question at this point in the decision-making process is whether the cost of carrying out a covert action is justified. Cost becomes especially important when looking at covert actions that may last for months or longer.

Alternatives to covert action are a key issue. If overt means of producing a similar outcome are available, these will almost certainly be preferable. Using them does not preclude the use of covert action later if the overt means fail, or in conjunction with overt means, but the overt means should be tried first.

Policymakers and intelligence officials examine at least two levels of risk before approving a covert action. The first is the risk of exposure.

Former DCI William Colby—perhaps reflecting the large-scale investigations of intelligence that dominated his tenure as DCI (1973–1976)—said a director should always assume that an operation will become known at some point. Clearly, there is a difference between an operation that is exposed while under way or shortly after its conclusion and one that is revealed years later. Nonetheless, even a long-postponed exposure may prove to be embarrassing or even very costly politically.

The second risk to be weighed is failure of the operation. Failure may be costly at several levels: in human lives and as a political crisis for the nation carrying out the operation, as well as for those it may be trying to help. Decision makers must weigh the relative level of risk against the interests that are at stake. An extremely risky operation may still be worth undertaking if the stakes are high enough and there are no alternatives. In other words, the ends may justify the means, or at least the risks. For example, in the 1980s the United States was looking for ways to aid the Mujaheddin rebels in Afghanistan who were fighting Soviet invaders. One option was to arm the rebels with Stinger antiaircraft missiles, which would counter the successful Soviet use of helicopters. But policymakers were concerned that some Stingers would fall into the wrong hands or even be captured by the Soviets. Ultimately, the Reagan administration decided to send the Stingers, which helped alter the course of the war. It also left Stingers in the hands of the Mujaheddin after their victory, but policymakers deemed that a smaller risk than Soviet victory in Afghanistan.

Even though intelligence analysis and operations exist only to serve policy, intelligence officers may be eager to demonstrate their covert action capabilities. Several factors may drive officers to do so: a belief that they can deliver the desired outcome, a bureaucratic imperative to prove their value, their professional pride in doing this type of work. However, unless the operation is closely tied to agreed-upon policy goals and is supported as a viable option by the policy community, it starts off severely hampered. Covert action planners must therefore closely coordinate their plans and actions with policy offices.

Covert actions are extraordinary steps, something between the states of peace and war. That alone is enough to raise broad ethical questions, although the policymakers' willingness to maintain a covert action capability indicates some agreement among them on the propriety of its use. The specific details of an operation are likely to raise ethical issues as well. Should a democratically elected but procommunist government be subverted and overthrown (Guatemala, 1954)? Should a nation's economy be disrupted—with attendant suffering for the populace—to overthrow the government (Cuba, 1960s)? Should a group opposed to a hostile government be armed, with a view toward fomenting an insurgency

(Nicaragua, 1980s)? These issues are important not only intrinsically but also because of the risk of exposure. How do these actions fit with the causes, standards, and morals that the United States supports?

In evaluating proposed covert actions, policymakers should examine analogous past operations. Have they been tried in this same nation or region? What were the results? Are the risk factors different? Has this type of operation been tried elsewhere? Again, with what results? Although these are common-sense questions, they run up against a fascinating governmental phenomenon: the inability to use historical examples. Decision makers are so accustomed to concentrating on near-term issues that they tend not to remember accurately past analogous situations in which they have been involved. They move from issue to issue in rapid succession, with little respite and even less reflection. Or, as Ernest R. May and Richard Neustadt pointed out in *Thinking in Time: The Uses of History for Decision Makers* (1988), they "learn" somewhat false lessons from the past, which are misapplied to new circumstances.

Legislative reaction to covert actions is a bigger issue for the United States than it is for other democracies. The congressional committees that oversee the intelligence community are an integral part of the process, not only for funding but as decision makers who need to be apprised of a planned operation; although their support is important, it is not mandatory. The process by which covert actions are ordered in the United States is worth describing. To repeat, covert actions should be closely tied to agreed policy goals, and they are usually not planned overnight. The long lead times required for these operations also mean that they can be put into the budget process in advance, so that funds can be allocated for them.

Assuming that all of the questions raised above have been successfully answered, the action still requires formal approval. The president must sign an order approving the operation, based on his finding that it is "necessary to support identifiable foreign policy objectives of the United States, and is important to the national security of the United States." In intelligence parlance, this document is called a "presidential finding." Congress and the American public did not know that the president signed off on each operation until Secretary of State Henry Kissinger was forced to reveal as much before a congressional committee in the mid-1970s. Presidential findings are now required by law and must be in writing (except for emergencies, in which case a written record must be kept and a finding produced within forty-eight hours).

The finding is transmitted not only to those responsible for the operation but also to Congress (the House and Senate Intelligence Committees or a more limited congressional leadership group). Often, because of the long timelines involved, the congressional committees will already have learned about the operation via the budget process, which includes a review of the year's covert action plan. Congress may wish to be briefed on the specifics of the finding and the operation as well. These briefings are advisory in nature. Other than denying funding during the budget process, Congress has no basis for approving or disapproving an operation, unless specific laws or executive orders ban them—such as the various acts passed by Congress in the 1980s limiting aid to the contras or the executive order banning assassination.

However, should committee members or the staffs raise serious questions, a prudent covert action briefing team will report that fact to the executive. This should be enough to cause the operation to be reviewed. The executive branch may still decide to go ahead, or it may make changes in the operation to respond to congressional concerns.

The covert action policy system, for all of its rules, remains fragile because of its inherent secrecy. The Iran-contra scandal underscored some of its weaknesses. A majority in Congress, opposed to support for the contras in Nicaragua, cut off funding. President Reagan, in his usual broad manner, urged his NSC staff to help the contras "keep body and soul together." NSC staffer Lt. Col. Oliver North did this by soliciting donations from private individuals and foreign governments, alleging that DCI Casey, who died just as the scandal broke, had approved these activities. North also argued that Congress's restrictions applied to Defense Department and intelligence agencies, not to the NSC staff. In a parallel activity, the NSC staff pursued clandestine efforts to improve ties to Iran and free hostages in the Middle East, despite earlier objections to this policy by the secretaries of state (George Shultz) and defense (Caspar Weinberger). Israel shipped antitank missiles to Iran at the behest of the NSC staff, with the United States replacing them. North also became involved in the Iranian initiative and suggested diverting to the contras the money that Iran had paid.

Iran-contra pointed up several problems in the covert action process:

- There were questionable delegations of authority to order and manage covert actions (the actions of North on the NSC staff).
- Presidential findings were postdated and signed ex post facto (the finding authorizing the sale of missiles to Iran).
- Disparate operations were merged (using the Iranian money to fund the contras).
- The executive branch failed to keep Congress properly informed (disregarding the laws restricting aid to the contras and not briefing on the finding to sell missiles to Iran).

Debates on the worthiness of the respective policies involved in Iran-contra notwithstanding, NSC staff and other executive branch officials violated a host of accepted norms and rules in managing the operations.

THE RANGE OF COVERT ACTIONS

Covert actions encompass many types of activities. Several of the main types will be discussed here, ranging from the least to the most violent.

Propaganda is the very old political technique of disseminating information that has been created with a specific political outcome in mind. Propaganda can be used to support individuals or groups friendly to you or to undermine your opponents. It can also be used to create false rumors of political unrest, economic shortages, or direct attacks on individuals, to name a few techniques.

Political activity is a step above propaganda, although they may be used together. But political activity enables an intelligence operation to intervene more directly in the political process of the targeted nation. As with propaganda, political activity can be used to help friends or to impede foes. For example, in the late 1940s the United States supplied scarce newsprint to centrist, anticommunist political parties in Italy and France during closely contested elections. The United States has also funneled money to political parties overseas to help during elections. Or a state can use political activity more directly against its foes, such as disrupting rallies or interfering with their publications.

The United States has tended to use economic activity against governments deemed to be hostile. Every political leadership—democratic or totalitarian—worries about the state of its economy because this has the greatest daily effect on the population: the availability of food and commodities, the stability of prices, the relative ease or difficulty with which basic needs can be met. Economic unrest often leads to political unrest. Again, other techniques may be used in conjunction with economic activity, such as propaganda to create false fears about shortages. Or the economic techniques may be more direct, such as attempts to destroy vital crops or to flood a state with counterfeit currency in order to destroy faith in the monetary system. For years, the United States attacked Cuba's economy directly as well as indirectly via a trade embargo. Economic unrest was also a key factor in U.S. efforts to undermine the government of Salvador Allende in Chile in the early 1970s. Interestingly, economic destabilization may be more effective against a more democratic rule, as in Chile, than against a dictatorship, as in Cuba, which has fewer qualms about inflicting want or privation on its people and will be much less responsive to—or even willing to tolerate—popular protests.

Coups, the actual overthrow of a government, either directly or through surrogates, are a further step up the covert action ladder (see Figure 8-1). Again, a coup may be the culmination of many of the other techniques—propaganda, political activity, economic unrest. The United States used coups successfully in Iran in 1953 and in Guatemala in 1954

FIGURE 8-1   The Covert Action "Ladder"

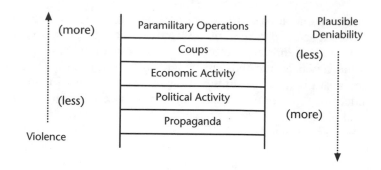

and was involved in undermining the Allende government in Chile, although the coup that brought down his government was indigenous.

Paramilitary operations are the largest, most violent, and most dangerous covert actions, involving the equipping and training of large armed groups for a direct assault on one's enemies. They do not involve the use of a state's own military personnel in combatant units, which technically would be an act of war. The United States was successful in this type of operation in Afghanistan in the 1980s but failed abysmally at the Bay of Pigs in 1961. The contra war against the Sandinistas in Nicaragua was neither won nor lost, but the Sandinistas were defeated at the polls when they held a free election in the midst of a deteriorating economy.

Some nations have also practiced a "higher" level of covert military activity—secret participation in combat. For example, Soviet pilots flew combat missions during the Korean War against UN (primarily U.S.) aircraft. This type of activity raises several issues: military action without an act of war and possible retaliation and the rights of combatants if captured. The United States has largely eschewed this practice because of these complications, preferring to allow intelligence officers to take part in paramilitary activities.

It is important to distinguish between paramilitary operations and the growing use of special operations forces, even before the war in Afghanistan. To repeat the most fundamental and important distinction, special forces are uniformed military personnel conducting a variety of combat tasks not performed by traditional military arms. The United States now has a Special Operations Command (SOCOM). Other such forces are the British Special Air and Special Boat Services (SAS and SBS). Paramilitary operations do not involve the use of one's own uniformed military personnel as combatants. In Afghanistan, the role of paramilitary personnel appears to have been closer to actual combat than was primarily the case in Nicaragua, but their main role remains training, helping supply, and offering leadership assistance to indigenous forces. The CIA's paramilitary forces in Afghanistan are part of the CIA/DO's Special Activities Division. According to press accounts, CIA paramilitary personnel were the first U.S. forces in Afghanistan, establishing contact with the Northern Alliance and preparing them for the offensive against the Taliban.

ISSUES IN COVERT ACTION

Covert action, both in concept and practice, raises a host of issues. This section will pose questions more than provide answers.

The most fundamental issue is whether such a policy option is "legitimate." Like most questions of this sort, there is no "correct" answer. The prevailing opinions can be divided into two schools—idealists and pragmatists. Idealists argue that covert intervention by one state in the internal affairs of another violates acceptable norms of international behavior. They argue that the very concept of a third option is illegitimate. Pragmatists may accept the arguments of the idealists but contend that the self-interest of a state occasionally makes covert action necessary and legitimate. Historical practice over several centuries would tend to favor the pragmatists. Idealists would respond that the historical record still does not justify covert intervention. (This debate took a curious turn with passage of the 1998 Iraq Liberation Act, in which Congress and the president agreed to spend $97 million to replace the regime of Saddam Hussein—an overt commitment to interfere in Iraq's internal affairs.)

We can move from this abstract argument on propriety and legitimacy to a more specific discussion about the U.S. use of covert action during the cold war. In several instances during the nineteenth and twentieth centuries the United States intervened in other nations, primarily in the Western Hemisphere, but these activities were largely overt and usually military in nature. The United States began to use covert action in the context of the cold war. Did the nature of the Soviet threat make covert action legitimate? Did the use of this option—not only directly against the Soviet Union but also in third world nations that were often the battlegrounds of the cold war—lessen the moral differences between the United States and the Soviet Union? Again, there are broad differences of opinion. To U.S. policymakers during the administrations of Harry S. Truman (1945–1953) and Dwight D. Eisenhower (1953–1961) the Soviet threat was so large and multifaceted that the question of the legitimacy of covert action never really arose. Indeed, they preferred covert action to the possibility of a general war in Europe or Asia. On the other hand, some people believe that the use of this option blurred distinctions between the two nations that should have been important.

Assuming that, in broad terms, covert action is an acceptable option, is it circumscribed by the nature of the state against which it is being carried out? Or does this question become irrelevant if one accepts the legitimacy of covert action? For example, the United States used covert economic destabilization against Castro's Cuba and Allende's Chile. Both were communists, but Castro had seized power after a guerrilla war; Allende never commanded an electoral majority, but he had been elected according to the Chilean constitution. Castro turned Cuba into a hostile Soviet base. Allende showed only disturbing signs of friendliness to Castro and to other Soviet allies. Rather than have a second Soviet satellite in the Western Hemisphere, the United States opted to destabilize Allende in the hope of fomenting a coup against him. Should the fact that Allende had been elected according to Chilean law have been sufficient to preclude covert action by the United States? Or were U.S. national security concerns of sufficient primacy to make the covert option legitimate? This was not the first time the United States had intervened in democratic processes. As noted, the United States gave covert assistance in a variety of forms to centrist parties in Europe in the late 1940s to preclude communist victories.

Central to the U.S. concept of covert action is "plausible deniability": that U.S. denials of a role in the events stemming from a covert action appear plausible. The need to mask its role stems directly from the idea that the action has to be covert. If the situation could be addressed overtly, the role of the United States would not be an issue.

Plausible deniability depends almost entirely on having the origin of the action remain covert. Once that is lost, deniability is barely plausible. Deniability may have been sustainable during the 1950s and 1960s, but this has become more difficult since the revelation that the president signs each finding to order a covert action.

The scale of the activity also matters. For example, in the aftermath of the Bay of Pigs debacle, President John F. Kennedy (1961–1963) sought counsel from his predecessor, President Eisenhower. Kennedy defended his decision not to commit air power to assist the invasion on the grounds of maintaining deniability of a U.S. role. Eisenhower scoffed, asking how—given the scale and nature of the operation—the United States could plausibly deny a role.

Plausible deniability also raises concerns about accountability. If one of the premises of covert action policy is the ability to deny a U.S. role, does this also allow officials to avoid responsibility for an operation that is controversial or perhaps even a failure? Or does the fact that the president must sign a finding put the responsibility on him?

The main controversy raised by propaganda activities is that of "blowback." The CIA is precluded from undertaking any intelligence activities within the United States. It is possible, however, for a story that is planted in a media outlet overseas to be reported in the United States. That is blowback. This risk is probably higher today with global twenty-four-hour news agencies than it was during the early days of the cold war. Thus, inadvertently, a CIA-planted story that is false can be reported in a U.S. media outlet. In such a case, does the CIA have a responsibility to inform the U.S. media outlet of the true nature of the story? Would doing so compromise the original operation? If such notification should not be given at the time, should it be given afterward?

Not all covert actions remain covert. One of the key determinants seems to be the scale of the operation. The smaller and more discreet the operation, the easier it is to keep secret. But as operations become larger, especially paramilitary operations, the ability to keep them covert declines rapidly. Two operations undertaken during the Reagan administration—aid to the contras in Nicaragua and to the Mujaheddin in Afghanistan—illustrate the problem. Should the possibility of public disclosure affect decision makers when they are considering paramilitary operations? Or should disclosure be accepted as one of the costs of undertaking this type of effort, with the understanding that it is likely to be something less than covert and not plausibly deniable?

Despite the desired separation of intelligence and policy, covert action blurs the distinction in ways that analysis does not. Instead of providing intelligence to assist in the making of decisions, through covert action the intelligence community is being asked to help execute policy. Of necessity, it will have a role in determining the scale and scope of an operation, about which it has the greatest knowledge. The intelligence community will also have a day-to-day role in managing an operation.

The distinction blurs further because the intelligence community has a vested interest in the outcome of a covert action in ways that are vastly different from its interest in the outcome of a policy for which it has provided analysis. Covert action is not just an alternative means of achieving a policy end; it is also a way for the intelligence community to demonstrate its capabilities and value.

Thus, covert action makes the policy and intelligence communities closer collaborators, as the separation between them diminishes. Conversely, the intelligence community takes on additional responsibilities in the eyes of the policy community. The intelligence community will bear a greater burden for a less-than-successful covert action than it will for less-than-perfect intelligence analysis.

Paramilitary operations raise numerous questions, some of which have been addressed above. In addition to the problem of keeping them covert and the strains they put on plausible deniability, paramilitary operations raise serious questions about the amount of time available to achieve their stated goals. Unless these operations appear to have a reasonable chance of success in a well-defined period of time, policymakers find their ensuing options rather limited. On the one hand, they can decide to continue the operation even if the chances of success—usually defined as some sort of military victory—appear slim. It may be that the paramilitary force is unlikely to be defeated but unlikely to win, offering the prospect of an open-ended operation. Alternatively, policymakers can decide to terminate the operation. U.S. abandonment of the Kurds in the 1970s is a case in point. The United States had been supporting the Kurds in their struggle against Iraq to create an independent homeland; covert aid was given to the Kurds via Iran, which also had an interest in weakening its neighbor. The Kurdish effort remained inconclusive. In the mid-1970s, however, the shah decided to resolve his differences with Iraq and ordered the operation to cease. The United States complied, abruptly leaving the Kurds to fend for themselves. But when an operation like this is shut down, it may not be possible to extricate all of the combatants. In such a case, what is the obligation of the power backing the operation to the combatants? Do the combatants understand the risks they have undertaken, or are they really assets of the power backing the covert action?

Within the United States debate continues about which agency should be responsible for paramilitary operations: the CIA or the Defense Department. The CIA has traditionally run paramilitary operations because, initially, the Defense Department wanted no involvement in them. If covert action is an alternative to military operations, the Defense Department might find it difficult to keep the two options separate. International law poses another difficulty. Although there is no international sanction for covert action, the target may consider the use of military personnel (in or out of uniform) in such an activity to be an act of war. Finally, the involvement of the Defense Department may undercut the effort to achieve plausible deniability.

On the other hand, the Defense Department has greater expertise than the CIA in the conduct of military operations as well as a greater infrastructure to carry them out, which might save some money. Removing paramilitary operations from the CIA might also save the intelligence community from some of the internal strains caused by having responsibility for both analysis and operations (see below). Of course, new strains might subsequently appear in the Defense Department.

One concern raised by the conduct of covert actions is their possible effect on intelligence analysis, which is carried out, in part, by the same agency conducting the operation. If the CIA is conducting an operation—

Assassination: The Hitler Argument

Adolf Hitler is often cited as a good argument in favor of assassination as an occasional but highly exceptional policy option. The arguments in favor of assassinating Hitler are fairly obvious, but when would a policymaker have made that decision? Hitler assumed power legally in 1933. Throughout the 1930s he was not the only dictator in Europe who repressed civil liberties or arrested and even killed large numbers of his own population. Indeed, Josef Stalin probably killed more Soviet citizens during collectivization and the great purges than the Nazis sent to death camps. Deciding to kill Hitler prior to his attacks on the Jews or the onset of World War II would have required a fair amount of foresight as to his ultimate purposes. Indeed, very little about Hitler was extraordinary until he invaded Poland in 1939 and approved the "final solution" against the Jews in 1942.

Interestingly, Britain revealed in 1998 that its intelligence considered assassinating Hitler during the war, even as late as 1945. The British abandoned the plan not because of moral qualms or concerns about success but because they decided that Hitler was so erratic as a military commander that he was actually an asset for the Allies!

particularly a paramilitary operation—is it reasonable to expect the analytical part of the CIA to produce objective reports on the situation in that country and the progress of the paramilitary operation? Or will there be a certain impetus, perhaps unstated, to be supportive of the operation? DCI Allen Dulles kept the Directorate of Intelligence—the CIA's analytical arm—ignorant of operations in Indonesia (1957–1958) and at the Bay of Pigs (1961) so as not to "contaminate" them with knowledge of these operations.

In seventeenth- and (to a lesser extent) eighteenth-century Europe, statesmen occasionally used assassination as a foreign policy tool. Heads of state, who were royalty, were exempt from this occasional use of officially sanctioned assassination, but their ministers and generals were not. Soviet intelligence occasionally undertook "wet affairs," as it referred to assassinations. Israeli intelligence has allegedly killed individuals outside of Israel on several occasions. The Church Committee, a Senate select panel formed in 1975 to investigate allegations that the CIA had exceeded its charter, found in 1976 that the United States was involved in several assassination plots in the 1960s and 1970s—the most famous being that against Fidel Castro—although none succeeded.

Since 1976 the United States has formally banned the use of assassination, either directly by the United States or through a third party. This

The Assassination Ban: A Modern Interpretation

In August 1998 the United States launched a cruise missile attack on targets in Afghanistan associated with Osama bin Laden. The United States believed that bin Laden was behind the terrorist attacks earlier that month on two U.S. embassies in East Africa.

The Clinton administration later stated that one goal of the raid was to kill bin Laden and his lieutenants. Administration officials also argued that their targeting of bin Laden did not violate the long-standing ban on assassinations. Their view was based on an opinion written by National Security Council lawyers that the United States could legally target terrorist infrastructures and that bin Laden's main infrastructure was "human."

After the September 2001 attacks, bin Laden and other terrorists were seen as legitimate combatant targets, as the United States was now at war against them.

ban has been written into three successive executive orders, the most recent signed by President Reagan in 1981.

Still, the policy remains controversial. Although support for the ban was fairly widespread when instituted by President Gerald R. Ford (1974–1977), debate over the policy has been growing. Opponents continue to hold that it is morally wrong for a state to target specific individuals. But proponents have argued that assassination might be the best option in some instances and might be morally acceptable, depending on the nature of the target. Drawing up such guidelines still appears to be so difficult as to preclude a return to the previous policy. In the aftermath of the September 11, 2001, terrorist attacks, debate over the assassination ban was renewed. The issue had changed somewhat, however, in that the United States now considered itself to be at war with terrorists, which altered the nature of the target and the legitimacy of using violent force. (See chap. 13 for a more detailed discussion of the ethical and moral issues raised by assassination.)

ASSESSING COVERT ACTION

In addition to raising ethical and moral issues, covert action faces the difficulty of assessing its operations. When assessing a covert action, what constitutes success? Is it just achieving the aims of the operation? Should human costs, if any, be factored into the equation? Is the covert action still a success if its origin has been exposed?

Some people also question the degree to which covert actions produce useful outcomes. Critics point, for example, to the 1953 coup against Mohammad Mossadegh in Iran and argue that it helped lead to the Khomeini regime in 1979. On the other hand, proponents can argue that an operation that put in place a regime friendly to the United States for twenty-six years, in a region as volatile as the Middle East, was very successful.

As with all other policies, the record of covert action is mixed, and there are no hard-and-fast rules for assessing them. Assistance to anticommunist parties in Western Europe in the 1940s was very successful; the Bay of Pigs was a fiasco. The view here is that the Mossadegh coup was a success, for the reasons noted above. But covert action is also subject to the law of unintended consequences. Abetting the fall of Allende helped lead to the regime of Gen. Augusto Pinochet. The average Chilean was probably better off, but many people suffered repression and a period of internal terror. Aid to the Mujaheddin in Afghanistan was highly successful and played an important role in the collapse of the Soviet Union. At the same time, Afghanistan remained mired in a civil war ten years after the last Soviet troops withdrew and was eventually ruled by the Taliban, who hosted the al Qaeda terrorists.

To repeat the two key points: covert action tends to be successful the more closely it is tied to very specific policy goals and the more carefully defined the operation is.

KEY TERMS

blowback
covert action
paramilitary operations
plausible deniability

presidential finding
propaganda
third option

FURTHER READINGS

The works selected here do not go into the details of specific operations. Rather, they focus on the major policy issues discussed in this chapter.

Barry, James A. "Covert Action Can Be Just." *Orbis* 37 (summer 1993): 375–390.
Berkowitz, Bruce D., and Allan E. Goodman. "The Logic of Covert Action." *National Interest* 51 (spring 1998): 38–46.
Chomeau, John B. "Covert Action's Proper Role in U.S. Policy." *International Journal of Intelligence and Counterintelligence* 2 (fall 1988): 407–413.
Godson, Roy S. *Dirty Tricks or Trump Cards: U.S. Covert Action and Counterintelligence*. Washington, D.C.: Brassey's, 1996.

Johnson, Loch K. "Covert Action and Accountability: Decision-Making for America's Secret Foreign Policy." *International Studies Quarterly* 33 (March 1989): 81–109.

Knott, Stephen F. *Secret and Sanctioned: Covert Operations and the American Presidency.* New York: Oxford University Press, 1996.

Prados, John. *Presidents' Secret Wars: CIA and Pentagon Covert Operations since World War II.* New York: William Morrow, 1986.

Reisman, W. Michael, and James E. Baker. *Regulating Covert Action: Practices, Contexts, and Policies of Covert Coercion Abroad in International and American Law.* New Haven: Yale University Press, 1992.

Rositzke, Harry. *The CIA's Secret Operations: Espionage, Counterespionage and Covert Action.* New York: Reader's Digest Press, 1977.

Shulsky, Abram N., and Gary J. Schmitt. *Silent Warfare: Understanding the World of Intelligence.* 2d rev. ed. Washington, D.C.: Brassey's, 1993.

Treverton, Gregory F. *Covert Action: The Limits of Intervention in the Postwar World.* New York: Basic Books, 1987.

Chapter 9

The Role of the Policymaker

Most authors and experts do not consider the policymaker to be part of the intelligence process. In their opinion, once the intelligence has been given to the policy client, the intelligence process is complete. As was stated in chap. 1, the view in this book is that policymakers play such a central role at all stages of the intelligence process that it would be a mistake to omit them. Policymakers do more than receive intelligence; they shape it throughout the entire process. Indeed, without a constant reference to policy, intelligence is rendered meaningless. Moreover, as this chapter states, policymakers can play a determining role at every phase of the intelligence process.

THE NATURE OF THE NATIONAL SECURITY
POLICY PROCESS IN THE U.S. GOVERNMENT

Although much of this book is intended to be a generic discussion of intelligence, the main reference point is the U.S. government. Therefore, a brief discussion of how national security policy is formed in the United States is appropriate.

STRUCTURE AND INTERESTS. The five main loci of the policy process are:

1. The president, as an individual

2. The departments, particularly the State Department and the Defense Department, which has two major components: the civilian (the Office of the Secretary of Defense) and the military (the Joint Chiefs of Staff and the Joint Staff). On certain issues, other departments may also be involved, including Justice, Commerce, Treasury, Agriculture, and, in the aftermath of the September 2001 attacks, those involved in homeland security or defense.

3. The National Security Council staff, which is the hub of the system

4. The intelligence community

5. Congress, which controls all expenditures, makes policy in its own right, and performs oversight.

The main national security structure has been remarkably stable since it was established by the National Security Act of 1947.

These five groups have somewhat varying interests. The president is a transient, mainly concerned about broad policy initiatives and, eventually, his place in history. Richard Nixon, who was intensely suspicious of the permanent bureaucracy, argued—correctly—that a gulf exists between the president's interests and those of the permanent bureaucracy. Sometimes they will work together; at other times they will be at odds. The bureaucracy tends to be more jaded and, on occasion, to take the view that it can outlast the president, his appointees, and their preferred policies.

The principal interest of the State Department is maintaining diplomatic relations as a means of furthering U.S. policy interests. Critics of the State Department argue that Foreign Service officers sometimes forget which nation they represent, becoming advocates for the nations on which they have expertise rather than for the United States.

The Defense Department is primarily concerned with having a military capability sufficient to deter hostile nations from using force or to defeat any threats as quickly as possible. Critics of the Defense Department hold that the department overestimates its needs and threats and requires too large a margin against any potential foe. In the aftermath of Vietnam, the unofficial but very influential rules for the use of force promulgated by Secretary of Defense Caspar Weinberger and JCS Chairman Gen. Colin Powell set very high requirements for domestic political support and force preponderance before any troops should be committed.

The National Security Council, as constituted by law, consists of the president, the vice president, and the secretaries of state and defense. The chairman of the Joint Chiefs of Staff serves as the military adviser; the director of central intelligence is subordinate to the NSC and serves as the intelligence adviser. As a corporate group, the NSC meets irregularly. (A Deputies Committee, below the NSC, meets more often.) The NSC staff consists of career civil servants, military officers, and political appointees who have day-to-day responsibility for conveying the wishes of the president to the policy and intelligence communities and for coordinating among the various departments and agencies. The NSC staff is primarily interested in the execution of policy as defined by the president and senior presidential appointees.

The intelligence community has no policy interests per se, although it wants to be kept informed about the course of policy in order to make a contribution to it.

POLICY DYNAMICS—"THE INTERAGENCY." Policymakers often refer to the "interagency process," or "the interagency." The term reflects the involvement of any and all necessary agencies and players in the process. The ultimate goal of the U.S. policy process is to arrive at a consensus that all parties can support. But consensus in the U.S. bureaucratic system means agreement down to the very last detail of any paper being considered.

The process has no "override mechanism," that is, no way of forcing agreement, of isolating an agency that refuses to go along. This safeguards the rights and interests of all agencies, because the agency that is isolated on an issue today may not be the one that is isolated tomorrow. To ensure that an agency is not coerced, the interagency process emphasizes bargaining and negotiation rather than majority rule. Bargaining has three immediate effects. First, it can require a great deal of time to arrive at positions that everyone can accept. Second, this system gives tremendous leverage to any agency that refuses to reach an agreement. In the absence of any override process, the agency that "just says 'no'" can wield enormous power. Third, the necessity of reaching agreement generates substantial pressure in favor of lowest-common-denominator decisions.

On controversial issues, the system can suffer inertia, as agencies constantly redraft papers that never achieve consensus or that one agency refuses to support, effectively bringing the system to a halt. The only way to break such logjams is for the NSC staff or someone higher, meaning the president and his senior appointees, to apply pressure from above. Without their intervention, the system will spin endlessly if an agency continues to hold out. Senior pressure renews the impetus to reach a conclusion or raises the prospect that officials in the holdout agency will be told to support what the president wants or to resign. But without pressure from above, holdouts suffer no penalty.

Neither the policy community nor the intelligence community is a monolith. Each has multiple players with multiple interests, which do not always coincide with one another.

THE ROLE OF THE INTELLIGENCE COMMUNITY IN THE SYSTEM. Policymakers accept the intelligence community as an important part of the system. But the role of intelligence varies with each administration and sometimes with each issue within an administration. The way in which an administration treats intelligence is the key determinant of the role it plays.

Everyone accepts the utility of intelligence as part of the basis upon which decisions will be made. Again, translating this generality into practice is the important issue. Policymakers have many reasons to find fault with or even ignore intelligence. They do not necessarily view intelligence in the same way as those who are producing it.

Policymakers also accept that the intelligence community can be called upon to carry out certain types of operations. Again, the willingness to use this capacity and the specific types of operations that are deemed acceptable vary with the political leadership. These elected or presidentially appointed leaders are the ones who must make the final decisions on operations and who will be held accountable, in a political sense, if the operations fail. To be sure, intelligence officers can and do get their share of the blame, but policymakers perceive that their own costs are much greater.

WHO WANTS WHAT?

The fact that the government is not a monolithic organization helps explain why policymakers and intelligence officers have different interests. At a very high macro level, everyone "wants the same thing"—successful national security policy—but this statement is so general that it is misleading. Success can mean quite different things to policymakers and intelligence officials.

Policymakers (the administration's senior political appointees and the president) define success as the advancement of their agenda. Even though there is broad continuity in U.S. foreign policy, each administration interprets goals individually and fosters initiatives that are uniquely its own. The success of an administration's agenda must be demonstrable in ways that are easily comprehended, because its successes are expected to have a political dividend. This is not as crass as it sounds. It is important to remember that national security policy is created within a political system and process, the ultimate rewards of which are election and reelection to national office. Finally, policymakers expect support for their policies from the permanent bureaucracy.

The intelligence community defines its goals differently. As noted in chap. 6, Sherman Kent said that intelligence officers have three wishes: to know everything, to be listened to, and to influence policy for the good, as they understand it. The intelligence community also wants to maintain its objectivity regarding policy. Intelligence officials do not want to become, or even to be seen as becoming, advocates for policies other than those that directly affect their activities. Only by maintaining their distance from policy can they hope to produce intelligence that is objective.

But objectivity is not always easily achieved. To cite a fairly recent example, Director of Central Intelligence George Tenet (1997–) was intimately involved in the Israeli-Palestinian negotiations in October 1998. The CIA took responsibility for creating a security relationship between the two sides. As a result, the CIA now had a vested interest in the outcome of the agreement, not because of any intelligence it had produced but because it had become a participant. In this sort of case, legitimate questions can be raised about the potential effect on subsequent analyses of the implementation of the agreement. Will analysts feel free to report that security arrangements are failing, if that is the case, knowing that their own agency is charged with implementing these same arrangements? The answer may be yes, but it is subject to serious question.

The intelligence community also wants to be kept informed about policy directions and preferences. Although this would seem obligatory if the intelligence community is expected to provide relevant analysis, it does not always happen. All too often, policymakers do not inform intelligence, either by design or oversight. Such behavior not only makes the role of intelligence more difficult but can lead to resentment that may be played out in other ways.

Finally, the policymakers' expectation of support from the permanent bureaucracy extends to the intelligence community. But they may be seeking intelligence that supports known policy preferences, thus running the risk of politicization. Politicization can also work in the other direction. The intelligence officer's desire to be listened to (Kent's second wish) may lead to analysis that is meant to please the policymakers, either consciously or unwittingly. In either case, the desire for a good working relationship can directly undermine the desired objectivity of intelligence.

THE INTELLIGENCE PROCESS: POLICY AND INTELLIGENCE

The differences between the policy and intelligence communities—and the potential for tension—appear at each stage of the intelligence process.

REQUIREMENTS. Requirements are not abstract concepts. They are, in reality, the policymakers' agenda. All policymakers will have certain areas on which they must concentrate as well as others on which they would like to concentrate. There will also be areas that are of no interest to them but that require their attention either occasionally or regularly. This mixture of preferences will be very important in forming the agenda and thus the requirements. For example, Secretary of State James Baker was very clear, upon taking office in 1989, that he was not going to spend a lot of time on the Middle East. His decision was not based on a view that the region was unimportant but rather that he was unlikely to achieve much in the Middle East and therefore his time would be better spent elsewhere. Senior subordinates could handle the Middle East. Iraq's invasion of Kuwait undermined his choice. Ironically, it also helped lead to the Madrid conference—presided over by Secretary Baker—at which Israel and its Arab foes met together for the first time.

The intelligence community wants guidance on the priorities of the agenda so that its collection and reporting can be as helpful as possible. At the same time, the community tends to understand that it rarely has the luxury of ignoring a region or issue entirely, even if it is not high on the agenda. Sooner or later, one of them is likely to blow up. That said, the intelligence community regularly makes resource choices that lead to some regions or issues receiving very little attention.

This difference in the approaches of policymakers and intelligence officials to requirements is not played out entirely in formulating the requirements themselves, but in the ensuing parts of the intelligence process.

COLLECTION. Policymakers tend to be uninvolved in the details of collection unless they involve political sensitivities. In such cases, policymakers can have direct and dramatic effects. (*See box, "Policymakers and Intelligence Collection."*) Their practical concerns lie, first, in the budget, as collection is one of the major intelligence costs, particularly technical intelligence. But policymakers also tend to assume, incorrectly, that "everything" is being covered, at least at some minimal level. Thus, when one of the low-priority issues explodes, they expect that a certain low level of collection and on-the-shelf intelligence already exists and that collection can be quickly increased. Both assumptions may be strikingly false. As was noted above, collection priority decisions tend to be zero-sum games, and not all collection assets are easily fungible.

The intelligence community would rather collect more than less, although officials recognize that they cannot cover everything and hope to get policymakers to concur in the areas left uncovered. Still, collection is the bedrock of intelligence. But when policymakers place limits on collection, the intelligence community obeys, even if its preference is to collect. Like the policymakers, intelligence officials are aware of the costs of collection, but they cannot spend more on collection than the policy community is willing to allocate. The customary practice is for the policy community to set limits on collection resources that are lower than the intelligence community would like.

Finally, the intelligence community has a greater understanding, as would be expected, of the limits of collection at any given time. Intelli-

Policymakers and Intelligence Collection

In several instances, policymakers have intervened in intelligence collection for political reasons.

In Cuba, at the onset of the missile crisis in 1962, Secretary of State Dean Rusk opposed sending U-2s over the island because a Chinese Nationalist U-2 had recently been shot down over China and an Air Force U-2 had accidentally violated Soviet air space in Siberia. The need for imagery of possible Soviet missile sites in Cuba was great, but Rusk had other—also legitimate—concerns.

In Iran, several successive U.S. administrations imposed limits on intelligence collection. Basically, intelligence officers were not allowed to have contact with the opposition to the shah in the souks (the markets and bazaars), since this would offend the shah's regime. Instead, U.S. intelligence had to rely on the shah's secret police, Savak, which had an institutional interest in denying that any opposition existed. Thus, as the shah's regime unraveled in 1978–1979, policymakers denied U.S. intelligence the sources and contacts it needed to better analyze the situation or to influence the opposition.

Again, in Cuba, President Jimmy Carter unilaterally suspended U-2 flights as a gesture to improve bilateral relations. Carter came to regret his decision in 1980, when he faced the possibility that a Soviet combat brigade was in Cuba and he required better intelligence on the issue.

In each case, responsible political leaders made decisions that directly affected intelligence collection.

gence officials know that they are not collecting everything. Indeed, they make decisions on a regular basis to exclude certain regions or issues. In their own budget requests, intelligence officials also determine how much of the collection will be processed and exploited, which is always far less than is collected. The intelligence community sees no reasons to convey these facts to the policymakers. At one level, doing so is unnecessary. An uncovered region may stay quiet, which is the bet that the intelligence managers are making. At another level, it may undermine their relationship with policymakers. Why arouse concerns about collection coverage over an issue that is not expected to be a significant priority? Obviously, their choices can lead to even worse relations should one of the regions suddenly become a concern and collection be found wanting.

ANALYSIS. Policymakers want information that will enable them to make an informed decision, but they do not come to this part of the process as blank slates or wholly objective observers. Already in favor of

Intelligence Uncertainties and Policy

In 1987 U.S.-Soviet negotiations were drawing to a close on the Intermediate Nuclear Forces (INF) Treaty. The U.S. intelligence community had three different methods for estimating the number of Soviet INF missiles that had been produced—all of which had to be accounted for and destroyed. Any final number given by the Soviet Union would be suspect.

Each of the three major intelligence agencies advocated its methodology and its number as the one that should go forward. But the senior intelligence officer responsible for the issue decided, correctly, that all three numbers had to go to President Reagan. Some agency representatives argued that this was simply pusillanimous hedging. But the intelligence officer argued that the president had to be aware of the intelligence uncertainties and the possible range of missile numbers before he signed the treaty. That was the right answer, rather than choosing, perhaps arbitrarily, among the methodologies.

certain policies and outcomes, they would like to see intelligence that supports their preferences. Again, this is not necessarily as crass as it sounds. It is only natural for policymakers to prefer intelligence that will enable them to go where they want. This attitude becomes problematic only when they ignore intelligence that is compelling but contrary to their preferences.

Some policymakers also want to keep their options open for as long as possible. Indeed, they may resist making important decisions. (President Franklin D. Roosevelt often exhibited this behavior.) Intelligence can occasionally serve to limit options by indicating that some options are either insupportable or may have dangerous consequences. This may serve as yet another area of friction.

Intelligence often deals in ambiguities and uncertainties. If a situation were known with certainty, there would be no need for intelligence. Honestly reported intelligence highlights uncertainties and ambiguities. (See box, "Intelligence Uncertainties and Policy.") However, these may prove to be discomforting to policymakers for several reasons. First, if their goal is intelligence that will help them make decisions, anything that is uncertain and ambiguous is going to be less helpful or perhaps even a hindrance. Second, some policymakers cannot appreciate why the multibillion-dollar intelligence community cannot resolve issues. Many of them assume that important issues are ultimately "knowable," when in fact many are not.

Setting the Right Expectations

During the briefings that each new administration receives, an incoming under secretary of state was meeting with one of his senior intelligence officers on the issue of narcotics. The intelligence officer laid out in detail all the intelligence that could be known about narcotics: amounts grown, shipping routes, street prices, and so forth. "That said," the intelligence officer concluded, "there is very little you will be able to do with this intelligence."

The under secretary asked why the briefing had ended in that manner.

"Because," the intelligence officer replied, "this is an issue where the intelligence outruns policy's ability to come up with solutions. You are likely to grow frustrated by all of this intelligence while you have no policy levers with which to react. I want to prepare you for this at the outset of our relationship so as to avoid problems later on."

The under secretary understood.

Policymakers may also be suspicious of intelligence that supports their rivals in the interagency policy process. They may suspect that rivals have consorted with the intelligence community to produce intelligence that undercuts their position. Finally, policymakers are free to ignore, disagree with, or even rebut intelligence and offer their own analyses. This is inherent in a system that is dominated by the policymakers.

All of the behaviors noted above undermine Kent's second and third wishes (for the intelligence community to be listened to and to influence policy for the good). The intelligence community also tries to maintain its objectivity. Some policymakers raise questions that can undermine the ability of the intelligence community to fulfill Kent's two wishes and be objective. Some of the conflicts or disconnects noted above can be avoided or ameliorated if the intelligence community makes an initial effort to convey to policymakers as early as possible the limits of intelligence analysis. The goal should be to establish realistic expectations and rules of engagement. *(See box, "Setting the Right Expectations.")*

COVERT ACTION. Covert action can be attractive to policymakers, because it increases available options and theoretically decreases direct political costs. Policymakers may assume that an extensive "on the shelf" operational capability exists and that the intelligence community can mount an operation on fairly short notice. These assumptions are, in effect, the operational counterpart to the assumption that all areas of the world are receiving some minimal level of collection coverage.

Obviously, policymakers want covert actions that will be successful. As has been seen, success is easier to define for short-term operations, but it may be elusive for those of longer duration. This can be a source of tension between the two communities, as the most senior policymakers tend to think in blocks of time no longer than four years—the tenure of a single administration. The intelligence community, as part of the permanent bureaucracy, can afford to think in longer periods of time. It does not face the deadline that elections impose on the administration.

The intelligence community harbors a certain ambivalence about covert action. A covert action gives the intelligence community an opportunity to display its capabilities in an area that is of extreme importance to policymakers. Covert action is also an area where the intelligence community's skills are unique and are less subject to rebuttal or alternatives than is the community's analysis. However, disagreement over covert action is highly probable if policymakers request an operation that intelligence officials believe to be unlikely to succeed or inappropriate. Once the intelligence community is committed to an operation, it does not want to be left in the lurch by the policymakers. For example, in paramilitary operations, the intelligence community will likely feel a greater obligation to the forces it has enlisted, trained, and armed than will the policymakers. The two communities will not view in similar ways a decision to end the operation.

POLICYMAKER BEHAVIORS. Just as certain analyst behaviors matter, this is also true of certain policymaker behaviors. Not every policymaker consumes intelligence in the same way: some like to read, while others prefer being briefed. Policymakers are better served if they convey their preferences early on rather than leave them to guesswork.

Policymakers do not always appreciate the limits of what can be collected and known with certainty, the reasons behind ambiguity, and, occasionally, the propriety of intelligence. They will sometimes confuse the lack of a firm estimate with pusillanimity when that may not be the case.

Given the range of issues on which they must work, senior policymakers will probably not be fully conversant with every issue. The best policymakers will know what they do not know and take steps to learn more. Some will be less self-aware and either learn as they go along or fake it.

The most dreaded reaction to bad news is "killing the messenger," referring to the practice of kings who would kill the herald who brought bad news. Of course, messengers—including intelligence officers—are no longer killed for bringing bad news, but bureaucratic deaths do occur. An intelligence official can lose access to a policymaker or be cut out of important meetings. Both consequences befell DCI John McCone

(1961–1965) when he took issue with President Lyndon Johnson's strategy for the Vietnam War. Policymakers have also been known to badmouth intelligence officers behind their backs.

THE USES OF INTELLIGENCE. One of the divides between policymakers and intelligence officers is the actual use to which the intelligence will be put. Policymakers want to take action; intelligence officers, although sympathetic and sometimes supportive, are also concerned about safeguarding sources and methods and maintaining the community's ability to collect intelligence.

For example, suppose there is intelligence suggesting that officials in a ministry in Country A have decided to arrange a clandestine sale of high-technology components to Country B, whose activities are a proliferation concern. The intelligence community has intelligence strongly suggesting that the sale is going forward, although it is not clear whether Country A's leadership is fully aware of the sale. The State Department, or other executive agencies, believe that the situation is important to U.S. national interests and want to issue a demarche to Country A in order to stop the sale. The intelligence community, however, may argue that this will alert Country A—and perhaps Country B as well—to the fact that the United States has some very good intelligence sources. Thus, the intelligence community may oppose issuing a demarche. At a minimum, it will insist on having a hand in drafting the demarche so as to obscure its basis. This can result in a new bureaucratic tug of war, because the State Department will want the demarche to be as strong as possible in order to get the preferred response, cessation of the sale.

This type of situation arises so frequently that it is accepted by both sides—policy and intelligence—as one of the normal aspects of national security. This struggle is analogous to the divide between intelligence officers and law enforcement officials: intelligence officers want to collect more intelligence, whereas law enforcement officials seek to prosecute malefactors and may need to use the intelligence to support an indictment and prosecution. On occasion, policy officials may cite a piece of open-source intelligence that makes the same case that the classified intelligence does, and argue that this can be used as the basis of the demarche. However, the intelligence officers may not agree, contending that it is only because the same information is known via classified sources that the open-source intelligence is validated. Thus, the intelligence officers may argue that even using open-source intelligence can serve to reveal classified intelligence sources and methods. In the case of imagery, at least, the greater availability of high-quality commercial imagery may obviate this entire debate.

There is no correct answer to this debate. On the one hand, the intelligence exists solely to support policy. If it cannot be used, it begins to lose its purpose. On the other hand, officials must balance the gain to be made by a specific demarche versus the gains that may be available by not revealing intelligence sources and methods. "Usable intelligence" is a constant general goal, but which intelligence gets used when and how is open to debate.

OTHER ISSUES. Ideally, the relationship between policymakers and the intelligence community should be symbiotic: policymakers should rely upon the intelligence community for advice, which is a major rationale for the existence of the intelligence community. In order for the community to produce good advice, policymakers should keep intelligence officers informed about the major directions of policy and their specific areas of interest and priority. That said, the relationship is not one of equals. Policymakers can exist and function without the intelligence community, but the opposite is not true. Intelligence is dependent on policy for its existence; policy can exist without the support of intelligence.

The line that divides policy and intelligence—and the fact that policymakers can cross it but intelligence officers cannot—also affects the relationship. Policymakers tend to be vigilant in seeing that intelligence does not come too close to the line. However, they may ask intelligence officers for advice in choosing among policy options—or for some action—that would take intelligence over the line. If intelligence officers decline, as they should to preserve their objectivity regardless of the outcome, policymakers may become resentful. It is also important to remember that the line blurs at the very highest levels of the intelligence community, and the DCI may be asked for advice that is, in reality, policy.

In the United States, partisan politics has also become a factor in the policy–intelligence relationship. Although differences in emphasis developed from one administration to another (such as the greater emphasis on political covert action in the Eisenhower administration), there was general continuity in intelligence policy. Moreover, until 1976, intelligence was not seen as part of the "spoils" of an election victory. DCIs were not automatically replaced with each new administration, as were the heads of virtually all other agencies and departments. President Richard Nixon (1969–1974) tried to use the CIA for political ends in an attempt to curtail the Watergate investigations. But it was the Carter administration (1977–1981) that ended the political separateness of the intelligence community. Jimmy Carter, in his 1976 campaign, lumped together Vietnam, Watergate, and the recent investigations of U.S. intelligence. When Carter won the presidency, DCI George H.W. Bush (1976–1977) offered to stay on and eschew all partisan politics, saying that the CIA needed some continuity after the investigations and four DCIs in as many years. President-elect Carter said he wanted a DCI of his own choosing. This was the first time a serving DCI had been asked to step down by a new administration. Similarly, Ronald Reagan made "strengthening the CIA" part of his 1980 campaign and also brought in a new DCI, William Casey (1981–1987). In a presidential transition within the same party, President Bush kept on DCI William Webster (1987–1991) for most of his term, but Bill Clinton replaced DCI Robert Gates (1991–1993) with James Woolsey (1993–1995). Thus, a partisan change in the White House came to mean a change in DCIs as well. However, in 2001, President George W. Bush retained DCI George Tenet, who had been appointed by Clinton, despite some advice from within Bush's own party to remove him. Tenet thus became the first DCI since Helms to survive a party change in the presidency, but it is not clear that a new practice has been established.

The argument made in favor of changing DCIs when a new administration takes office is that presidents must have a DCI with whom they are comfortable. But in the days of a nonpartisan DCI, many people in Washington emphasized the professional nature of the DCI (even those DCIs who were not career intelligence officers) and had the sense that intelligence is in some way "different" from the rest of the structure that each president inherits and fills with his own appointees. An objective intelligence community was not to be part of the partisan spoils of elections. The shift since 1977 has affected the policy–intelligence relationship by tagging DCIs with a partisan coloration that they did not have in the past. The shift has also meant a movement away from professional intelligence officers serving as DCIs. Although professionals were not the only people selected in the past, their selection is less likely in the future.

Finally, one must note the potential effect of external intrusions on the relationship, particularly that of the electronic news media. Contrary to popular belief, television news does not foster major changes in policy. It does serve as a means of communication for states and their leaders, and it competes with the intelligence community as an alternative source of information. The media do occasionally "scoop" the intelligence community. This is not because they know things that the intelligence community does not. Rather, the electronic media—especially the twenty-four-hour operations such as CNN—put a premium on speed and have the capacity and willingness to provide updates and corrections as necessary. The intelligence community does not have the same luxury and tends to take more time in preparing its initial report. Being scooped by the media can lead policymakers to believe mistakenly that the media offer much the same coverage as the intelligence community—and at greater speed and less cost.

This chapter has emphasized those issues that are likely to create conflict between policymakers and the intelligence community. It would be incorrect to suggest that conflict is the mainstay of the policy–intelligence relationship. Close and trusting working relationships prevail between policymakers and intelligence officers at all levels. But a good working relationship is not a given, and it cannot be fully appreciated without understanding all of the potential sources of friction.

FURTHER READINGS

Despite its centrality to the intelligence process, the policymaker–intelligence relationship has not received as much attention as other parts of the process.

Betts, Richard K. "Policy Makers and Intelligence Analysts: Love, Hate, or Indifference?" *Intelligence and National Security* 3 (January 1988): 184–189.

Heymann, Hans. "Intelligence/Policy Relationships." In *Intelligence: Policy and Process*. Ed. Alfred C. Maurer et al. Boulder: Westview Press, 1985.

Hulnick, Arthur S. "The Intelligence Producer–Policy Consumer Linkage: A Theoretical Approach." *Intelligence and National Security* 1 (May 1986): 212–233.

Kovacs, Amos. "Using Intelligence." *Intelligence and National Security* 12 (October 1997): 145–164.

Lowenthal, Mark M. "Tribal Tongues: Intelligence Consumers and Intelligence Producers." *Washington Quarterly* 15 (winter 1992): 157–168.

Poteat, Eugene. "The Use and Abuse of Intelligence: An Intelligence Provider's Perspective." *Diplomacy and Statecraft* 11 (2000): 1–16.

Thomas, Stafford T. "Intelligence Production and Consumption: A Framework of Analysis." In *Intelligence: Policy and Process*. Ed. Alfred C. Maurer et al. Boulder: Westview Press, 1985.

Chapter 10

Oversight and Accountability

"*Sed quis custodiet ipso custodes?*" (But who will guard the guards?), the Roman poet and satirist Juvenal asked. The oversight of intelligence has always been a problem. The ability to control information is an important power in any state, whether democratic or despotic. Information that is unavailable by any other means and whose dissemination is often restricted is the mainstay of intelligence. By controlling an important body of information; by having expertise in surveillance, eavesdropping, and other operations; and by operating behind a cloak of secrecy, an intelligence apparatus always has the potential to threaten heads of government. Thus, government leaders' ability to oversee intelligence effectively is important.

In democracies, oversight tends to be a responsibility shared by the executive and legislative powers. The oversight issues are somewhat generic: budget, responsiveness to policy needs, control of operations, propriety of activities. This chapter, like the others in the book, will concentrate on the United States, which is unique in giving extensive oversight responsibilities and powers to the legislative branch. Other parliaments have committees devoted to intelligence oversight, but none have the same broad oversight powers.

EXECUTIVE OVERSIGHT ISSUES

Many of the oversight issues that concern the executive branch have been discussed in earlier chapters. The core question is whether the intelligence community is properly carrying out its functions, that is, whether the community is asking the right questions, responding to policymakers' needs, being rigorous in its analysis, and having on hand the right operational capabilities (collection and covert action). Policymakers cannot trust the intelligence community to answer these questions alone. At the same time, senior officials outside the intelligence community (the national

---

A Linguistic Aside: The Two Meanings of Oversight

Oversight has two definitions that are distinct, if not opposites:
- supervision; watchful care (as in "We have oversight of that activity.")
- failure to notice or consider (as in "We missed that. It was an oversight.")

In overseeing intelligence, Congress and the executive try to carry out the first definition and to avoid the second.

---

security adviser, the secretaries of state or defense, the president) cannot maintain a constant vigil over these matters. Outside of the intelligence community itself, the NSC Office of Intelligence Programs is the highest-level organization within the executive branch that provides day-to-day oversight and policy direction of intelligence.

Since the administration of Dwight D. Eisenhower (with two brief lapses), presidents have relied on the President's Foreign Intelligence Advisory Board (PFIAB) to carry out higher-level and more objective oversight than the NSC Office of Intelligence Programs does. PFIAB members are appointed by the president and usually include former senior intelligence and policy officials and individuals with relevant commercial backgrounds. (In the 1990s some people were appointed to PFIAB largely as political favors.) PFIAB can respond to problems (such as the investigation of alleged Chinese spying at Los Alamos National Laboratory) or can initiate activities (such as the Team A–Team B competitive analysis on Soviet strategic capabilities and intentions).

The executive branch tends to focus its oversight on issues related to espionage and covert action. Espionage oversight is inclined to concentrate on lapses, such as the Ames case or allegations of Chinese espionage. For example, in 1999 PFIAB issued a scathing report on Department of Energy security practices related to the Chinese espionage. As with all other activities, executive branch organizations divide responsibility for overseeing covert action. The president is responsible for approving all covert actions, but the day-to-day responsibility for managing them resides with the DCI and the Directorate of Operations.

One oversight issue relating to covert action centers on the operating concept of "plausible deniability." In the case of large-scale paramilitary operations—such as the Bay of Pigs or the contras—deniability is somewhat implausible. But many covert actions are much smaller in scale, making it possible to deny plausibly any U.S. role. Some critics of covert action argue that plausible deniability undermines accountability by giving operators an increased sense of license. Since the president will deny any connection to their activities, they operate under less constraint. The critics raise an interesting point but overlook the professionalism of most officers.

Another oversight issue relating to covert action has to do with broad presidential findings, sometimes called global findings, versus narrow ones. These tend to be drafted to deal with transnational issues, such as terrorism or narcotics. The broader the finding, and thus the less specificity it contains, the greater is the scope for the intelligence community to define the operations involved. This is not to suggest that the president should precisely define covert actions, but a broad finding does run a greater risk of disconnecting policy preferences from operations.

Policymakers must also be concerned about the objectivity of the intelligence community when it is asked to assess or draw up a covert action. Once again, intelligence officers who feel a need to demonstrate their capabilities may not be able to assess in a cold-eyed manner the feasibility or utility of a proposed action.

Similar concerns may arise when assessing the relative success of an ongoing covert action. Have policymakers and intelligence officials agreed on the signs of success? Are these signs evident? If not, what are the accepted timelines for terminating the action? What are the plans for terminating it?

Finally, can intelligence analysts offer objective assessments of the situation in a country where their colleagues are carrying out a major covert action, particularly a paramilitary one? This issue may be of heightened concern in view of the closer partnership forged between the Directorate of Operations and Directorate of Intelligence in the mid-1990s.

The propriety of intelligence activities is also an aspect of oversight. Are the actions being conducted in accordance with law and executive orders? All intelligence agencies have inspectors general and general counsels. In addition, the President's Intelligence Oversight Board (PIOB), a subset of PFIAB, can investigate in this area. However, the PIOB is a reactive body, with no power to initiate investigations or to subpoena. It is dependent on referrals from executive branch officials. Nonetheless, the PIOB has carried out some useful classified investigations.

CONGRESSIONAL OVERSIGHT

Congress approaches intelligence oversight—and all oversight issues, whether national security or domestic—from a different but equally legitimate perspective from that of the executive branch.

The concept of congressional oversight is established in the Constitution. Article I, section 8, paragraph 18, states: "Congress shall have Power . . . To make all Laws which shall be necessary and proper for carrying into Execution the foregoing Powers, and all other Powers vested by this Constitution in the Government of the United States, or in any Department or Officer thereof." Courts have found that this includes the power to require reports from the executive on the various issues subject to legislation. The essence of congressional oversight is the ability to gain access to information, usually held by the executive, that is relevant to the functioning of the government.

Apart from its constitutional mandate, a major factor driving Congress in all matters of oversight is the desire to be treated by the executive as an equal branch of government. This is not always easy to achieve, as the executive branch ultimately speaks with one voice, that of the president, while Congress has 535 members. Indeed, this significant difference leads some people to question whether Congress's constitutional authority works in reality.

Moreover, in the area of national security, Congress has often given presidents a fair amount of leeway to carry out their responsibilities as commander in chief. This is not to suggest that partisan debates do not arise over national security or even intelligence issues, such as the missile gap or the window of vulnerability. To the contrary, debate has become more partisan in the post–cold war period, despite the fact that threats to U.S. national security have greatly decreased.

Congress has several levers that it can use to carry out its oversight functions.

BUDGET. Control over the budget for the entire federal government is the most fundamental lever of congressional oversight. Article I, section 9, paragraph 7, of the Constitution states: "No Money shall be drawn from the Treasury, but in Consequence of Appropriations made by Law; and a regular Statement and Account of the Receipts and Expenditures of all public Money shall be published from time to time."

The congressional budget process is complex and duplicative. It comprises two major activities: authorization and appropriation. Authorization consists of approving specific programs and activities that will be funded. During this process, authorizing committees suggest dollar amounts for the various programs. The House Permanent Select Committee on Intelligence and the Senate Select Committee on Intelligence are the primary authorizers of the intelligence budget. The House and Senate Armed Services Committees authorize some defense-related intelligence programs. Appropriation consists of allocating specific dollar amounts to authorized programs. The defense subcommittees of the

---

Congressional Humor: Authorizers versus Appropriators

The tension between those who sit on authorizing committees and those who sit on appropriations committees is pithily characterized by the following joke often heard on Capitol Hill:

"Authorizers think they are gods; appropriators know they are gods."

House and Senate Appropriations Committees perform this function for intelligence.

Technically speaking, Congress may not appropriate money for a program that it has not first authorized. If authorizing legislation does not pass before a congressional session ends (to date, this has not happened for intelligence), the appropriations bills contain language stating that they will also serve as authorizing legislation until such legislation is passed. (President George H. W. Bush once vetoed an intelligence authorization bill because Congress had included a requirement that the president give Congress forty-eight hours' prior notice of covert actions, but Congress ultimately passed a new authorization bill omitting that language.)

There is usually some tension between the authorizers and the appropriators. Authorization and appropriations bills sometimes vary widely. For example, authorizers may approve a program that is not given significant funds by the appropriators. This is called "hollow budget authority." Or appropriators may vote money for programs or activities that have not been authorized. These funds are called "appropriated but not authorized" (or "A not A"). In both cases, the appropriators are calling the tune and taking action that disregards the authorizers. (See box, "Congressional Humor: Authorizers versus Appropriators.")

When funds are appropriated but not authorized, the agency receives the money but may not spend it until Congress passes a bill to authorize spending. Sometimes, however, an agency will submit a reprogramming request to Congress, asking permission to spend the money, and Congress can informally approve it. If Congress does not pass a new authorization bill or approve a reprogramming request, the money reverts to the Treasury at the end of the fiscal year.

The centrality of the budget to oversight should be obvious. In reviewing the president's budget submission and crafting alternatives or variations, Congress gets to examine the size and shape of each agency, the details of each program, and the plans for spending money over the next year. No other activity offers the same degree of access or insight.

Moreover, given the constitutional requirement for congressional approval of all expenditures, in no other place does Congress have as much leverage as in the budget process.

Critics of the annual budget process argue that it not only gives Congress insights and power but also subjects the executive to frequent fluctuations in funding levels, since they can vary widely from year to year. Every executive agency dreams of having multiyear appropriations or "no year" appropriations, that is, money that does not have to be spent by the end of the fiscal year. Although some funds are allocated in these ways, Congress resists doing so on a large scale, since this would fundamentally undercut its power of the purse.

The budget gives Congress power over intelligence. In the 1980s, for example, Congress used the intelligence budget to restrict Reagan administration policy in Nicaragua, passing a series of amendments, sponsored by the chairman of the House Permanent Select Committee on Intelligence, Edward Boland, D-Mass., that denied combat-support funds for the contras. Efforts to circumvent these restrictions led to the Iran-contra scandal.

HEARINGS. Hearings are also essential to the oversight process as a means of requesting information from responsible officials and obtaining alternative views from outside experts. Hearings can be open to the public or closed, depending on the subject under discussion. Given the nature of intelligence, a majority of the hearings of the two intelligence committees are closed.

Hearings are not necessarily hostile, but they are adversarial; they are not objective discussions of policy. Each administration uses hearings as a forum for advancing its specific policy choices and as opportunities to "sell" policy to Congress and to interested segments of the public. Congress understands this and is a skeptical recipient of information from the executive branch, regardless of party affiliation. Intelligence officials are somewhat exempt from "selling" policy, in that they often give Congress the intelligence community's views on an issue without supporting or attacking a given policy. They gain some protection from congressional recriminations because of the line separating policy and intelligence. (Executive branch policymakers may perceive the intelligence community's congressional testimony as unsupportive or as undermining policy, even if that was not the intelligence community's intent.) However, when intelligence officials testify about intelligence policies—capabilities, budgets, programs, intelligence-related controversies—they are also in a "sales" mode vis-à-vis Congress.

NOMINATIONS. The power to confirm or reject nominations is an extremely important political power, which resides in the Senate. Nominations for the DCI were not controversial until 1977, when President Jimmy Carter's nominee, Theodore Sorensen, withdrew his nomination after appearing before the Senate Select Committee on Intelligence and responding to a number of issues that had been raised publicly about him. The issues included Sorensen's World War II status as a conscientious objector, which raised questions about his willingness to use covert action; and the possible misuse of classified documents in his memoirs, as well as his defense of Daniel Ellsberg, the man who leaked to the press the so-called *Pentagon Papers* (a Defense Department study of the Vietnam War), which raised concerns about his ability to protect intelligence sources and methods.

Since 1977 the Senate has held several other controversial DCI-nominee hearings. Robert Gates withdrew his first nomination in 1987 as the Iran-contra scandal unfolded. His second nomination, in 1991, featured a detailed investigation of charges that Gates had politicized intelligence in order to please policymakers. In 1997 Anthony Lake withdrew his nomination at the onset of what promised to be a grueling and perhaps unsuccessful series of hearings.

Critics of the nomination process—not just for intelligence positions but across the board—charge that it has become increasingly political and personal, delving into issues that are not germane to a nominee's fitness for office. Defenders of the process respond that it is a political process, that the Senate is not supposed to be a rubber stamp, and that careful scrutiny of a nominee may preclude embarrassments later on. Regardless of which view is correct, it is fair to say that the nomination process has become so formidable that it has convinced some potential nominees to decline office.

TREATIES. Advising and consenting to an act of treaty ratification is also a power of the Senate. Unlike nominations, which require a majority vote of the senators present, treaties require a two-thirds vote of those present. Intelligence became a significant issue in treaties during the era of U.S.-Soviet arms control in the 1970s. The ability to monitor adherence to treaty provisions was and is an intelligence function. U.S. policymakers also called upon the intelligence community to give "monitoring judgments" on various treaty provisions—that is, to adjudge the likelihood that "significant" cheating would be detected. The Senate Select Committee on Intelligence, created in 1976, was later given responsibility for evaluating the intelligence community's ability to monitor arms control treaties. This committee gave the Senate another lever with which to influence intelligence policy. In 1988, for example, the Senate Select Committee on Intelligence, upon evaluating the Intermediate Nuclear Forces (INF) Treaty, and concerned about the upcoming Strategic Arms Reduction Treaty

(START), demanded the purchase of additional imagery satellites. The Reagan administration, which had not been averse to spending money on intelligence, argued that the additional satellites were unnecessary. However, the chairman of the Senate committee, David Boren, D-Okla., made it clear that purchase of the satellites was a price of Senate consent to the treaties.

REPORTING REQUIREMENTS. The separation of powers between the executive branch and Congress puts a premium on information. The executive tends to forward information that is supportive of its policies; Congress tends to seek fuller information in order to make decisions based on more than just the views that the executive volunteers. One of the ways Congress has sought to institutionalize its broad access to information is to levy reporting requirements on the executive branch. Congress often mandates that the executive report on a regular basis (often annually) on specific issues, such as human-rights practices in foreign nations, the arms-control impact of new weapons systems, or, during the cold war, Soviet compliance with arms control and other treaties.

Reporting requirements, which grew dramatically in the aftermath of the Vietnam War, raise several issues. Does Congress require so many reports that it cannot make effective use of them? Do the reports place an unnecessary burden on the executive branch? Would the executive branch forward the same information if there were no reporting requirements?

INVESTIGATIONS AND REPORTS. One of Congress's functions is to investigate, which it may do on virtually any issue it desires. The modern intelligence oversight system evolved from the congressional investigations of intelligence in the 1970s. Investigations tend to result in reports that summarize findings and offer recommendations for change, thus serving as effective tools in exposing shortcomings or abuses and in helping craft new policy directions. Every year the two intelligence committees report publicly on issues that have come before them. These reports may be brief because of security concerns, but they assure the rest of Congress and the public that effective oversight is being carried out, and they create policy documents that the executive must consider.

HOSTAGES. If the executive branch balks on some issue, Congress may seek means of forcing it to agree. One way is to "take hostages"—that is, to withhold action on issues that are important to the executive until the desired action is taken. This type of behavior is not unique to Congress; it was used as a bargaining tactic by intelligence agencies in formulating NIEs and other interagency products.

During the debate on the INF Treaty, the demands of the Senate Select Committee on Intelligence for new imagery satellites was one case of hostage taking. In 1993, Congress threatened to withhold action on the intelligence authorization bill until the CIA provided information on one of the Clinton administration's Defense Department nominees, Morton Halperin. Halperin eventually withdrew his nomination. In 2001 the Intelligence Committees "fenced" (that is, put a hold on) certain funds for intelligence to prod the Bush administration into nominating a new CIA inspector general. Critics argue that hostage taking is a blunt and unwieldy tool; supporters of Congress argue that it is used only when other means of reaching agreement with the executive have failed.

PRIOR NOTICE OF COVERT ACTION. One of Congress's main concerns is that it not be surprised by presidential actions, that it receive prior notice of them. Most members understand that prior notice is not the same as prior congressional approval, which is required for very few executive decisions. Covert action is one of the areas where prior notice has been a contentious issue. As a rule, Congress receives advance notice of covert action in a process that has been largely institutionalized, but successive administrations have refused to make prior notice a legal requirement. A congressional demand for at least forty-eight hours' notice led to the first veto of an intelligence authorization bill, by President George H. W. Bush in 1990.

ISSUES IN CONGRESSIONAL OVERSIGHT

Oversight of intelligence raises a number of issues that are part of the "invitation to struggle," as the separation of powers has often been called.

HOW MUCH OVERSIGHT IS ENOUGH? From 1947 to 1975—the first twenty-eight years of the modern intelligence community's existence—the atmosphere of the cold war promoted fairly lax and distant congressional oversight. A remark by Sen. Leverett Saltonstall, R-Mass., a member of the Senate Armed Services Committee, characterized that viewpoint: "There are things that my government does that I would rather not know about." This attitude was partly responsible for some of the abuses that investigators uncovered in the 1970s.

Working out the parameters of the new oversight system has not been easy. Successive administrations, regardless of party affiliation, have tended to resist what they have seen as unwarranted intrusions.

There is no objective way to determine the "proper" level of oversight. On the budget, Congress reviews each line item. No other way exists to make informed judgments on how to allocate funds, which ulti-mately is Congress's decision. Reviewing specific covert actions may seem intrusive, but it also represents an important political step. If Congress allows the operation to proceed unquestioned, the executive branch can claim political support should problems arise later. Similarly, serious questions raised by Congress are an important signal to rethink the oper-ation, even if the ultimate decision is to go ahead as planned.

Does rigorous oversight require just detailed knowledge of intelli-gence programs, or does it require something more, such as information on alternative intelligence policies and programs? Congress has on occa-sion taken issue with the direction of intelligence policy and acted either to block the administration, such as the Boland amendments that blocked military support to the contras, or to demand changes, such as the pur-chase of the INF satellites.

SECRECY AND THE OVERSIGHT PROCESS. The high level of security that intelligence requires imposes costs on congressional oversight. Mem-bers of Congress have security clearances by virtue of having been elect-ed to office. Members must have clearances to carry out their duties. Only the executive branch can grant security clearances, but there is no basis for its granting or denying clearances to members of Congress, as this would violate the separation of powers. At the same time, member clear-ances do not mean full access to the entire range of intelligence activities. Congressional staff members who require clearances receive them from the executive branch after meeting the usual background checks and demonstrating a need to know. Congressional staff are not polygraphed as a prerequisite for clearances.

Although all members are deemed to be cleared, both the House and Senate limit the dissemination of intelligence to members who are not on the Intelligence Committees. Although this limitation replicates the acceptance of responsibility that all congressional committees have, in the case of intelligence it entails additional burdens for the committees, as their information cannot be easily shared. Thus, the Intelligence Com-mittees require special offices for the storage of sensitive material and must hold many of their hearings in closed session. Both houses have also created different levels of notification, depending on the sensitivity of the information. Intelligence officials may brief only the leadership, or the leaders and the chairman and ranking member of the Intelligence Com-mittee, or some additional committee chairmen as well, or the full Intel-ligence Committees.

Despite these precautions and the various internal rules intended to punish leaks by members or staff, Congress as an institution has the rep-utation of being a fount of leaks. This image is propagated mainly by the executive branch, which believes that it is much more rigorous in handling classified information. In reality, most leaks of intelligence and other national security information come from the executive, not from Congress. (In 1999 DCI George Tenet admitted before a congressional committee that the number of leaks from executive officials was higher than at any time in his memory.) This is not to suggest that Congress has a perfect record on safeguarding intelligence material, but it is far better than that of the CIA, the State or Defense Departments, or the staff of the NSC. The reason is not superior behavior on the part of Congress so much as it is relative levers of power. Leaks occur for a variety of reasons: to show off some special knowledge, to settle scores, or to promote or stop a policy. Other than showing off, members of Congress and their staffs have much better means than leaks to achieve ends two and three. They control spending, which is the easiest way to create or terminate a policy or program. Even minority members and staff can use the legislative process, hearings, and the press to dissent from policies or attempt to slow them down. Officials in the executive branch do not have the same leverage and therefore resort to leaks more frequently. However, the perception of Congress as a major "leaker" persists.

The other issue raised by secrecy is Congress's effectiveness in acting as a surrogate for the public. The U.S. government ostensibly operates on the principle of openness: its operations and decisions should be known to the public. (There is nothing in the Constitution about "the public's right to know." The Constitution safeguards freedom of speech and of the press, but these are not the same as a right to information.) In the case of intelligence, the principle of openness does not apply. Some people accept the reasons for secrecy and the limitations that it imposes on public accountability. Others have concerns about the role of Congress as the public's surrogate in executive oversight. Their reasons vary, from doubts about the executive branch's willingness to be forthcoming with Congress to concerns about Congress's readiness to air disquieting information.

CONGRESS AND THE INTELLIGENCE BUDGET. A recurring issue for Congress has been whether to reveal some aspects of the intelligence budget. As noted above, Article I, section 9, paragraph 7, of the Constitution requires that accounts of all public money be published "from time to time." This phrase is vague, which allowed successive administrations to argue that their refusal to disclose the details of intelligence spending was permissible. Critics contended that this interpretation vitiated the constitutional requirement to publish some account at some point. Most advocates of publication were not asking for a detailed publication of the entire budget but wanted to know at least the total spent on intelligence annually. (See box, "Intelligence Budget Disclosure: Top or Bottom?")

Intelligence Budget Disclosure: Top or Bottom?

One of the curiosities of the debate over intelligence budget disclosure was the term used for the number most at issue. The overall spending total for intelligence was alternatively described as the "top line number" or the "bottom line number." It sometimes sounded as if people on the same side—those in favor of or opposed to disclosure—were at odds with themselves.

The argument over publishing some part of intelligence spending appeared to have ended effectively in 1997, when DCI George Tenet revealed that overall intelligence spending for fiscal 1998 was $26.6 billion. He provided the number in response to a Freedom of Information Act suit, acting to end the suit and to limit the information that the intelligence community revealed. Tenet later refused to divulge the amount requested or appropriated for fiscal 1999, arguing that to do so would harm national security interests and intelligence sources and methods.

Nonetheless, it is instructive to review the arguments that both sides raised in the debate. Proponents of disclosure cited, first and foremost, the constitutional requirement for publication. They also argued that disclosure of this one number posed no threat to national security, since it revealed nothing about spending choices within the intelligence community.

Proponents of continued secrecy tended not to cite the "time to time" language of the Constitution, which was a weak argument at best. Rather, they argued that Congress was privy to the information and was acting on behalf of the public. They also raised concerns that disclosure of the overall amount was just the beginning of demands for more detailed disclosure. Noting how little this one number revealed (and implicitly accepting their opponents' argument that its disclosure would not jeopardize security), they contended that this initial disclosure would inexorably lead to pressure for more detailed disclosures about specific agency budgets or programs and that these disclosures would have security implications.

DCI Tenet's disclosure revealed that many public estimates of the size of the intelligence budget were fairly accurate, as was the estimate that the intelligence budget is roughly one-tenth the size of the defense budget. As disclosure proponents had long argued, national security did not unravel. However, as disclosure opponents maintained, many who had advocated disclosure were dissatisfied because this one number provided so little information.

Disclosing the overall number entails political risks for U.S. intelligence. Relating spending to outputs is more difficult for intelligence than it is for virtually any other government activity. How much intelligence should we get for $26.6 billion? Do we quantify output by the number of reports produced? Number of covert actions undertaken? Number of spies recruited? Moreover, the overall number—which will not strike many people as a small sum—will inevitably lead some people to question intelligence community performance. Statements along the lines of "How could they miss that coup (or lose that spy) when they have $26.6 billion?" will ensue. Such sentiments would add little to a meaningful debate about intelligence.

REGULATING THE INTELLIGENCE COMMUNITY. The National Security Act of 1947 remains the most important piece of legislation passed by Congress on the subject of intelligence. Although the act has been amended several times, it retains the basic provisions regarding the NSC, DCI, and CIA. Since the 1975–1976 investigations of intelligence, congressional efforts at major legislative change have not been notably successful. Small changes have been made, but larger legislative efforts have faced executive opposition, minimal interest in Congress, and opposition from other congressional committees. (See chap. 14, Intelligence Reform.) Three presidents have since issued extensive executive orders on intelligence—Gerald R. Ford in 1976, Jimmy Carter in 1978, and Ronald Reagan in 1981.

The major advantage of executive orders (or E.O.s, as they are known) is that they give presidents the flexibility to make changes in the intelligence community to meet changing needs or to reflect their own preferences about how the intelligence community should be managed or its functions limited. The major disadvantages of executive orders are that they are impermanent, subject to change by each president (or even by the same president); they are not statutes and therefore are more difficult to enforce; and they give Congress a limited role. (As a rule, the executive branch has made Congress privy to drafts of executive orders in advance of their promulgation and has given Congress opportunities to comment on them.)

Despite the difficulty that Congress and the executive branch have experienced in making legislative changes, they offer the advantages of being permanent, of being statutes in law and therefore more enforceable, and of allowing Congress a major and proper role. On the other hand, legislation is more likely to raise major disputes between Congress and the executive branch and thus is more difficult to enact. Congress is also more likely to harbor several points of view on major intelligence issues than is the executive branch, where the major issues tend to be agency-parochial in nature.

Given the permanent nature of legislation, some people question whether certain regulations should not be made statutory largely because the actions they cover are embarrassing or inappropriate, such as assassinations. However, if legislation lists proscribed activities, does it implicitly permit those activities that are not listed?

THE ISSUE OF CO-OPTION. As eager as Congress is to be kept informed about all aspects of policy, a cost is incurred when it accepts information. Unless members raise questions about what they are told, they are, in effect, co-opted. Their silence betokens consent, as the maxim of English law says. They are free to dissent later on, but the administration will be quick to point out that they did not raise any questions at the time they were briefed. Having been informed before the fact will tend to undercut Congress's freedom of action after the fact.

This dynamic is not unique to intelligence, but intelligence makes it somewhat more pointed. The nature of the information, which is both secret and usually limited to certain members, makes co-option more easily accomplished and has more serious consequences. It also puts additional pressure on the members of the Intelligence Committees, who are privy to the information and are acting on behalf of their entire body.

Congress has no easy way to avoid the inherent exchange of foreknowledge and consent. It is unlikely to revert to the trusting attitude expressed by Senator Saltonstall, nor is it reasonable to expect Congress to raise serious questions about every issue just to establish a record that will allow it to dissent later on.

WHAT PRICE OVERSIGHT FAILURES? Even when the intelligence oversight system is working well, most members and congressional staff have difficulty running the system so as to avoid all lapses. Most members and staff involved in the process understand the difference between small lapses and large ones. Some of the larger lapses for which Congress has taken the intelligence community to task include:

- Failure to inform the Senate Intelligence Committee that CIA operatives were directly involved in mining Corinto, a Nicaraguan port, during the contra war. The CIA let it appear that the contras had carried this out on their own. When the truth became known, not only did Vice Chairman Daniel Patrick Moynihan, D-N.Y., resign—though he later changed his mind—Chairman Barry Goldwater, R-Ariz., also reprimanded DCI William Casey in harsh and public terms.
- Failure to inform Congress on a timely basis when agents in Moscow began to disappear, which was later presumed to be the

result of the espionage of Aldrich Ames. (This may change as a result of the damage assessment from the Robert Hanssen case.) The House Intelligence Committee issued a public report critical of the CIA, with which the CIA agreed.

Congress has at hand some real levers to enforce its oversight. It can reduce the intelligence budget, delay nominations, or, in the case of a serious lapse, demand the resignation of the official involved. If the lapse is serious enough and can be traced back to the president, impeachment might be an option. In the two cases cited above, Congress did not impose any of these penalties.

But even without inflicting concrete penalties of the sort noted above, Congress can enforce its oversight. The loss of officials' credibility before their major committees is serious in and of itself. As hackneyed as it sounds, much of Washington runs on the basis of trust and the value of one's word. Once credibility and trust are lost, as happened to Casey in the Corinto affair, they are very difficult to regain.

INTERNAL DYNAMICS OF CONGRESSIONAL OVERSIGHT OF INTELLIGENCE

Even though oversight is inherent in the entire congressional process, the way Congress organizes itself to handle intelligence oversight is somewhat peculiar.

WHY SERVE ON AN INTELLIGENCE OVERSIGHT COMMITTEE? Members of Congress take office with specific areas of interest, derived either from the nature of their district or state or their personal interests. Most members, at least early in their legislative careers, also tend to focus on issues that are most likely to enhance their careers. For most members, intelligence is unlikely to fit any of these criteria. Therefore, why would members spend a portion of their limited time on intelligence?

At first blush, the disadvantages are more apparent than the advantages. Intelligence is, for most members, a distraction from their other duties and from those issues likely to be of greatest interest to their constituents. Very few districts have a direct interest in intelligence. The main ones are those in the immediate Washington, D.C., area, where the major agencies are located, and those where major collection systems are manufactured. But these are a very small fraction of the 435 House districts in the fifty states.

Once involved in intelligence issues, members cannot discuss much of what they are doing or what they have accomplished. Co-option is also a danger. Should something go wrong in intelligence, committee members will be asked why they did not know about it in advance. If they did know in advance, they will be asked why they did not do something about it. If they did not know, they will be asked why not. These are all difficult questions to answer.

Finally, the intelligence budget is remarkably free of "pork," that is, budget projects that are earmarked to benefit a member's district or state. Therefore, members on the committees have few opportunities to help their constituents.

With all of those disadvantages, why serve? Because some advantages accrue from membership. First, service on the Intelligence Committees allows members to perform public service within Congress, to serve on a committee where they have few, if any, direct interests. Second, their service gives members a rare opportunity to have access to a closed and often interesting body of information. Third, it gives members a role in shaping intelligence policy and, given the relatively small size of the two committees (in the 106th Congress—1999–2001—sixteen members on the House Intelligence Committee and nineteen on the Senate Intelligence Committee), perhaps a greater role than they would have on many of the other oversight committees. Fourth, it may offer opportunities for national press coverage on high-profile issues about which very few people will be conversant. Finally, since members of the two intelligence committees are selected by the majority and minority leadership of the House and Senate, being chosen is a sign of favor that can be very important to a member's career. (Select committees usually have limited life spans, especially in the House. The House Intelligence Committee is called "permanent select" to denote its continued existence, even though it remains "select.")

THE ISSUE OF TERM LIMITS. Unlike other committees, service on the House and Senate Intelligence Committees is limited, currently to eight years. Congress adopted term limits for committee membership based on the view that the pre-1975 oversight system had failed, in part, because the few members involved became too cozy with the agencies they were overseeing.

The major advantage of term limits is the distance that they promote between the overseers and the overseen. Limited terms also make it possible for more members of the House and Senate to serve on the Intelligence Committees, thus adding to the knowledgeable body necessary for informed debate.

Term limits also carry disadvantages. Few members come to Congress with much knowledge of, and virtually no experience with, intelligence. Because it can be arcane and complex, requiring some time to master, members are likely to spend some portion of their tenure on the committee simply learning about intelligence. Once they have become knowledgeable and effective, they are nearing the end of their term. Term limits also make service on the Intelligence Committees less attractive, since they reduce the likelihood that a member can become chairman through seniority.

In 1996 Larry Combest, who was then chairman of the House Intelligence Committee, testified that he thought it was time to consider longer tenure on the committee, which would be to Congress's advantage.

BIPARTISAN OR PARTISAN COMMITTEES? The Senate and House Intelligence Committees are distinctly different in composition. Typically, the ratio of seats between the parties on committees roughly reflects the ratio of seats in each chamber as a whole. The Senate Intelligence Committee has always been exempt from this practice, with the majority party having just one more seat than the minority. Moreover, the ranking minority member is always the vice chairman of the Senate committee. The Senate leadership took these steps in 1976 to minimize the role of partisanship in intelligence. When the House Intelligence Committee was formed in 1977, the House Democratic leadership rejected the Senate model, insisting that membership on the committee be determined by the parties' ratio in the House, which reflected the will of the people in the last election.

A bipartisan committee offers opportunities for a more coherent policy, because the committee is removed—as far as is possible—from partisanship. A committee united on policy and not divided by party may also have more influence with the executive branch. In the case of the Corinto mining, Chairman Goldwater and Vice Chairman Moynihan agreed that the intelligence community was guilty of a significant and unacceptable failure. Thus, the DCI had no political refuge for his failure to keep the committee informed.

A partisan committee, the House Democratic leadership believed, is a reflection of the political will of the people. But partisanship runs counter to the preferred myth that U.S. national security policy is bipartisan or nonpartisan. A partisan committee has the potential to be more dynamic than a bipartisan committee, where political compromise is more at a premium. In many ways, the compromise that a bipartisan committee engenders is equivalent to the lowest-common-denominator dynamic that one sees in intelligence community estimates.

In its own accidental way, Congress may have achieved the right balance, with a bipartisan intelligence committee in one chamber and a partisan committee in the other.

HOW DOES CONGRESS JUDGE INTELLIGENCE? An important but little-discussed issue is how Congress views and judges intelligence, as opposed to the criteria used by the executive branch. No matter how much access Congress has to intelligence, it is not a client of the intelligence community in the same way that the executive branch is. Congress never achieves the same level of intimacy in this area and does not have the same requirements or demands for intelligence.

The budget is one major divide. There is no set pattern as to which branch wants to spend more or less. The Reagan administration favored spending more on intelligence than Congress did and was allowed to, up to a point, after which Congress began to resist. However, the Reagan administration did not want to buy the additional imagery satellites demanded by the Senate Intelligence Committee. In the Clinton administration, it was Congress, after the Republican takeover in 1995, that was willing to spend more than was requested. Congress takes the firm view that all budget requests from the executive are just that—requests. They are nonbinding suggestions for how much money should be spent. To put it succinctly, the executive has programs, Congress has money.

The second major divide is the intimacy of the relationship that each branch has with intelligence. Executive officials may have unrealistic expectations of intelligence, but over time they will have far greater familiarity with it than will the majority of members. Thus, the possibility of even larger false expectations looms in Congress. Moreover, having provided the money, members may have higher expectations of intelligence performance. At the same time, members may also tend to be more suspicious of intelligence analysis, fearing that it has been written largely to support administration policies. Members and staff rarely hear of intelligence that questions administration policies, even when such intelligence exists. Thus, the Congress–intelligence relationship is fertile ground for doubts, whether justified or not.

Another major divide is partisanship. Whether it is the majority or the minority, a substantial group in Congress always opposes the administration on the basis of party affiliation as well as policy. Partisanship inevitably spills over into intelligence, often in the form of concerns that the executive branch has "cooked" intelligence to support policy. There may be dissent about intelligence policy within the executive, but it is inconceivable that this would be based on partisanship.

Thus, for a variety of reasons that are largely inherent in the U.S. system, the two branches do not view intelligence in quite the same way.

EXTERNAL FACTORS. The intelligence oversight system does not take place in a vacuum. Among the many factors that come into play to affect oversight, the press is a major one. The lingering effects of Watergate, including the search for scoops and major scandals, have influenced reporting on intelligence. The press, as an institution, gets more mileage out of reporting things that have gone wrong than it does from bestowing kudos for those that are going right. The fact that intelligence correctly predicts some major event is hardly news; after all, that is its job. Moreover, in the aftermath of the 1975–1976 investigations, the intelligence community found it impossible to return to its previous state of being largely ignored by the press. The greater coverage given to intelligence and the press's emphasis on flaws and failures influence how some in Congress approach oversight.

Finally, even intelligence has partisans who appear in the guise of lobbyists. There are groups made up of former intelligence community employees and groups that advocate strong stances and spending on national security. There are also groups that oppose certain aspects of intelligence, usually covert action, as well as some aspects of espionage; groups concerned about U.S. policy in every region of the world; and groups that would prefer to see some portion of the funds devoted to intelligence spent elsewhere. Finally, there are some firms that derive large amounts of their income from the work they do for the intelligence community. All of these groups are legitimate within the U.S. political system and must be taken into account when considering how Congress oversees intelligence.

COMPETITION WITHIN THE CONGRESSIONAL AGENDA. The final issue that influences intelligence oversight is a series of debates that recur in every Congress, with varying degrees of strength. One is the debate between domestic and national security concerns, which is especially important when dealing with the budget. During the cold war, national security rarely suffered. In the post–cold war period, with national security concerns more difficult to define, the intelligence community had difficulty—until the terrorist attacks in 2001—maintaining level spending, let alone winning increases.

Another debate is that between civil liberties and national security. This debate is almost as old as the republic, dating back to the Alien and Sedition Acts of 1798. Other instances of civil liberties clashing with national security concerns predate the advent of the intelligence community: President Abraham Lincoln's suspension of habeas corpus during the Civil War, the arrest of antiwar dissidents during World War I, the mass arrests and detention of Japanese-Americans during World War II, and various acts aimed at rooting out communist subversion during the cold war. In each case, political leaders cited national emergencies to place temporary limitations on civil liberties. This debate resumed in 2001 in the aftermath of the terrorist attacks, as the Bush administration sought increased powers for surveillance, nonjudicial trials (the proposed use of military tribunals), and other types of authority.

These precedents notwithstanding, the intelligence investigations of the mid-1970s revealed several instances in which intelligence agencies violated constitutional guarantees, laws, and their own charters. The violations included surveillance of dissident groups, illegal mail openings, illegal wiretaps of U.S. citizens, and improper use of the Internal Revenue Service. Some of these actions were known by presidents at the time; some were not. The revelation of these activities underscored concerns about the ability of secret agencies to act without safeguards and the need for strong executive and congressional oversight.

A third perennial congressional debate focuses on the level and range of U.S. activism abroad. From World War I through the cold war, the Democrats were largely the interventionist party and the Republicans the noninterventionists. During World War II and the cold war, an interventionist consensus formed, although a Republican faction remained noninterventionist. The damage that the Vietnam War inflicted on the cold war consensus fostered a shift in the positions of the two parties. The Democrats largely became the noninterventionist party and the Republicans the interventionist. In the post–cold war period, a renascent noninterventionist faction grew within the Republican Party. After September 2001, there was broad support for both military and intelligence operations abroad, although it is too soon to tell how long this support will last or what range of intelligence or military activities it will support.

Finally, the immigrant basis of the U.S. population is reflected in foreign policy debates. Every region of the world and virtually every nation are represented within the U.S. population. U.S. policies or actions around the world—real, planned, or rumored—are likely to stir reactions from some segment of the population and perhaps even different reactions. Members of Congress having ethnic ties to a region or representing constituents who do are also likely to voice opinions.

CONCLUSION

The nature of congressional oversight of intelligence changed dramatically in 1975–1976. Although Congress may go through periods of greater or lesser activism, it is unlikely to return to the laissez-faire style of oversight. Congress has become a consistent player in shaping intelligence policy.

This seems novel in the case of intelligence only because it is relatively recent. Congress has played the same activist role in all other areas of policy since adoption of the Constitution, and its role is inherent in the checks and balances system that the Framers of the Constitution created. The willful division of power creates a system that is a constant "invitation to struggle."

The oversight system is, of necessity, adversarial but not necessarily hostile. Any system that divides power is bound to have debates and friction. But they do not have to be played out in an antagonistic manner. When antagonism arises, it is more often the effect of personalities, issues, and partisanship rather than the oversight system per se.

KEY TERMS

appropriated but not authorized
  (A not A)
appropriation
authorization

executive order
hollow budget authority
oversight

FURTHER READINGS

The expansion of the role of Congress as an overseer has been matched by an increasing number of books and articles on the topic. This chapter also discusses executive oversight issues, which are covered in the first entry below.

Adler, Emanuel. "Executive Command and Control in Foreign Policy: The CIA's Covert Activities." *Orbis* 23 (1959): 671–696.
Cohen, William S. "Congressional Oversight of Covert Actions." *International Journal of Intelligence and Counterintelligence* 2 (summer 1988): 155–162.
Colton, David Everett. "Speaking Truth to Power: Intelligence Oversight in an Imperfect World." *University of Pennsylvania Law Review* 137 (December 1988): 571–613.
Conner, William E. *Intelligence Oversight: The Controversy Behind the FY1991 Intelligence Authorization Act.* McLean, Va.: Consortium for the Study of Intelligence, 1993.
Currie, James. "Iran-Contra and Congressional Oversight of the CIA." *International Journal of Intelligence and Counterintelligence* 11 (summer 1998): 185–210.
Gumina, Paul. "Title VI of the Intelligence Authorization Act: Fiscal Year 1991: Effective Covert Action Reform or 'Business as Usual'?" *Hastings Constitutional Law Quarterly* (fall 1992): 149–205.
Jackson, William R. "Congressional Oversight of Intelligence: Search for a Framework." *Intelligence and National Security* 5 (July 1990): 113–147.
Johnson, Loch K. "The CIA and the Question of Accountability." *Intelligence and National Security* 12 (January 1997): 178–200.
———. "Controlling the Quiet Option." *Foreign Policy* 39 (summer 1980): 143–153.
———. "The U.S. Congress and the CIA: Monitoring the Dark Side of Government." *Legislative Studies Quarterly* 5 (November 1980): 477–499.
Latimer, Thomas K. "United States Intelligence Activities: The Role of Congress." In *Intelligence Policy and National Security.* Ed. Robert L. Pfaltzgraff Jr. et al. Hamden, Conn.: Archon Books, 1981.
Pickett, George. "Congress, the Budget and Intelligence." In *Intelligence: Policy and Process.* Ed. Alfred C. Maurer et al. Boulder: Westview Press, 1985.

Simmons, Robert Ruhl. "Intelligence Performance in Reagan's First Term: A Good Record or Bad?" *International Journal of Intelligence and Counterintelligence* 4 (spring 1990): 1–22.

Smist, Frank J., Jr. *Congress Oversees the United States Intelligence Community.* 2d ed. Knoxville: University of Tennessee Press, 1994.

Snider, L. Britt. *Sharing Secrets with Lawmakers: Congress as a User of Intelligence.* Washington, D.C.: Central Intelligence Agency, Center for the Study of Intelligence, 1997.

Treverton, Gregory F. "Intelligence: Welcome to the American Government." In *A Question of Balance: The President, the Congress and Foreign Policy.* Ed. Thomas E. Mann. Washington, D.C.: Brookings Institution, 1990.

U.S. Senate Select Committee on Intelligence. *Legislative Oversight of Intelligence Activities: The U.S. Experience.* Report, 103d Cong., 2d sess., 1994.

Chapter 11

The Legacy of the Cold War

Although the intelligence community was not created specifically to prosecute the cold war, the community's development, forms, structures, and practices were largely influenced by that nearly fifty-year struggle. To understand how the intelligence community developed and its nature as it seeks to transform itself to address twenty-first-century issues, it is important to understand the cold war's influence on the community.

THE PRIMACY OF THE SOVIET ISSUE

The "Soviet issue"—actually a series of related issues, including the Soviet Union, Soviet satellites and third world allies, and communist parties in some Western nations—was the predominant issue in U.S. national security and foreign policy from 1946 to 1991, when the Soviet Union ceased to exist. This meant that the requirements for intelligence were never in doubt. Although other issues might occasionally and temporarily supplant the Soviet issue during this period, it remained predominant.

There was also great clarity and continuity in the policy that intelligence was expected to support. Inspired by the career diplomat George Kennan, the United States developed a policy of containment vis-à-vis the Soviet Union. Kennan argued, first in his famous "long telegram" from Moscow in February 1946 and then in his "Mr. X" article in *Foreign Affairs* (July 1947), that the Soviet Union was, by its nature, an expansionist state. If the Soviet Union were contained within its own geographic limits, it would eventually be forced to deal with the inconsistencies and shortcomings of its communist system and either change or collapse. Kennan viewed the struggle between the United States and the Soviet Union as largely political and economic. But others responsible for shaping policy, particularly Paul Nitze, who played a key role in drafting the planning guidance document NSC-68 in early 1950, gave containment a more military dimension, as did the outbreak of the Korean War in June of that year.

THE INTELLIGENCE IMPLICATIONS OF CONTAINMENT. The containment policy included a role for intelligence analysis and operations. Analytically, the intelligence community was expected to know or be able to predict:

- Likely areas of Soviet probes or expansion
- Imminence and strength of the probes
- Overall Soviet strength—military, economic, and social
- Likely Soviet allies or surrogates
- Strength of U.S. allies or surrogates
- Signs of relative Soviet strength or weakness (signs of the "contradictions" predicted by Kennan)

This is a long list and an ironic reflection of Sherman Kent's desire to "know everything."

In terms of intelligence operations, containment required:

- An ability to collect intelligence on the Soviet target to enable analysts to fulfill their requirements
- An operational ability to help blunt Soviet expansion
- An ability to weaken the Soviet Union and its allies and surrogates
- A counterintelligence capability to deal with Soviet espionage and possible subversion

Neither set of tasks, analytical or operational, arrived full-blown with the acceptance of the containment policy. Both sets evolved over time as the United States dealt with the Soviet problem.

THE DIFFICULTY OF THE SOVIET TARGET. The Soviet Union was a uniquely difficult target for intelligence collection and analysis. First, it was a very large nation with a remote interior, providing the Soviet leaders with a vast amount of space in which to hide capabilities they preferred to keep secret. Moreover, large portions of the Soviet Union were subject to adverse weather conditions that impeded overhead collection. Second, it was a closed and heavily policed society, which meant that large areas of the Soviet state—even in its more developed regions—were inaccessible to foreigners, even to diplomats legally posted to the Soviet Union.

Long-standing Russian traditions compounded the geographic difficulties. Russians traditionally have been suspicious of foreigners. Prior to the reign of Peter the Great (1682–1725), foreigners were often sequestered in special areas of the Russian capital, where they could be easily watched and their contact with Russians kept limited and controlled. Russians also have a tradition of obscuring the physical realities of the Russian state, which came to be known as *maskirovka*, whose roots go back to the tsars.

The most famous instance of obscuring reality occurred during the reign of Catherine the Great (1762–1796). Her minister of war, Grigory Potemkin, built what appeared to be villages but, in reality, were merely facades to impress Catherine with the success of his policies. These "Potemkin villages" presaged *maskirovka.*

As the scope of the cold war expanded from the Soviet Union to Europe, Asia, and then globally, the field within which intelligence had to be collected and analyzed and within which operations might be required expanded as well. The bilateral cold war was, in intelligence terms, a global war.

For all of these reasons, but primarily because of the size and inaccessibility of the Soviet Union, the intelligence community developed technical means to collect the required intelligence remotely. The United States continued to pursue HUMINT operations as well, both in the Soviet Union and against Soviet diplomats posted around the world, but the technical INTs predominated. The applicability of these technical INTs to post–cold war issues is uncertain. In effect, some aspects of the collection system are a legacy that cannot simply be scrapped or easily modified.

THE EMPHASIS ON SOVIET MILITARY CAPABILITIES

The predominant question within the Soviet issue was that nation's military capabilities, which posed a threat to the United States and its allies.

Capabilities refer to the current forces or those being planned. The U.S. intelligence community sought information about the quantity and quality of Soviet armed forces across the board; the directions of Soviet military research and development and new capabilities they might be pursuing; the degree to which current and planned capabilities posed a threat to U.S. and allied interests; and Soviet doctrine, that is, how they planned to employ forces in combat.

With the right collection systems, much of a potential adversary's capabilities can be known. This is particularly true of deployed forces, which are difficult to conceal, as they tend to exist in identifiable garrisons and must exercise from time to time. Indeed, the regularity and precision that govern each nation's military make it susceptible to intelligence collection. Forces tend to exercise in regular and predictable patterns, which also reveals how they are intended to be employed in combat. Research and development may be more difficult to track up to a point, but systems must be tested before they are deployed, again exposing them to collection.

Although the intelligence community made mistakes, such as overestimating and underestimating missile forces, overall Soviet capabilities were fairly well known in detail. There may even have been some level of comfort in tracking these hard objects. As one senior military intelligence officer put it, "The Soviet Union was the enemy we came to know and love." Some people dismissed the bean counts, arguing that they were undertaken largely to justify bigger defense budgets. The logic of this view was difficult to follow, since the intelligence community had little institutional interest in larger military forces. Indeed, within the national security sector of the budget, every dollar that went to defense was one dollar less that was available for intelligence, which was always funded at significantly lower levels than defense.

Intentions—the plans and goals of the adversary—are a more amorphous subject and pose a much more difficult collection problem. They need not be demonstrated, exercised, or exposed in advance, and they may not even be revealed by regular military exercises. Stand-off or remote collection systems, which may be useful for collecting against capabilities, may reveal nothing about intentions. That collection task may require espionage.

During the mid-1970s a capabilities-versus-intentions debate about the Soviet Union took place, largely among policymakers and influential individuals outside of government, but involving the intelligence community as well. U.S. intelligence was fairly well informed about Soviet military capabilities, but not Soviet intentions. The question at issue was whether these intentions mattered. U.S. officials engaged in long and sometimes heated debates about whether the Soviet Union planned to conduct large-scale offensive conventional operations preemptively or at the very outset of a war with NATO; whether it could carry out such operations from a "standing start," that is, with forces already deployed and supplied, without bringing up telltale reserves and additional supplies, thus with little or no warning; and whether the Soviet Union thought a nuclear conflict was "winnable."

Those who believed that intentions mattered argued that simply keeping track of the number of military forces was not enough to gauge the threat they posed. Only intentions made it possible to gauge the true level of threat. For example, Britain has a substantial nuclear force but is of no concern to the United States because the two nations are close allies. By taking into account Soviet intentions, the United States would have a much clearer picture of the true nature of Soviet policy, which was central to U.S. and Western security concerns. Proponents of this view believed that the Soviet threat was being underestimated because intentions were not a factor in national estimates.

Those who were less concerned about intentions argued that if one was aware of a certain level of hostility and also knew the adversary's capabilities, then knowing specific intentions was not that important.

Indeed, they argued that a "worst case" based on capabilities could serve as a planning yardstick. Finally, intentions (that is, plans) may be changed at will, making them a highly elusive target. Differences over the importance of intentions led to the Team A–Team B competitive analysis discussed earlier.

The track record for Soviet intentions is much less certain. The United States was never able to ascertain, for example, whether the Soviets subscribed to the nuclear doctrine of mutual assured destruction (MAD), which provided the basis for the size of U.S. strategic nuclear forces. MAD was based on the view that nuclear devastation was such an awesome prospect that it made nuclear forces almost unusable, the two forces holding each other in check. The United States spent many rounds of the early strategic arms-control talks proselytizing the Soviets on the importance of MAD. Did the Soviets really agree at last or give lip service to the idea of MAD merely as a way to get on to negotiations? Did it matter? Similarly, did the Soviets think that nuclear war was winnable? Did they plan to invade Western Europe? Soviet doctrine certainly emphasized keeping war away from the homeland, but this is true of most doctrines.

Mirror imaging underlay some of the debate over Soviet intentions. Did U.S. analysts impose their own views of Soviet intentions in lieu of knowing them? Another question was the utility of worst-case planning. Is it a useful analytical tool? For defense planners, the answer is yes. If they are going to commit forces to combat, they need to be able to gauge the worst level of threat they are likely to face. For other planners and analysts, the worst case may be an overestimate that is much less useful.

Finally, some people question whether the intelligence products themselves affected the intelligence process. Each year the intelligence community completed a national estimate on Soviet strategic military capabilities (NIE 11-3-8). U.S. policymakers viewed this estimate as necessary for strategic planning, including preparation of forces and budgets. But did the preparation of an annual major estimate also affect intelligence? Did it lock intelligence into set patterns, making it more difficult for the community to effect major changes or shifts in analyses? In other words, once the community had produced NIE 11-3-8 for several years, how easy was it for analysts to propose dissenting, iconoclastic, or wholly new views? One remedy for these possible flaws was competitive analysis, tried most prominently in the Team A–Team B exercise.

Direct comparison of forces, a legitimate intelligence activity, often took place in a politicized atmosphere. Policymakers in successive administrations and Congresses tended to have preconceptions about the nature of the Soviet threat and thus viewed intelligence as being either supportive or mistaken. They engaged in long debates about quality (a U.S. advantage) versus quantity (a Soviet advantage) of weapons systems. The inconclusive nature of the debates led many to seek other means of comparison. One means was defense spending, both in direct costs and in the percentage of GNP devoted to defense, which were taken as signs of intentions as well as capabilities.

THE EMPHASIS ON STATISTICAL INTELLIGENCE

Much of the intelligence that was produced (as opposed to collected) about the Soviet Union was statistical, including:

- The size of Soviet and Soviet-satellite forces in terms of manpower and all levels of weaponry
- The size of the Soviet economy and its output
- The amount/percentage of the Soviet economy devoted to defense
- A variety of demographics about life in the Soviet Union

Not all areas of inquiry were equally successful. As noted above, the capabilities of the Soviet military were tracked quite well. Analysis of the Soviet economy was less successful. Ultimately, the intelligence community both overestimated the size of the Soviet economy and underestimated that portion of it devoted to defense, which probably totaled 40 percent of GDP annually—a staggering level. Demographic data in the late 1980s and early 1990s pointed to a steady decline in the quality of Soviet life.

As important as these data were, the overall effort to quantify aspects of the Soviet issue was also important. Although there was much about this issue that remained intangible, the intelligence community emphasized its ability to track these various attributes in detail.

Looking back, one finds some of these efforts a bit comical. For example, the U.S. intelligence community devoted a great deal of time and energy—perhaps too much—to a variety of efforts to compare Soviet defense spending with that of the United States. Some analysts converted the cost of U.S. defense into rubles; others converted assessed values for the Soviet defense establishment into dollars. Each of these methodologies was artificial, and their respective proponents usually ended up preaching to the converted or to the stubbornly unbelieving regarding the Soviet threat.

What was often missing in this wealth of detailed data was the intangibles: the solidity of the Soviet state, the depth of support for it in the general population, and the degree of restiveness among the satellite populations. Very few analysts questioned the stability or viability of the Soviet Union in the near term. Discussions about the possible collapse of the Soviet Union tended to be mostly hypothetical in nature as opposed to a potential policy problem.

THE INTELLIGENCE RECORD—COLLAPSE
OF THE SOVIET UNION

Much of the controversy surrounding the U.S. intelligence record on the Soviet Union stems from the sudden Soviet collapse. Critics of intelligence performance argue that this demise deeply surprised the intelligence community, which had overestimated the strength of the Soviet state and thus "missed" the biggest story in the community's history. Some people even contended that this intelligence "failure" was sufficient reason for a profound reorganization of U.S. intelligence. Defenders of intelligence performance argue that the community had long reported the inner rot of the Soviet system and its weak hold on its own people and the satellite states.

The defenders of U.S. intelligence performance are, in part, correct. Intelligence provided numerous stories about the gross inefficiencies of the Soviet system, many of them anecdotal but too many to ignore. Insights into the sad realities of the Soviet system grew with the beginning of on-site inspections of Soviet INF bases in 1988. But few, if any, analysts compiled these anecdotal accounts into a prediction that the Soviet state was nearing collapse. It was weak; it might even be tottering. But no one expected that the Soviet Union would suddenly—and, most importantly, peacefully—pass from the scene. At least two factors were at work. First, most U.S. analysts working on the Soviet Union could not bring themselves to admit that the center of their livelihood might disappear, or that it was as weak politically as it turned out to be. Such a conclusion was inconceivable. They concentrated on the perils and pitfalls of reform but did not consider the possibility of collapse. Second, analysts failed to factor into their calculations the role of personalities, particularly that of Mikhail Gorbachev.

The difficulty in assessing Gorbachev should not be underestimated. He came to power through the usual Politburo selection process. Like each new Soviet leader, Gorbachev promised reforms to make the admittedly inefficient state work more effectively. Eduard Shevardnadze, Gorbachev's foreign minister, reveals that at a certain point they both admitted that fixing the economy would require something more basic than tweaking reforms. Even while accepting this fact, Gorbachev remained committed to the basic forms of the Soviet state, not understanding that any true reform was, by definition, revolutionary. Only over time did Gorbachev come to these conclusions, and he could not accept their ultimate implications. In other words, he did not know where his reforms would lead. Should the intelligence community have known better than Gorbachev himself?

Many intelligence analysts were also slow to pick up on Gorbachev's approach to most of his foreign policy problems—arms control, Angola, even Afghanistan—which was to liquidate them as quickly as possible in order to be free to concentrate on more pressing domestic problems. Nor did many correctly analyze that the Soviet Union would acquiesce in the collapse of its European satellite empire. Czechoslovakia, maybe. But East Germany? Never! Again, the degree to which this was knowable remains uncertain. Ironically, Gorbachev succumbed to the premises of containment as described by George Kennan forty years earlier. Stymied abroad, Gorbachev had to face the manifold problems he had at home.

We still do not know all of the factors that went into Gorbachev's thinking or into the sudden Soviet collapse. Did the U.S. defense buildup convince Gorbachev that he needed to strike some deals with the United States or be outpaced and outspent and face even deeper economic ruin? Shevardnadze suggests that the answer is yes. There is reason to believe that President Reagan's Strategic Defense Initiative was an important spur to arms control, not because of any near-term change that SDI might effect in the military balance but because it brought home to the Soviet leadership all of their weaknesses in technology, in computers, in wealth. One of the ways to avoid economic ruin was to strike arms-control deals.

We also do not know whether the so-called Reagan Doctrine—a U.S. effort to aid anti-Soviet guerrillas—had any effect on Soviet thinking. The effort to aid the contras became a political liability for the Reagan administration. But aid to the Mujaheddin in Afghanistan and the stalemate of that war shook the Soviet leaders. They were unable to win a war just over their border. All of their military prowess was meaningless. Some analysts believe that a rift developed between the General Staff in Moscow and the Afgantsy—Soviet field commanders in the war, many of whom rallied to Boris Yeltsin in August 1991, when opponents of radical reform attempted to overthrow Gorbachev.

Gorbachev clearly thought that the price of empire was too high, not only overseas but even in Eastern Europe. What neither Western analysts nor Gorbachev himself understood was that piecemeal liquidation of these problems could not save the Soviet state.

CONCLUSION—INTELLIGENCE AND THE SOVIET PROBLEM

No U.S. intelligence estimate boldly predicted the peaceful collapse of the Soviet Union and its dissolution into several independent republics. Indeed, U.S. intelligence assumed that the Soviet state would go on, perhaps ever weaker but still intact. At the same time, the community produced numerous reports about how inefficient, weak, and unsustainable (over some unknown period of time) the Soviet Union was.

There are two key questions. Should intelligence have done better? Did intelligence matter in our final cold war victory?

Those who argue that intelligence should have done better do so on the grounds that the Soviet Union was the central focus of U.S. intelligence and that all of the expertise and spending over five decades should have provided greater insight into the true state of affairs. But there is a large gap between knowing that a state has fundamental weaknesses and foreseeing its collapse. To a large extent, the collapse of the Soviet Union was unprecedented. (In the past, some once-great empires, such as the Ottoman Empire, had suffered long, lingering demises. Other great empires had suffered sudden collapses, but usually in the context of war, as did the German, Austrian, and Russian empires after World War I.) Nor was there anything in Soviet behavior—which had shown its brutal side often enough—to lead analysts to expect that the nation's elite would acquiesce to their own fall from power without a struggle. Indeed, it is one of the ironies of history that an attempt by the so-called power ministries of the Soviet state (the military, the defense industrial complex, the KGB) to derail Gorbachev revealed how little support the Soviet system really had. (Rumors persist that Gorbachev knew about the coup or actually abetted it as a means of isolating his opposition.)

The debate about the performance of U.S. intelligence in the final stages of the cold war continues. Perhaps some analyst should have made the leap from the mountain of anecdotal evidence to a better picture of the true state of Soviet staying power. But much that happened from 1989 to 1991 was unknowable, both to U.S. analysts and to those taking part in the events.

How do we assess the role of intelligence overall on the Soviet problem? In collection, U.S. intelligence performed some remarkable feats, finding sophisticated technical solutions to the problems posed by the remote and closed Soviet target. In analysis, U.S. intelligence very accurately tracked Soviet military numbers and capabilities. This was important not only on a day-to-day basis but during periods of intense confrontation, such as in Cuba in 1962, when President John F. Kennedy acted confidently, because he knew a great deal about the true state of the U.S.-Soviet military balance. Discussion of Soviet intentions veered quickly to the political realm, where equally adamant hawks and doves dominated the debate, often freed from the constraints of intelligence by its unavailability. Operationally, the record is much less clear. Early efforts to foment rebellion within Soviet domains were disasters. Operations to limit Soviet expansion were uneven. U.S. intelligence operations were successful in Western Europe, Guatemala, and Iran but were failures in Cuba and Southeast Asia. The contra war probably could have been dragged out inconclusively forever. But the intervention against Soviet forces in Afghanistan was a major and telling success. In espionage, U.S. intelligence scored major successes, such as Col. Oleg Penkovsky, and suffered a number of Soviet penetrations as well, some of which, notably Aldrich Ames and Robert Hanssen, bridged the Soviet and post–Soviet Russian states.

In short, the record of intelligence in the cold war is mixed. Perhaps a better way to pose the original question might be: Would the United States have been better off or more secure without an intelligence community during the cold war?

Finally, it is important to understand that in the early twenty-first century the intelligence community continues to be influenced by its performance vis-à-vis the Soviet Union. The clarity of requirements and the emphasis on remote technical collection, military capabilities, and other statistical intelligence are all cold war intelligence legacies. Their applicability to current intelligence issues will be discussed in chap. 12.

KEY TERMS

bean counting
capabilities versus intentions
containment
maskirovka

Potemkin villages
Reagan Doctrine
worst-case analysis

FURTHER READINGS

As might be expected, the literature on U.S. intelligence vis-à-vis the Soviet Union is rich. The readings listed here include some older pieces that are of historical value.

Berkowitz, Bruce D., and Jeffrey T. Richelson. "The CIA Vindicated: The Soviet Collapse Was Predicted." *National Interest* 41 (fall 1995): 36–47.

Burton, Donald F. "Estimating Soviet Defense Spending." *Problems of Communism* 32 (March–April 1983): 85–93.

Firth, Noel E. *Soviet Defense Spending: A History of CIA Estimates, 1950–1990.* College Station: Texas A&M University Press, 1998.

Freedman, Lawrence. "The CIA and the Soviet Threat: The Politicization of Estimates, 1966–1977." *Intelligence and National Security* 12 (January 1997): 122–142.

———. *U.S. Intelligence and the Soviet Strategic Threat.* Boulder: Westview Press, 1977.

Koch, Scott A., ed. *Selected Estimates on the Soviet Union, 1950–1959.* Washington, D.C.: History Staff, U.S. Central Intelligence Agency, 1993.

Lee, William T. *Understanding the Soviet Military Threat.* New York: National Strategy Information Center, 1977.

Lowenthal, Mark M. "Intelligence Epistemology: Dealing with the Unbelievable." *International Journal of Intelligence and Counterintelligence* 6 (1993): 319–325.

MacEachin, Douglas J. *CIA Assessments of the Soviet Union: The Record vs. the Charges.* Langley, Va.: Central Intelligence Agency, Center for the Study of Intelligence, 1996.

Moynihan, Daniel Patrick. *Secrecy: The American Experience.* New Haven: Yale University Press, 1998.

Pipes, Richard. "Team B: The Reality Behind the Myth." *Commentary* 82 (October 1986): 25–40.

Prados, John. *The Soviet Estimate: U.S. Intelligence and Russian Military Strength.* New York: Dial Press, 1982.

Reich, Robert C. "Re-examining the Team A–Team B Exercise." *International Journal of Intelligence and Counterintelligence* 3 (fall 1989): 387–403.

Steury, Donald P., ed. *CIA's Analysis of the Soviet Union, 1947–1991.* Washington, D.C.: History Staff, U.S. Central Intelligence Agency, 2001.

———. *Intentions and Capabilities: Estimates on Soviet Strategic Forces, 1950–1983.* Washington, D.C.: History Staff, U.S. Central Intelligence Agency, 1996.

U.S. Central Intelligence Agency, History Staff. *At Cold War's End: U.S. Intelligence on the Soviet Union and Eastern Europe, 1989–1991.* Washington, D.C.: CIA, 1999.

U.S. Congress. Senate Select Committee on Intelligence. *The National Intelligence Estimate A–B Team Episode Concerning Soviet Strategic Capability and Objectives.* 95th Cong., 2d sess., 1978.

U.S. General Accounting Office. *Soviet Economy: Assessment of How Well the CIA Has Estimated the Size of the Economy.* GAO Report NSIAD 910274. Washington, D.C., September 1991.

Chapter 12

The New Intelligence Agenda

The end of the cold war was not the end of history, as political scientist Francis Fukuyama suggested. (Fukuyama posited that, since the struggle to advance democratic values had been the major development of the last several centuries, the collapse of the Soviet Union would bring an "end" to "history.") But the end of the cold war did remove the most central national security issue that the United States faced. In the aftermath of the cold war, the role of intelligence and the issues that it should be tracking in support of U.S. policymakers did not seem entirely clear. After September 2001, terrorism became the primary issue, raising a new set of questions about the intelligence agenda.

U.S. NATIONAL SECURITY POLICY AFTER THE COLD WAR

The cold war gave U.S. national security policy an easily understood point of reference. Diplomacy, defense policy, intelligence, and all else followed from the fundamental bilateral struggle with the Soviet Union. Admittedly, serious debates arose in the United States over the nature of the Soviet threat, how the United States should deal with the threat overseas, defense spending levels, arms-control agreements, and other major facets of the bilateral competition. But there was little doubt that the antagonistic and hostile relationship with the Soviet Union was the foremost issue in U.S. national security policy. As the previous chapter indicated, U.S. analyses of the subtler aspects of the Soviet problem suffered significant flaws. But the issues of what the intelligence community should be doing and why were rarely in doubt.

The post–cold war period offered no such clarity. The administrations of George H. W. Bush (1989–1993) and Bill Clinton (1993–2001) either failed or did not try to define U.S. national security interests in the aftermath of the cold war. The Bush administration tried the concept of "new world order," which was never clearly defined and became irrelevant after President Bush's defeat at the polls in 1992. The Clinton administration largely avoided such grandiose concepts—despite brief forays into the concepts of "preventive diplomacy," "engagement," and "enlargement"—taking a more ad hoc approach to shaping policy. Some people suggested that the concept of national security, which had been comfortably vague to most of its practitioners, should be redefined, although few offered concrete, useful suggestions. In short, the core of U.S. national security policy remained vague after the fall of the Soviet Union. This vagueness raised several questions for U.S. intelligence that remain pertinent even after the September 2001 attacks: Has the mission of the intelligence community changed? How do policymakers and intelligence officials create and define intelligence requirements—and all that flows from them—in the absence of guiding national security concepts or policies? The terrorist attacks did not wholly answer these questions. As horrible as those attacks were, terrorism does not represent the same level of threat to the nation's existence as did the Axis in World War II or the Soviet Union. Terrorism may be the primary national security issue for years to come, but it is unlikely to assume the position of overwhelming dominance that the Soviet Union did. Thus, the questions posed above remain important.

At a basic level, the answer to the question of whether the mission of the intelligence community has changed in the aftermath of the cold war is no. Its mission remains what it was: to collect and analyze information that policymakers need and to carry out covert actions as lawful authorities direct. This mission is—or should be—independent of any particular target, relationship, or crisis. It is the reason for having an intelligence community and should not be subject to the vagaries of international politics. U.S. intelligence targets and priorities have changed, but the community's mission has not.

Agenda and priorities are much more vexing questions. DCI Robert Gates (1991–1993) estimated that at the height of the cold war, some 50 percent of the intelligence budget was earmarked for the Soviet Union and related issues. Everything else was secondary. That clarity of priorities is gone.

From 1991 to 2001 numerous issues jostled for top priority on the U.S. national security agenda: international economics, proliferation of weapons of mass destruction, narcotics, crime, terrorism, ecological and health issues, the post–Soviet transition in Russia, peacekeeping operations, and a variety of regional issues—the Balkans, the Middle East, central Africa, North Korea, and so on. Any one of these issues could be the most important for some period of time, but none of them maintained the dominance within the intelligence agenda that the Soviet Union once had.

The lack of a clear focus posed a severe problem for policymakers and intelligence managers. Requirements were uncertain or subject to rapid shifts. A greater diversity of talent was required. Very few of these issues are new to the U.S. national security agenda. Economic issues, narcotics, terrorism, proliferation, and regional stability were all being addressed during the cold war. Health and ecological issues are somewhat new. All of these issues are more difficult to analyze than were the cold war political–military issues, and they are much less susceptible to "bean counting."

In most cases, policymakers also found these issues more difficult to deal with than the old Soviet issues. The cold war had a certain comforting pattern of action/reaction. The United States and the Soviet Union each assumed, often correctly, that it could influence the behavior of the other through certain actions. On many of these new issues, there are no clear actions to take and sometimes no actors whom one can hope to influence. In some cases, the available intelligence outruns available or acceptable policy options. This often leads to frustration on the part of policymakers because they seek intelligence that is "actionable," that is, intelligence with which they can "do something." But this proves difficult when they do not know what they want to do.

Finally, several of these issues spill over into the domestic realm—economics, narcotics, crime, and terrorism—thus curtailing the activities of much of the intelligence community and creating confusion and competition between intelligence and law enforcement agencies. This problem is unique to the United States; most countries, even other democracies, have a domestic intelligence service (see chap. 15). As has been noted, the CIA and kindred agencies are limited in their work to foreign intelligence issues. The FBI, however, is not a domestic intelligence agency. Rather, it is a law enforcement agency, responsible for capturing criminals or spies and helping bring them to a successful prosecution. This division of responsibilities and limitations on roles has even extended to the capture of individuals overseas, a practice known as "rendition," because the subject is "rendered up" to justice. Renditions require the presence of U.S. law enforcement personnel even if the operation is primarily an intelligence operation. (This legal requirement does not extend to captured al Qaeda or Taliban members, who are considered combatants.) Thus, in responding to the post-2001 terrorist threat there was an organizational gap.

George W. Bush's proposal, in June 2002, to create a Department of Homeland Security recognized the problem. The president's proposal included creation of a division for Information Analysis and Infrastructure Protection, envisioned as a clearinghouse for all intelligence related to homeland security. This unit, which would receive terrorist-related intelligence from the CIA, the FBI, and other agencies, would be responsible for analyzing data and making sure that important items did not slip through the foreign intelligence–domestic intelligence divide. Officials also stated that the new unit would not receive raw intelligence, which implied that at least a "first order" analysis would be performed by the traditional agencies. In another break from past practice, the new division would also be charged with devising strategies to respond to specific threats.

Although many observers first noted that there would be little effect on the CIA or the FBI, the new department, when implemented, undoubtedly will bring some changes, if only minimally at the level of coordination and intelligence sharing. Larger issues likely loom, such as staffing to help set up the new analytical unit. There is also the question of how FBI-derived information will be used for intelligence and prevention of terrorism. The FBI and the Justice Department traditionally have been wary about sharing information needed for criminal prosecutions, lest its use taint the information and render it unusable.

The most recent authoritative attempt to define intelligence priorities was Presidential Decision Directive 35 (PDD-35), promulgated by the Clinton administration in 1995. PDD-35 divided intelligence priorities into two groups: hard targets and global coverage. Hard targets (or upper-tier issues) are the most pressing priorities: the so-called rogue states (Iran, Iraq, Libya, Cuba, North Korea), and the transnational issues (terrorism, weapons proliferation, narcotics, international crime, ecological issues). Global coverage (the lower tiers) includes everything else.

Clinton administration officials envisioned PDD-35 as a way of allocating resources across all intelligence needs. Critics argued that, inevitably, the lion's share of resources would go to the hard targets, leaving little at all for global coverage. This proved to be the case; the intelligence community admitted that it had the resources to cover the hard targets but not global coverage.

The other flaw in PDD-35 derives from the fact that over the course of a year some global-coverage issues would inevitably become more critical, moving into the upper tier. Although the intelligence community regularly checks the status of issues to determine if they are becoming more pressing, issues still receive significant attention only when they have moved into the upper tier. Moreover, the absence of a collection or analytical surge capacity in the intelligence community means that when an issue moves from global coverage to hard targets, it sets off a sudden scramble for resources.

In December 2000 the National Intelligence Council (NIC) published a study titled *Global Trends 2015*, looking at likely future trends and "drivers" of those trends, such as technology, natural resources, and demographics. Many experts beyond the intelligence community were consulted for this report, which is interesting both intellectually and in terms of process, but it did not serve to alter more near-term intelligence priorities.

INTELLIGENCE AND THE NEW PRIORITIES

An examination of several of the issues that have risen in priority in the post–cold war period reveals some of the difficulties that the intelligence community faces.

TERRORISM. The September 2001 attacks led to the beginning of a U.S. war against terrorism, which became the primary national security issue.

Terrorism had long been seen as a very demanding issue for intelligence because of the belief that the political system would not tolerate even one terrorist attack on U.S. interests, either within the United States or overseas. The reaction to the September 2001 attacks proved this view to be false. Although many people requested reviews of intelligence, both generally and with respect to the attacks, and some called for the resignation of senior officials, the political costs to the intelligence community were surprisingly mild.

To understand the difficulties inherent in tracking and forestalling terrorism, one must recall the various intelligence legacies of the cold war. Terrorist groups, unlike the Soviet Union, do not operate from large, easily identifiable infrastructures and do not rely on extensive communications networks. Indeed, as more and more becomes known publicly about U.S. intelligence sources and methods, terrorists have made greater efforts to avoid detection. For example, it has been widely reported that Osama bin Laden gave up the use of cell phones and fax machines to avoid being located by the United States. Also, terrorist groups do not conduct large-scale repetitive exercises, as do organized military forces. Thus, the visible "signature" of terrorists is much smaller than is that of the Soviet Union or any nation-state. But, as noted, the intelligence community is to some extent a cold war legacy system developed to track a large political-military structure.

In the aftermath of the September 2001 attacks there were the familiar claims that the United States was overly reliant on technical intelligence and needed more HUMINT. Although it is true that HUMINT can, theoretically, collect terrorist-related intelligence that TECHINT cannot, one must again examine the realities of terrorism. Terrorist groups, and certainly their leadership cells, tend to be very small and very well known to one another. They have tended to operate in parts of the world where the United States does not have ready access. Even if one did have available trained agents who knew the required language and could be provided with a plausible cover story for their presence in one of these areas, penetrating the terrorist organization would remain problematic at best. One does not simply show up in Kabul and ask for the local al Qaeda recruiting office and then ask to see the top man. (The press has made much in this regard of the activities of the American John Walker Lindh in Afghanistan. Lindh was captured fighting for the Taliban, not for al Qaeda. Recruitment into the Taliban was fairly simple. One had to be a self-professed Muslim willing to carry a gun—a far easier task than joining al Qaeda.) Finally, if HUMINT penetration were to be achieved, the new recruit would likely be asked to take part in some operation to prove his commitment to the cause. This raises important moral and ethical issues for intelligence. How far would we be willing to go in that direction to sustain a HUMINT penetration? Would we be willing to have an agent put his life at risk and possibly take part in a terrorist operation?

A more plausible HUMINT scenario will likely arise as the United States continues to attack terrorist groups. Some terrorists will decide that they want to get out and may make overtures to the United States or a friendly state. The price of a safe exit may be to remain in place for a while as a human source.

Finally, it is important to recall that much of U.S. HUMINT against the Soviet Union was carried out in foreign diplomatic posts outside of the Soviet Union, where Soviet officials were present and more accessible. Terrorists do not have this same overseas presence and thus present a smaller target.

State sponsorship of, or at least acquiescence to, terrorists also makes the intelligence issue more complicated. The intelligence community must collect not only against the terrorists but also against other governments and their intelligence services. At one level this is easier than is the terrorist collection itself, as it falls within more common intelligence practice. However, it also puts a further strain on intelligence resources. Liaison relationships may be questionable in such cases. For example, the government of Pakistan has been very supportive of U.S. operations in Afghanistan, but the Pakistani intelligence service has been a longtime sponsor of the Taliban.

Closely related to state sponsorship is the even murkier question of relations between and among terrorist groups. For example, members of one of the Irish Republican Army factions were arrested after spending time with the FARC guerrillas in Colombia. Obviously, these ties are both important and very difficult to track or disrupt.

The war on terrorism adds another intelligence burden: support to military operations. This requirement encompasses both the usual military-related support and new activities. For example, the press has reported that the CIA has a Special Activities Division in the Directorate of

Operations that was engaged in operations against the Taliban and al Qaeda. Although little is known publicly about this division, it would appear to occupy a niche between Special Forces and the DO's paramilitary activities in support of indigenous groups, such as the contras or the Mujaheddin. Also, as noted, some important developments have been made in IMINT in the use of both UAVs and commercial imagery.

The September 2001 attacks raised new questions about intelligence-law enforcement coordination and cooperation. As noted, President Bush's Homeland Security Department proposal is, to some extent, an attempt to rectify identified problem areas.

Finally, officials have raised concerns about cyberattacks on the United States as part of a terrorist campaign. The main fear is that such actions could affect vital parts of the U.S. infrastructure. The intelligence issues inherent in these circumstances are discussed below in the section on Information Operations.

PROLIFERATION. Preventing the proliferation of weapons of mass destruction (WMD) has been a long-standing goal of U.S. policy, but it is now a more important issue with added dimensions. The United States has always given primary emphasis to nuclear weapons, given their lethal capability and the fact that they were central to the U.S.-Soviet relationship. But even during the cold war, the United States also worked to contain the spread of chemical and biological weapons (CBW or CW and BW).

Three major shifts have occurred in U.S. nonproliferation policy in the post–cold war era. First, policymakers and intelligence officials have given CW and BW increased attention. These concerns increased dramatically after the spate of anthrax mailings shortly after the September 2001 attacks, although it remains unclear as to whether these were of foreign or domestic origin. Second, the collapse of the Soviet Union has added the problem of "loose nukes," a catch phrase for the weapons and associated expertise in former Soviet states that might be acquired by nations eager to create an indigenous nuclear weapons capability. Third, the explosion of nuclear weapons by India and Pakistan in 1998 represented a setback for nonproliferation policy and added new concerns about relations between these two nations; these fears were heightened after a terrorist attack on the Indian parliament in 2002, which India blamed on Pakistani citizens, leading to a new confrontation.

The role of intelligence in this policy area is fairly obvious: identify proliferation programs early enough to stop them before they are completed. Intelligence also targets the clandestine international commerce in some of the specialty items required to manufacture weapons of mass destruction. This entails obvious problems. Proliferation programs are, by their very nature, covert. Thus, the types of collection that the United

Iraq's Nuclear Program—A Cautionary Tale

During the 1980s, Iraq was one of the nations whose nuclear weapons program was closely watched by U.S. experts. The existence of a program was not in question; its status was.

On the eve of the Gulf War, the considered analytical judgment, according to subsequent accounts, was that Iraq was at least five years away from a nuclear capability. After Iraq's defeat in the Persian Gulf War, analysts learned that Iraq had been much closer to success, even though Israel had attacked and destroyed some of its facilities some years earlier.

What had gone wrong with U.S. estimates?

Iraq was and is a closed target, one of the most repressive and heavily policed states in the world. The state's nature makes collection more difficult, but that is not the answer to the question.

The answer lies again in an analytical flaw, namely, mirror imaging. In order to manufacture the fissionable material it required, Iraq chose a method abandoned by the United States in the early days of its own nuclear program after World War II. The method works, but it is a very slow and tedious way to produce fissionable material.

For Iraq, however, it was the perfect method, not because it was slow, but because foreign analysts disregarded it. The method allowed Iraq to procure materials that were more difficult to associate with a nuclear weapons program, to mask its actual status. A program of this sort was also more difficult for Western analysts to spot because they largely dismissed this approach out of hand, assuming that Iraq would want—just as the United States and others had—to find the fastest way to produce fissionable material.

States must undertake tend to come from the clandestine side of the intelligence community. The evidence of nascent programs that U.S. intelligence might obtain may be ambiguous. Indeed, this may also be true of mature programs. Fuzzy information complicates the ability of policymakers to confront potential proliferators with confidence or to convince other nations that a problem exists.

Beyond the problem of amassing convincing evidence lies the policy question: How do you stop a would-be proliferator? The preferred means is diplomacy, but the track record in this area is unimpressive. No nation has been talked out of developing nuclear weapons by diplomacy alone. The United States has used its influence, and its leverage as the guarantor of a state's national security, to pressure a state into desisting from nuclear weapons development. Press accounts allege that the United States used this method with Taiwan in the 1980s. Some other nations—for reasons of their own—decided to abandon nuclear programs. Sweden and Japan chose not to develop programs. Argentina and Brazil agreed bilaterally to abandon their fledging efforts. The white South African government gave up its nuclear weapons and its capabilities on the eve of the black majority's advent to power. But many other states—Israel, Iran, Iraq, and, reportedly, North Korea—remain unconvinced by U.S. diplomacy. Given the minimal success of moral suasion, some people have argued that the only workable solution is an active nonproliferation policy—intervening to destroy the capability, as both Israel and the Gulf War allies did with Iraq. (See box, "Iraq's Nuclear Program—A Cautionary Tale.")

As noted, the Indian and Pakistani tests represented a setback for nonproliferation; the Indian test was also an intelligence setback, in that political signs were ignored and technical collection was "looking" elsewhere.

The "loose nukes" aspect of the issue adds a new and more difficult complication. The Soviet Union agreed with the goal of nuclear nonproliferation, recognizing that it could be a target of would-be proliferators. But far more daunting is the prospect of tracking unknown quantities of weapons-grade material (which even Russian and other authorities have been unable to account for with accuracy) and the international movement of experts from former Soviet states. The collapse of the post–Soviet economy and the end of the privileged status these scientists once enjoyed are incentives to would-be proliferators.

CW and BW proliferation requires much less expertise and technical capability than nuclear proliferation requires. CW and BW weapons are far less accurate than nuclear weapons, but the random terror they portend is part of their appeal to nations and terrorists. These types of programs are more difficult than nuclear programs to identify and track. The anthrax scare of late 2001 underscores all of these points and also indicates how difficult it is to detect this type of attack in advance or to stop it once under way.

NARCOTICS. Narcotics policy is a difficult area in which to work. The main goal is to prevent individuals, by a variety of means, from using drugs that the government deems addictive and harmful. As almost everyone who has ever worked on this issue has said, it is a domestic issue, not a foreign policy issue. Also, given the fact that individuals use drugs for a variety of reasons, preventing their use is a very difficult goal to attain. For both practical and political reasons, narcotics has become, in part, a foreign policy problem, since the United States attempts to reduce the overseas production of illegal drugs and to intercept them before or just as they arrive in this country.

The intelligence community is quite capable of collecting and analyzing intelligence related to the illicit trade in narcotics. The plants from which certain narcotics are derived can be grown in large quantities only in certain parts of the world. Coca is produced in the Andean region of South America. Poppies, from which heroin is made, are grown predominantly in two parts of southern Asia, centering roughly on Afghanistan and Myanmar (formerly Burma). Areas where these plants are processed into narcotics are also fairly well known, as are the routes customarily used to ship the finished products to customer areas.

The real problem lies in converting this intelligence into successful policy. Efforts at crop eradication and substitution stumble on the simple economic choices facing local farmers. Narcotics crops pay more than food crops do. Processing facilities, although U.S. intelligence can locate them, tend to be small and numerous. Drugs are so profitable that small amounts, which are easily shipped, are economically attractive. This fact allows shippers to use a variety of routes, which they can change in response to pressure and efforts at interdiction. Finally, narcotics activities yield money in sufficient amounts to subvert the local authorities—civil, military, and police.

All experienced policymakers point to the importance of a domestic answer. If people do not have an interest in using illegal drugs, then everything else—growth, processing, shipping, and even price—becomes irrelevant. The drugs become valueless commodities. But the elusiveness of a successful domestic response leads policymakers back to foreign policy. (Legalizing drugs might not have the same effect on production and distribution as eliminating demand, since a black market might arise to compete with government-approved providers.)

The conjunction of the narcotics trade with international crime and possibly with terrorism as well adds a new dimension to the intelligence-gathering and policymaking problem. The profits from sales of narcotics, rather than being an end in themselves, now become the means to fund a different end. This also puts new and more difficult demands on intelligence, since terrorists and criminals operate clandestinely. The United States must be able to establish intelligence about networks, contacts, relationships among individuals and groups, flows of capital, and so forth. For example, various guerrilla and right-wing paramilitary groups in Colombia have used cocaine to finance their operations. Ironically, the Taliban in Afghanistan had made some progress against poppy crops (as opposed to the processed opium, much of which simply remained in storage), which now may be reversed under the successor regime in Afghanistan in a classic case of competing priorities.

Finally, narcotics crosses the line established in the United States between foreign and domestic intelligence and between intelligence and law enforcement. As noted earlier, the point at which an issue is handed from one agency to another is not always clear but is important, raising both practical and legal questions, some of which can impede prosecution.

ECONOMICS. Economics can be subdivided into several issues: U.S. economic competitiveness overseas, U.S. trading relations, foreign economic espionage and possible countermeasures, and the intelligence community's ability to forecast major international economic shifts that may have serious consequences for the U.S. economy.

During the late 1980s some people maintained that several of these issues (overseas competitiveness, trading relations, foreign economic espionage, industrial espionage undertaken by businesses, and possible countermeasures) could be addressed, in part, through a closer connection between intelligence and U.S. businesses. Few advocates of closer intelligence–business collaboration, however, had substantial answers for some of the more compelling questions that it raised (which is one reason why this approach was quickly rejected):

- If the intelligence community were to share intelligence with businesses, how would they safeguard the sources and methods used in obtaining the information? If the underlying sources and methods could not be shared, would businesses accept the intelligence?
- With whom would the intelligence be shared, or, in other words, what constitutes a "U.S. company"? In an age of multinational corporations, the concept is not easy to define.
- Given that every business sector has many competitive businesses, which ones would the community provide with intelligence? What would be the basis for selecting recipients and nonrecipients of the intelligence?
- Would providing intelligence be part of an implicit quid pro quo on the part of the government—that some action should or should not be taken by industry in exchange for access to intelligence?

The collection of foreign economic intelligence by other nations was also very controversial. An aggressive collection policy was at the heart of the concept of greater intelligence support to business. Supporters of the policy cited cases in which supposed "friends" of the United States, such as France, were caught engaging in such activity. Advocates saw similar activity by the United States as "fighting fire with fire." Critics argued that to do so would justify the initial hostile action. They also raised some of the arguments noted above about the limits on how such information might be used. But DCI Robert Gates put it best when he said that no U.S. intelligence agent was "willing to die for General Motors."

Allegations of U.S. economic espionage arose in the late 1990s concerning an NSA program called ECHELON. In simplest terms, NSA uses this program to search through collected SIGINT, using key words via a computer. Key-word searching allows more material to be processed and exploited. Some European officials claimed that ECHELON was being used to steal advanced technology secrets, which were then being passed to U.S. firms to enhance their competitiveness. Former DCI James Woolsey (1993–1995), in a stinging article, held that ECHELON was used to detect attempts by European firms to bribe foreign officials in order to make sales and to detect the illicit transfer of dual-use technologies—technologies that have both commercial and WMD applications, such as supercomputers and some chemicals.

U.S. policymakers viewed foreign economic counterintelligence as largely noncontroversial. Most of them considered it a proper response to foreign economic intelligence, although questions were raised about the extent of the problem. Press accounts of the issue often cited the same shopworn cases, creating "echo"—the impression of a larger problem through repetition. But the problem may actually be underreported, since many businesses do not want to admit that they have been the victims of successful foreign intelligence operations. There are also people who argue that foreign economic counterintelligence, although necessary, treats the symptom but not the cause. They acknowledge that blunting attempts at economic intelligence collection may be important but contend that the issue should be addressed at a political level—perhaps by negotiations that offer nations the choice of cessation or countermeasures.

Legislation passed during the 105th Congress (1997–1999) extended the role of FBI counterintelligence in the business information area, which has been very controversial. This legislation also reflects a continuing expansion of FBI authority in the gray areas between foreign and domestic intelligence and between intelligence and law enforcement.

Finally, at least three serious currency-related crises have occurred since the end of the cold war. In 1995 there was a peso "meltdown" in Mexico, which the intelligence community apparently handled well, giving policymakers significant advance warning. In 1998 the two-year Thai economic crisis turned into a full Asian meltdown, encompassing Malaysia, the Philippines, Indonesia, and South Korea. Little has been said about intelligence performance in this crisis. The 2000–2001 Argentine financial collapse was long evident. The likelihood that other such crises will occur in years to come underscores the importance of economic intelligence in this area, especially given the greater interrelatedness of the global financial market.

HEALTH AND ENVIRONMENT. These issues are relatively new to the intelligence agenda. They are sometimes treated as one issue and sometimes separately. The health issue has gained increasing prominence

A New Intelligence Task: Environmental Verification

One of the most compelling and difficult tasks of the intelligence community during the cold war was monitoring Soviet compliance with arms-control agreements. With the advent of the Kyoto treaty on the environment, the intelligence community now faces the prospect of a similar, if not more, daunting task.

The Kyoto treaty establishes levels of pollution that nations are allowed to generate via their industrial activities. The limitations are more onerous for the industrialized nations. However, nations may "buy" the pollution rights of other nations—presumably the less industrialized ones.

The United States will "self-police," that is, voluntarily keep within its limits. But U.S. policymakers are likely to want to know whether other nations are also complying. The issue will take on a regional aspect in the United States, since states in the so-called Rust Belt face the loss of jobs.

It will fall to the intelligence community to track other nations' compliance, but doing so will be even more difficult than tracking the production and deployment of nuclear systems. As with arms control, policymakers will have to decide how and when to use intelligence indicating noncompliance. The call will never be straightforward. Other factors—the state of relations, trade issues, national security issues, to name a few—will also intrude.

because of the AIDS pandemic and smaller outbreaks of deadly diseases such as the one caused by the ebola virus. The intelligence task is largely one of tracking patterns of infection, but there is a large gap between intelligence and policy. Take AIDS as an example. The causes, means of infection, and results of AIDS are very well known. Although the disease strikes people worldwide, some areas, notably eastern and central Africa, have extremely high concentrations of AIDS cases. The intelligence community's ability to track rates of infection and mortality has little effect on any useful international policy. Many of the African governments that face the highest rates of AIDS infection have chosen, for a variety of reasons, to ignore or even to deny their health crisis; this is also true of the government of China. In the case of Africa, local culture is a major factor in the spread of AIDS: toleration of polygamous relationships; low literacy rates, thus making even minimal efforts at education about prevention more difficult; and minimal use of prophylactics. Nor is it clear what these nations or the international community should be doing in the absence of any cure for the disease. Outsiders' attempts to change the cultural factors that facilitate the spread of AIDS would not only be difficult to make but also would probably be resisted as interference.

The environment issue is also somewhat amorphous. The basic goal—preserving a healthier global ecology—stumbles when it comes down to practicalities. As has been the case with international efforts to deal with AIDS, the nations at the center of the issue have different interests and preferences. The international community may believe that it has a vested interest in the preservation of some local ecological habitat, such as a rain forest. However, the nation whose land it is may be more interested in its own economic development than in the stewardship of a world ecological resource.

The basic intelligence tasks are identifying major threats to the environment, identifying states whose policies may be harmful to the environment, and tracking major changes in the environment. Again, a gap separates intelligence from what policymakers are supposed to do with it. Substantial intelligence community involvement in this issue dates back only to the very late stages of the cold war. *(See box, "A New Intelligence Task: Environmental Verification.")*

Much of the intelligence about the health and environment issues can be carried out by means of open sources. Commercial infrared satellites can track environmental changes. The spread of disease also can be tracked overtly. Intelligence on these issues has tended to suffer from the inattention of policymakers and from the fact that overt means of collecting intelligence have been less fully developed than the clandestine means.

The anthrax attacks in the autumn of 2001 may have added a further dimension to the health issue—the ability to determine the cause of a serious outbreak of disease in order to differentiate between natural occurrences and terrorism. If it is believed to be terrorism, the source of the attack and the prevention of future attacks must also be undertaken. These are daunting tasks and would have to be carried out under conditions of extreme pressure in terms of time and political requirements.

PEACEKEEPING OPERATIONS. Since the end of the cold war, international peacekeeping operations have expanded dramatically. Regional outbursts of violence, most of them within the borders of one country (or former country), have required the imposition of external troops to restore and then maintain peace. These external troops have customarily been formed into multinational units. Although many of these nations have experience in allied operations—at least training operations—the participants tend to cross the boundaries of old alliances. UN-mandated forces in Bosnia, for example, include NATO allies (United States, Britain, France, Italy, Spain) and their former Warsaw Pact foes (Russia, Ukraine), along with other nations. A similar array has been formed in Afghanistan. Successful military operations require strong intelligence support; multinational operations require intelligence sharing. But even in the aftermath of the cold war, some U.S. policymakers and intelligence officials are reluctant to share intelligence with former foes, non-allies, and even some allies. Responsible civil and military officials may find themselves torn between the need to keep peacekeeping partners well informed in order to carry out successful operations and the recognition that sources and methods may be compromised even beyond the limited peacekeeping theater of operations.

The use of peacekeeping or other internationally sanctioned operations for unilateral intelligence purposes became an issue in 1999. A former member of UNSCOM—the UN group responsible for monitoring Iraqi destruction of its weapons of mass destruction—alleged that the United States used an UNSCOM inspection team to plant intelligence collection devices. Some saw the U.S. action as a necessary precaution against a hostile state; others believed it violated the basis of the UNSCOM mission.

INFORMATION OPERATIONS. This is a new issue on the intelligence agenda, dealing with the use of computer technology to wage war and also to protect the United States from similar attacks. The Gulf War gave a great boost to this operational concept. Intelligence officers find that information operations allow them to be combatants rather than just combat supporters.

The parameters of information operations have yet to be fully defined. The technology to disrupt communications and infrastructure, send false messages, and destroy vital information exists; firm operational concepts for using the technology do not. The same was true of virtually every other military technology—firearms, tanks, airplanes, and so on. Only through operations do military and intelligence officials learn the best ways to employ—and defend against—new technologies.

The widespread use of computers and the increasing dependence on them by all nations and their militaries underscore the appeal and the threat of information operations, which can weaken an opponent and lessen the chance of U.S. casualties in combat.

At this point, the doctrinal questions outnumber the accepted precepts. Should information operations be used preemptively, before hostilities begin? This would tend to preempt potential diplomatic solutions, which depend on the ability of leaders and diplomats to communicate authoritatively between capitals. One can easily envision heated debates between diplomats seeking to forestall information operations in order to keep lines of communications open and military officers arguing about the need to begin preparing the electronic battlefield. On the other hand, a broad and successful information operation might induce a hostile state to agree to end a crisis. It would not entail civilian casualties, as would a classic military attack. But is this the way the United States wants to behave? Would U.S. leaders feel compelled, for legal reasons, to regard an information operation as a covert action, launched with a presidential finding, rather than a military operation? The agency largely responsible for information warfare, the National Security Agency, is both an intelligence agency and a combat support agency, so it bridges the gap. But this fact does not, in and of itself, answer the question.

Battle damage assessment (BDA), which became a major intelligence issue during the Gulf War, would be difficult to perform in an information operation. Analysts in Washington (mostly at the CIA) differed with analysts in the field as to the efficacy of the air campaign in the Gulf War. How would you carry out BDA in the even more opaque area of information operations? How would you know if an enemy's computer system had been successfully disrupted, or if the enemy had just shut it down when it recognized that an attack was under way? How would you know if the enemy had backup systems? If a successful information warfare attack is a precondition for some type of overt military operation, can we be sure that the precondition has been satisfied? How much disruption do we want to cause? Disrupting enemy communications is useful, but do we want to preclude, for example, the ability of an enemy headquarters to signal its troops authoritatively that hostilities are to cease? Or, having disrupted the enemy's ability to communicate, how do we verify an enemy's offer to cease hostilities, to negotiate, and so on.

As the United States learned in Afghanistan, there will be targets in the third world for which information operations are useless and unnecessary. Under the Taliban, the electronic infrastructure of Afghanistan had been allowed to deteriorate to the point where few suitable information operations targets existed.

Turning to the defensive problem, how do we verify the state or group responsible for an information operations attack on the United States? As with terrorism and retaliation, the source of the attack is an important question. Moreover, if the United States were subject to such an attack, what should be the proper response? Do we retaliate via computers or with weapons? Again, is our response an intelligence action or a military one?

DOMINANT BATTLEFIELD AWARENESS. As noted earlier, support to military operations (SMO) is one of the highest intelligence priorities under PDD-35. Operations in Afghanistan and any that follow elsewhere underscore this point. A key aspect of SMO is the concept of dominant battlefield awareness (DBA). At the National Defense University in June 1995, former DCI John Deutch (1995–1997) defined DBA as the integration of

IMINT, SIGINT, and HUMINT to give "commanders real-time, or near real-time, all-weather, comprehensive, continuous surveillance and information about the battlespace in which they operate. . . . Dominant battlefield awareness, if achieved, will reduce—never totally eliminate—the 'fog of war,' and provide you, the military commanders, with an unprecedented combat advantage."

DBA reflects at least two impulses. The first is the very great strides that U.S. intelligence has made in collecting and disseminating intelligence to military commanders in the field. Commanders believe that this superiority will allow them to use forces more effectively, so as to achieve ends more quickly and with fewer casualties. The second impulse behind DBA is the so-called lessons learned from the Gulf War about the problems in bringing intelligence to the field and getting the right intelligence to the right military user.

Although Deutch raised the caveat that the "fog of war" (a term coined by nineteenth-century Prussian general Karl von Clausewitz for the confusion and uncertainty that are inevitable in any combat) will never be totally eliminated, many advocates of DBA seem not to have heard him. DBA is often oversold as the ability to bring near-total intelligence to commanders. This hyperbole puts intelligence on the spot for capabilities it does not have. Unrealistically high expectations may lead commanders to place greater reliance on intelligence (which may not be forthcoming) and less on their own instincts when dealing with the fog of war, which is the ultimate skill of a combat commander. (Gen. William T. Sherman observed that Gen. Ulysses S. Grant was the superior commander because he was unconcerned about what the enemy was doing when out of sight.)

Defense Department official statements on the topic are somewhat confusing. The two key documents are *Joint Vision 2010* and *Joint Vision 2020*. Both documents emphasize the importance of DBA and the role of intelligence but tend to use intelligence and information technology interchangeably; however, information technology is a means to but is not the same thing as intelligence.

Another problem with DBA is that delivering on its promise could require the intelligence community to allocate a very large percentage of collection assets to the task, to the detriment of other priorities elsewhere in the world. As with SMO, the question "How much is enough?" is pertinent. Finally, an essential ingredient in successful DBA is getting the right type and amount of information to the right user. An army commander's intelligence needs differ from those of an infantry squad leader or a combat pilot. Some critics are concerned that too much information will be pushed down to users who have no need for it, flooding them with irrelevant intelligence simply because we have the means to do so and making their jobs more difficult.

As with intelligence operations, much in DBA remains to be worked out.

CONCLUSION

In the first decade after the end of the cold war (using as a benchmark the breaching of the Berlin Wall in 1989), the U.S. national security agenda remained largely unformed, not in terms of which issues mattered but rather which of them mattered the most, which would receive the highest priority over time (as opposed to immediate reactions to events), and what the United States would be willing to do to achieve its preferred ends. In the absence of clear definition, the intelligence community found it difficult to perform. Intelligence officials have a broad understanding of policymakers' preferences and immediate interests, but these do not provide the basis for making a coherent set of plans for investments, collection systems, personnel recruitment, and training. The war on terrorism offered some clarity in that it has given one issue priority over all the others, although not to the same extent as the old Soviet issue. Moreover, the terrorism issue is different from the Soviet issue in many important respects, thus emphasizing the importance of the cold war legacy for the intelligence community, as well as the need to transcend this legacy.

Many of the issues discussed in this chapter share an important hallmark: the gap between the intelligence community's ability to provide intelligence and the policymakers' ability to craft policies to address the issues and to use the intelligence. This gap may even be seen in the war against terrorism. If this disparity persists, it has the potential to disaffect the intelligence community and its policy clients. These clients want to be more than just informed; they want to act. And intelligence is not meant to be collected and then filed away; it is intended to assist people in making decisions or taking action. This is not to suggest that the intelligence community will suddenly disappear. But it may come to be seen as less central and necessary—a provider of information that is interesting but not as useful as it has been in the past because of the changed nature of the issues.

KEY TERMS

actionable intelligence	hard targets
battle damage assessment	industrial espionage
dominant battlefield awareness	information operations
ECHELON	key-word search
foreign economic espionage	surge capacity
global coverage	

FURTHER READINGS

Writings on the post–cold war intelligence agenda remain somewhat scattered across issue areas, reflecting the nature of the debate itself.

General

Colby, William. "The Changing Role of Intelligence." *World Outlook* 13 (summer 1991): 77–90.

Goodman, Allan E. "The Future of U.S. Intelligence." *Intelligence and National Security* 11 (October 1996): 645–656.

Goodman, Allan E., and Bruce D. Berkowitz. *The Need to Know.* Report of the Twentieth Century Fund Task Force on Covert Action and American Democracy. New York: Twentieth Century Fund, 1992.

Goodman, Allan E., et al. *In from the Cold.* Report of the Twentieth Century Fund Task Force on the Future of U.S. Intelligence. New York: Twentieth Century Fund, 1996.

Johnson, Loch K. *Bombs, Bugs, Drugs, and Thugs: Intelligence and America's Quest for Security.* New York: New York University Press, 2000.

Johnson, Loch K., and Kevin J. Scheid. "Spending for Spies: Intelligence Budgeting in the Aftermath of the Cold War." *Public Budgeting and Finance* 17 (winter 1997): 7–27.

U.S. National Intelligence Council. *Global Trends 2015.* Washington, D.C.: National Intelligence Council, 2000.

Economics

Fort, Randall M. *Economic Espionage: Problems and Prospects.* Washington, D.C.: Consortium for the Study of Intelligence, 1993.

Hulnick, Arthur S. "The Uneasy Relationship between Intelligence and Private Industry." *International Journal of Intelligence and Counterintelligence* 9 (spring 1996): 17–31.

Lowenthal, Mark M. "Keep James Bond Out of GM." *International Economy* (July–August 1992): 52–54.

Woolsey, R. James. "Why We Spy on Our Allies." *Wall Street Journal,* March 17, 2000, A18.

Zelikow, Philip. "American Economic Intelligence: Past Practice and Future Principles." *Intelligence and National Security* 12 (January 1997): 164–177.

Information Operations and Dominant Battlefield Awareness

Aldrich, Richard W. *The International Legal Implications of Information Warfare.* Colorado Springs: U.S. Air Force Institute for National Security Studies, 1996.

Deutch, John M. Speech at National Defense University, Washington, D.C., June 14, 1995. Transcript at *http://www.fas.org/irp/cia/product/dci—speech—61495.html.*

Law Enforcement

Hulnick, Arthur S. "Intelligence and Law Enforcement." *International Journal of Intelligence and Counterintelligence* 10 (fall 1997): 269–286.

Snider, L. Britt, with Elizabeth Rindskopf and John Coleman. *Relating Intelligence and Law Enforcement: Problems and Prospects.* Washington, D.C.: Consortium for the Study of Intelligence, 1994.

Narcotics

Best, Richard A., Jr., and Mark M. Lowenthal. "The U.S. Intelligence Community and the Counternarcotics Effort." Washington, D.C.: Congressional Research Service, 1992.

Peacekeeping

Best, Richard A., Jr. "Peacekeeping: Intelligence Requirements." Washington, D.C.: Congressional Research Service, 1994.
Johnston, Paul. "No Cloak and Dagger Required: Intelligence Support to UN Peacekeeping." *Intelligence and National Security* 12 (October 1997): 102–112.
Pickert, Perry L. *Intelligence for Multilateral Decision and Action.* Edited by Russell G. Swenson. Washington, D.C.: Joint Military Intelligence College, 1997.

Terrorism

Cilluffo, Frank J., Ronald A. Marks, and George C. Salmoiraghi. "The Use and Limits of U.S. Intelligence." *The Washington Quarterly* 25 (winter 2002): 61–74.

Chapter 13

Ethical and Moral Issues
in Intelligence

The title of this chapter is not as much of an oxymoron as some people may consider it. Important ethical standards and moral dilemmas challenge intelligence officers and policy officials and must be dealt with. As with most discussions of ethics and morality, some of the questions have no firm or agreed-upon answers.

GENERAL MORAL QUESTIONS

The very nature of intelligence operations and issues and the basis upon which they are created raise a number of broad moral questions.

SECRECY. At the outset of this book, it was acknowledged that much intelligence work is done in secret, although the definition of intelligence in chap. 1 did not include secrecy as a necessary precondition. The question remains: Is secrecy necessary in intelligence? If so, how much secrecy? And at what cost?

If secrecy is necessary, what causes or drives the need? Governments have intelligence services because they seek information that others would deny them. Thus, secrecy is inherent not only in what our intelligence service is doing (collection and covert action) but also in the information that others withhold from us. We also do not want the other state to know our areas of interest. Is this second level of secrecy necessary? After all, those keeping information from us often know—or at least presume—that we want it. That is one reason for hiding it from us (although many dictatorial states attempt to control all information, understanding that it poses a threat to their regime). Or is secrecy driven primarily by our attempts to gain access to hidden information? Is it based on not allowing those who are attempting to deny us information to know that, to some degree, they have failed? How necessary is that? After all, we will act on the intelligence collected, although we will attempt to mask the reasons for our actions. Won't our opponents at least guess, based on our decisions and actions, that we have gained some access to the information they were safeguarding?

Beyond the motivations for secrecy are the costs it imposes. This does not refer to the monetary costs—background checks, a variety of control systems for access, and so forth—which are quite real. The issue here is how operating in a secret milieu affects people. Does secrecy inherently lead to a temptation or willingness to cut corners or take steps that might be deemed unacceptable if they were not cloaked in secrecy? This is not to suggest that thousands of people are morally compromised because they work in organizations that prize secrecy. But the nature of some aspects of intelligence—primarily collection and covert action—combined with the fact that they are undertaken in secret, may lower an intelligence official's inhibitions to commit questionable actions. These factors put a premium on the careful selection and training of officers and on vigorous oversight.

WAR AND PEACE. Moral philosophers and states have long presumed that the conditions of war and peace are different and allow different types of activity. The most obvious wartime activity is organized violence against the territory and citizens of other states. During peacetime, overt conflict is obviously precluded. Does this division between acceptable peacetime and wartime norms extend to intelligence activities? Are efforts to subvert and overthrow the governments of enemy states acceptable in peacetime, as they are in wartime?

Even during periods of peace, the United States has relations with states that are hostile. The cold war between the United States and the Soviet Union may have been the epitome of such relationships: hostile at virtually all levels but never reaching the point of overt conflict between the two primary antagonists (as opposed to some of their surrogates).

A relationship such as that between the two cold war antagonists occupies a gray middle ground between peace and war. Intelligence activities—both collection and covert action—became one of the principal means by which the two countries could attack each other. Even in this unique situation, however, the United States and the Soviet Union accepted some limits. The two sides did not kill each other's nationals who were caught spying. Rather, they jailed the spies and sometimes exchanged them, as was the case with Col. Rudolf Abel and U-2 pilot Francis Gary Powers. (One's own national caught spying for the other side could be executed, as were Julius Rosenberg and Col. Oleg Penkovsky.) The national leadership of each side was safe from physical attacks. But did these unwritten rules create necessary boundaries, or did they serve to allow a great many other activities, including propaganda and subversion?

If a country threatens to make war or this seems imminent, does the concept of self-defense allow states to engage preemptively in certain activities, including intelligence operations? As noted earlier, in an age of information operations, this question is increasingly important.

ENDS VERSUS MEANS. The usual answer to the question "Do the ends justify the means?" is no. But if the ends do not justify the means, what does? Policymakers face difficult choices when means and ends are in conflict. For example, during the cold war, was it proper for the United States, which advocated free elections, to interfere in Western European elections in the late 1940s in order to preclude communist victories? Which choice was preferable: upholding moral principles or allowing a politically unpalatable and perhaps threatening outcome? How does U.S. interference in postwar European elections compare with the subversion of the Chilean economy as a means of undermining the government of Salvador Allende?

Within the U.S. political experience, such questions represent two deeply rooted concepts: realpolitik and idealism. In the milieu of the cold war, realpolitik predominated. The moral aspect of the cold war (Western democratic ideals versus Soviet communism) made choices like those described above easy for policymakers. Would they make the same choices in the post–cold war world in the absence of such a moral imperative?

THE NATURE OF THE OPPONENT. For nearly half a century the United States faced successive totalitarian threats: the Axis and then the Soviet Union and its satellite states. A vast gulf existed between the accepted values and behavioral norms of the United States and its allies and their opponents. Do the actions of your opponents affect the actions you may undertake? Are they a useful guide to action?

"All's fair . . ." is one response. It would be foolish for a state to deny itself weapons or tactics that are being used by an opponent bent on the state's destruction. On the other hand, does a state not lose something important when it sinks to the level of an opponent who is amoral or immoral? John Le Carré, in his novels featuring the spy George Smiley, argued that there was little difference between the actions of the United States and the Soviet Union during the cold war, that a certain moral equivalence existed. Was Le Carré correct, or can one argue that the moral distinctions between the two states remained strong and important, even if there were similarities in some types of intelligence operations?

NATIONAL INTEREST. The concept of national interest is not new. In the period that historians refer to as "early modern Europe," roughly the seventeenth century, all statesmen agreed that *raison d'état*—literally "reason of state"—guided their actions. *Raison d'état* implied two tenets: first, that the state embodied its own ends, and, second, that the interests of the state were the only guides for actions, rather than resentments, emotions, or other subjective impulses. *Raison d'état*, as practiced in early modern Europe, also implied the use of intrigue by one state against another and the ultimate sanction: the use of force.

In the late seventeenth and eighteenth centuries, international relations were, beneath a refined veneer, rather brutal. One could argue that even the creation of an international body, the United Nations, has done little to modify the behavior of states in the late twentieth and early twenty-first centuries; for example, witness the brutality of many parties in the dismemberment of Yugoslavia, or of the Khmer Rouge in Cambodia. One can see a direct descent from seventeenth-century *raison d'état* to twentieth-first-century national interest.

Is national interest a sufficient guide to the ethics and morality of intelligence? On the one hand, it is the only guide. If intelligence activities are not undertaken in support of the policies of the legitimate government, then they are meaningless at best or dangerous rogue operations at worst. On the other hand, we know from experience that legitimate governments—even those that adhere to democratic ideals and principles—can sometimes reach decisions and take actions that are morally or ethically questionable.

Thus, national interest is a difficult guideline, both indispensable and insufficient at the same time.

CHANGES IN ETHICS AND MORALS. Ethics and morals change over time. For example, slavery was accepted in Britain as late as the 1830s, in some parts of the United States as late as the 1860s, and in Brazil as late as the 1880s. Slavery reportedly continued in Sudan in the late 1990s. As late as the 1910s the issue of women's suffrage was still being vigorously debated in Britain and the United States; in Switzerland, the debate continued into the 1960s.

Assuming, as we must, that intelligence activities are undertaken on lawful authority, should they keep abreast of changes in ethics and morality? As citizens, we want to say yes. But who decides when these changes have come? How quickly do changes in ethics and morals get translated into policies and actions? For example, political intervention of the sort undertaken in Europe during the cold war is probably insupportable today (with the 1998 Iraq Liberation Act, which publicly appropriated money to foster a change in the regime in Iraq, a notable exception to this view). But when did that change come? When the Soviet Union collapsed or earlier? In 1975 the United States faced the prospect of seeing one of its NATO allies, Portugal, elect a communist government. After a strenuous debate between the U.S. ambassador (who opposed covert intervention in the Portuguese elections) and the national security adviser (who advocated it), the United States opted not to intervene, and the episode turned out satisfactorily, from the U.S. perspective. This decision was based not on a new morality but on the view that the United States had more to lose by intervening and possibly being exposed than by allowing the elections to take their course, the outcome of which proved favorable, as the ambassador felt it would.

A second important question prompted by changes in values is whether new standards should be imposed after the fact. For example, during the cold war the United States often supported regimes that were undemocratic and sometimes brutal, but were anticommunist. Although some people in the United States found these relationships objectionable at the time, many accepted their apparent necessity. In the mid-1990s DCI John Deutch ordered the CIA to review all of its contacts and operations to see if any involved links to human-rights abuses. Many in the CIA felt that this review, and some of the actions that the CIA leadership took against some officers, was an unfair ex post facto imposition of standards. (Interestingly, the Constitution bars laws that are ex post facto in nature.) Was Deutch's action a necessary cleaning up of past errors or an unfair imposition of new standards on officers who had acted in good faith under old standards? As noted earlier, in the aftermath of the September 2001 attacks, many people felt that the so-called Deutch rules had placed hobbling limits on HUMINT. The CIA claimed that no useful contact had been turned away because of these rules, but critics argued that the mere existence of the rules and the threat of some later punishment bred extreme caution in the DO. At any rate, the Deutch rules were abandoned after the terrorist attacks.

Another interesting case is that of Markus Wolf. Wolf ran East German intelligence operations for years, successfully penetrating many levels of the West German government, including the chancellor's office. When East Germany collapsed and was absorbed by West Germany, the German government put Wolf on trial for treason. Its rationale for doing so ran as follows: according to the constitution of West Germany, it was the one legitimate government of all Germany, and Wolf had carried out espionage against that government. (Despite its constitutional claims, West Germany had granted East Germany diplomatic recognition, and the two states had exchanged ambassadors.) Wolf argued that he had been the citizen of a separate state and therefore could not be guilty of treason. In 1993 he was convicted of espionage, but in 1995 the highest German court voided the verdict, accepting Wolf's argument that the charge should not have been made in the first place since he had not broken the laws of the state he had served, East Germany. After receiving a suspended sentence for kidnappings carried out by agents under his authority, Wolf, in 1998, was jailed for refusing to identify an agent he had referred to in his memoirs.

ISSUES RELATED TO COLLECTION AND COVERT ACTION

Many ethical and moral issues arise from collection and covert action. As with the broad issues discussed above, there are many questions and few agreed-upon answers.

HUMINT. HUMINT collection involves the manipulation of other human beings as potential sources of information. The skills required to be a successful HUMINT collector are acquired over time with training and experience. They basically involve psychological techniques to gain trust, including empathy, flattery, and sympathy. There are also more direct methods of gaining cooperation, such as bribery, blackmail, or sex.

Two issues predominate. The first is the morality of the manipulation itself. One might argue that the various psychological techniques are used on someone who is already susceptible to manipulation. An unwilling subject will likely terminate the relationship. ("Walk-ins" are different by virtue of the fact that they volunteer their services.) Are these legitimate activities to be undertaken by a government against the citizens of another country, whether an enemy or not?

The second issue is the responsibility of the government doing the recruiting to the source:

- How far does the government's responsibility go?
- How deep an obligation, if any, does the government incur in the recruitment?
- If the HUMINT asset is compromised, how far should the recruiter go to maintain the asset's safety? Does this obligation extend to his or her family as well?
- What if the asset has not been productive for some time? For how long a period is the government obliged to protect the asset once the relationship has ended?
- What if the asset proves to be unproductive? Perhaps the asset has misrepresented his or her access and capabilities. Is there still an obligation?

One of the most compelling arguments in favor of strong and continued responsibility for recruited sources has little to do with morality and ethics. It is the more practical concern that recruitment of new sources will become more difficult if word gets out that current or former sources are not given the support and protection they need. In other words, failing to protect your sources is bad for business.

A third issue that arises in HUMINT tends to be specific to certain issues, such as terrorism and narcotics, that depend heavily on HUMINT for good intelligence. To collect that intelligence, U.S. officials must develop contacts with—and usually pay money to—members of terrorist or narcotics-trafficking organizations. After all, these are the people who have the needed intelligence. Such a case arose in 1995, when the press reported that a CIA-paid asset was instrumental in the arrest of the terrorist known as Carlos. The asset was also a terrorist, a member of Carlos's group. Penetration of a terrorist group may require the agent to "prove" himself or herself by taking part in a terrorist activity. This probably approaches a line that many would find impossible to cross. Thus, for very understandable reasons, it is again necessary to review our assumptions about the efficacy of HUMINT against terrorism.

Some people find these types of relationships morally objectionable because of the past activities of the sources, some of which may have been directed against U.S. interests. Policy and intelligence officials must make a difficult choice between access to useful information that cannot be obtained through other means and the distasteful prospect of paying money to a terrorist or narcotics trafficker.

COLLECTION. Beyond the recruiting of human assets, intelligence officials use a variety of techniques to collect intelligence, including the theft of material and various types of eavesdropping. These activities are deemed unlawful in everyday life. What legitimizes them as intelligence operations of the state? When operating within the United States, intelligence and law enforcement officials are required to have court orders for eavesdropping and other techniques, and various procedures are in place to prevent intelligence collections from including information about U.S. citizens, a category that includes legally resident aliens.

The same issues arise in counterintelligence when a potential suspect has been identified. In the United States, unlike many other countries, the law requires intelligence officials to obtain a court order before performing these activities against a possible spy.

Collection also raises the moral question of responsibility for the knowledge that has been gained. Do intelligence officials or policymakers incur any obligations by discovering some piece of intelligence? For example, during World War II, British and U.S. intelligence became aware, via SIGINT, of the mass killing of the Jews by the Germans. The Allies did not carry out military action (bombing rail lines and camps) for two reasons. One was the belief that attacking purely military targets would end the war sooner and thus save more people in the concentration camps than would direct attacks on the camps. Another reason was concern over safeguarding the sources and methods by which the Allies had learned about the camps. What are the ethical and moral implications of the decision to desist?

COVERT ACTION. Covert actions are interventions by one state in the affairs of another. The basic ethical issue is the legitimacy of such operations. As noted earlier, concepts of national interest, national security, or national defense are most commonly used to support these operations. But, taken to the extreme, *every* nation could be both a perpetrator and a target, creating Hobbesian anarchy. In reality, many states have neither the capability, the need, nor the will to carry out covert actions against other states. But those states that do have the need and the ability believe their covert actions to be legitimate.

Covert actions also may conflict with personal goals or beliefs. Across the range of covert actions, from purely political (electoral aid, propaganda) to economic subversion and coups, innocent citizens in the targeted state can be affected and perhaps put in jeopardy. We long ago accepted military attacks on civilians in wartime as a legitimate activity, such as the large-scale bombings of cities. Are peacetime covert actions different?

As discussed in chap. 8, propaganda operations raise concern in the United States over "blowback"—the danger that a false story planted in the foreign press by U.S. intelligence might be picked up by U.S. media outlets. If U.S. intelligence informs these outlets of the true nature of the story, it runs the risk of a leak, thus undoing the entire operation. How serious a concern should blowback be? Is it a major threat to the independence of the press?

What are the moral limits of operations? During the Soviet invasion of Afghanistan, some Soviet troops, dispirited by the interminable war, succumbed to the ready availability of narcotics, as had U.S. troops in Vietnam. The United States supplied arms to the anti-Soviet Mujaheddin, including sophisticated Stinger missiles. Would it have been legitimate and acceptable to take steps to increase drug use by the Soviet troops as a means of undermining their military efforts?

Paramilitary operations—the waging of war via surrogate forces, placing them somewhat beyond the norms of accepted international law—raise a number of ethical and moral issues. Are they legitimate? They raise the prospect of innocent civilians being put in jeopardy. Are there limits to paramilitary operations? For example, does the nature of the regime that is being fought matter? Are such operations legitimate against oppressive, undemocratic regimes but illegitimate against those with more acceptable forms of government? If there are differences, who determines which governments are legitimate targets and which are not?

As with HUMINT, paramilitary operations raise questions about the sponsoring power's obligations to the combatants. This is a problem particularly for operations that are unsuccessful or appear to be inconclusive. In the case of a failed operation, does the supporting power have an obligation to help extricate its surrogate combatants and move them to a safe haven? In the case of an inconclusive operation, the choices are even more difficult. The supporting state may be able to continue the paramilitary operations indefinitely, perhaps knowing that there is little chance of success, but also little prospect of defeat. Should the supporting power continue the operation despite its near-pointlessness? Or does it have a responsibility to terminate the operation? If it decides to terminate, does it have an obligation to extricate the fighters it has supported?

Even a successful operation can raise ethical and moral issues. In the aftermath of the Soviet withdrawal from Afghanistan, one faction, the Taliban, eventually took over much of the country. The Taliban imposed a strict Muslim regime on Afghanistan, much at odds with Western notions of civil liberties and the rights of women. Did the United States and its anti-Soviet partners in Afghanistan (Pakistan, Saudi Arabia, China) bear some responsibility to attempt to moderate the rule imposed by the Taliban? Eventually, of course, the Taliban played host to Osama bin Laden, raising further questions about the results of the earlier policy.

ASSASSINATION. The issues raised by assassination and the U.S. ban on its use were discussed in chap. 8. Most people would, and official U.S. policy does, draw a distinction between casualties inflicted as a result of military operations and the targeting of a specific individual. At the same time and even before the 2001 terrorist attacks, the formerly broad support for the assassination ban had apparently eroded among the general public and to some extent in the press, perhaps reflecting some of the difficulties the United States has encountered in imposing its will since the end of the cold war.

Even if the ban were to be lifted selectively, it is difficult to imagine how useful criteria for implementing assassination could be drawn up. What level of crime or hostile activity would make someone a legitimate target? As noted in the discussion about Adolf Hitler, it is not easy to identify a potential target at the right time. Also, some possible targets are former partners. Saddam Hussein, for example, received U.S. backing in his war with Iran (1980–1988), which was then seen as the bigger foe. His behavior became problematic only after Iraq invaded Kuwait.

In the case of Osama bin Laden and other terrorist leaders, the debate over assassination became irrelevant. The United States declared itself to be at war with terrorists, making these individuals legitimate military targets.

Assassination is also a remarkably sloppy tool. Without absolute assurances about who will follow the victim into power and how the successor will behave, assassination provides no guarantee of solving the problem. The leaders we would consider as targets are not in democracies; they are in states where the mechanisms for political succession are ill defined or subject to contest. It is entirely possible to replace one thug with another, gaining little while risking your international reputation.

Assassination also raises the risk of reprisal. An absence of rules cuts both ways.

A FINAL LOOK AT OPERATIONAL ETHICS. Author James Barry ("Covert Action Can Be Just") has argued that it is possible to establish criteria for making morally guided decisions about intelligence operations. Barry suggests the following:

- Just cause
- Just intention
- Proper authority
- Last resort
- Probability of success
- Proportionality
- Discrimination and control

In the abstract, this is a compelling list of checkpoints for a policymaker to consider before launching an operation. But policymakers do not act in the abstract. And once they have decided upon the necessity for an operation, they can find ways to rationalize each of the succeeding steps.

ANALYSIS-RELATED ISSUES

The ethical and moral issues surrounding analysis largely center on the many compromises that analysts must confront as they prepare their product and deal with policymakers.

IS INTELLIGENCE "TRUTH-TELLING"? One of the common descriptions of intelligence is that it is the job of "telling truth to power." (This sounds fairly noble, although it is important to recall that court jesters once had the same function.) Chap. 1 took issue with the idea that intelligence is about "truth." Yet the image persists and carries with it some important ethical implications. If truth is the objective of intelligence, does that raise the stakes for analysis? Are analysts working on more than a well-informed and, they hope, successful policy? Moreover, does a goal of truth allow them greater latitude to pursue and defend their views of likely outcomes?

A problem with setting truth as a goal is that it has a relentless quality. Most individuals understand the importance of being honest most of the time (and acknowledge the occasional need to at least shade the truth). But if an analyst's goal is to tell the truth—especially to those in power who might not want to hear it—then there is no room for compromise, no possible admission of alternative views. After all, if one has the truth, those who disagree must have falsehood. Thus, analysts cannot compromise with other analysts whose views may differ, even slightly. Moreover, what should a truth-teller do if the powerful reject his or her analysis, as they are free to do? Once the powerful have failed to accept the truth, is their legitimacy at stake?

These questions may seem farfetched, but they underscore the problems raised by truth-telling. As noble as it may be as a goal, as a practical matter truth-telling raises many problems in an already complex intelligence and policy process.

ANALYTICAL PRESSURES. Let us step back from truth-telling and ascribe to intelligence the role that we have assumed throughout this book: the providing of informed analysis to policymakers to aid their decision making.

Even with this less demanding role, analysts can reach judgments that are based on deep and strongly held beliefs. They may be convinced not only of the conclusions they have reached but also of the importance of the issue for the nation. What should they do if their views are rejected, disregarded, or ignored by their policy clients?

- Accept that this is the policymaker's prerogative and move on to the next issue?
- Attempt to raise the issue again with the policymaker, based on the possibility that the policymaker misunderstood the importance of the issue and the analysis? How often can analysts do this, either on one particular issue or as a regular practice? How does this behavior affect their credibility?
- Try to take their analysis to other policymakers, either going over the head of their original client or elsewhere in the policy process? Even if this ploy is successful, what is the cost to the analysts' relationship with the original and all other policy clients?
- Threaten to quit? Is the issue that important? Are the analysts willing to carry out the threat or risk the loss of credibility? What does quitting accomplish beyond a protest?

The multioffice or multiagency nature of intelligence analysis raises the many issues of group dynamics noted in chap. 6. Analyses are often the product of negotiation and compromise among several analysts with differing views, but:

- To what extent should an analyst be willing to compromise with other analysts? Which types of trades are acceptable and which are not?
- At what point do the compromises affect the integrity of the document? If the compromises appear to have jeopardized its utility or integrity, can an analyst go back on previous compromises?
- Can an analyst warn policymakers that, in his or her view, an analysis has been overly compromised? In other words, at what point should an analyst feel obligated to break free of the procedural constraints of the multiagency process and venture out as a "lone wolf"? What types of issues merit this behavior? What is the likelihood of efficacy? What are the costs in terms of future working relationships within this process, even if one wins his or her point? Will there be an inevitable and irreplaceable loss of trust that makes all future interactions difficult at best? The risk/benefit analysis in such cases is clearly complex.

Finally, the nature of the relationship between the intelligence officer and the policymaker is an issue. When Sherman Kent stated that the analyst wants to be believed or listened to, he was mainly referring to the quality of the analysis. However, an analyst's access also depends on the nature of the relationship itself.

- How great a concern, if any, should the relationship be for analysts? Should they avoid stands that would alienate policymakers in order to keep open the best lines of communication?
- What if the analyst strongly believes that he or she must take a stand? Again, should the stand be tempered for the sake of the long-term relationship with policymakers?
- Alternatively, what should an analyst do in the face of pressure to produce intelligence that is perhaps "more supportive" of policy? Such a request may be subtle, not overt. Can, and should, the intelligence officer resist outright? How many small compromises add up to large ones that politicize the product? What if the analyst knows that the policymaker will write a memo with contrary views and will ultimately prevail? Is it still worth resisting blandishments, knowing one will lose both the argument and perhaps access to a key policy client as well?

Many games are being played simultaneously. There is the intelligence process itself, the policy process, and the desire of the intelligence

---

Analysts' Options: A Cultural Difference

The two options for analysts who find they cannot compromise—fighting from within or quitting—tend to play out very differently in the bureaucracies of Britain and the United States. In Britain there is a strong tradition of quitting in protest. To cite a high-level example, Foreign Secretary Anthony Eden resigned in February 1938 when he disagreed with Neville Chamberlain's policy of appeasement toward Nazi Germany. In the United States resignation is more rare, with individuals opting instead to fight from within. There is no definitive way to account for this difference. Several U.S. civil servants did resign, however, during the early stages of the civil war in Bosnia to protest the lack of action by the United States.

---

officers to have access to policymakers and to keep their funding levels safe and preferably growing. It is easy, in the abstract, to declare that the integrity of the intelligence process is primary, but in the "trenches," this is not always so obvious or so appealing.

ANALYSTS' OPTIONS. An intelligence analyst may believe that something fundamental is at stake, that neither compromise nor silence is possible. What are his or her options then? They boil down to two: continue the struggle from within the system or quit. (*See box, "Analysts' Options: A Cultural Difference."*) Continuing the struggle from within is appealing in that one's professional standards are preserved. But is it a realistic choice or a rationalization? Are there real prospects of continuing to fight for that viewpoint from within the bureaucratic system? For whatever reason, the viewpoint did not prevail either in the intelligence community or with policymakers. Short of capitulation, the analyst is now tagged with a certain view that has been found wanting. How influential will he or she be on this issue in the future? Or is the analyst, not wishing to abandon a chosen career, simply putting the best gloss on having lost? If such choices must be made, the analyst can only hope that they come over an issue of some significance. Not every issue is worth engaging at this level.

Alternatively, the analyst can quit. Honor and professional standards are preserved intact. But by quitting, the analyst abandons all hope of further influencing the process. Yes, there are ways in which one can attempt to influence policy from outside the government, but they are rarely very effective. The analyst who quits has, in effect, conceded the field to those with a different viewpoint.

OVERSIGHT-RELATED ISSUES

The demands of oversight raise ethical issues for witnesses before Congress and for the members and staff as well.

THE HELMS DILEMMA. In 1973, while testifying before the Senate Foreign Relations Subcommittee on Multinational Corporations in an open session, DCI Richard Helms was asked if the CIA had been involved in operations to overthrow the Allende government in Chile. Helms said that the CIA had not been involved. In 1977 the Justice Department considered a charge of perjury against Helms for his false testimony. After negotiations, Helms agreed to plead guilty to a misdemeanor and was fined $2,000 and given a suspended two-year prison sentence.

Helms believed that his testimony was accurate, in that the CIA had tried to prevent Allende's election but had not been part of the plot to overthrow him once he was in office. This fine line notwithstanding, what options did Helms have when he was asked about CIA activity in Chile?

Under the National Security Act, the DCI is personally responsible for protecting the sources and methods of U.S. intelligence. Helms found himself caught between that obligation and his obligation to testify fully and honestly before Congress. If he had stated that the CIA was involved in some way, he would have revealed operations in an open, public hearing. Alternatively, had he expressed the wish to answer that question in private, or in a closed session, it would also have been tantamount to admitting CIA involvement. After all, if the CIA had not been involved, why not answer in public? Helms opted for a third choice: to view the question within very narrow bounds, preserve secrecy, and deny CIA involvement. There may have been a fourth choice: to respond as he did in public and then visit the senators privately to discuss the realities of CIA activity in Chile. Helms apparently did not consider this choice, since in 1973 oversight of CIA activity was the prerogative of a small group of members of the Senate Armed Services Committee, not those on Foreign Relations. Thus, he also construed his oversight responsibilities within a narrow spectrum.

Did Helms make the right choice? Should he have been prosecuted for perjury under these circumstances? How responsible were the senators for asking such questions in an open session (particularly Sen. Stuart Symington, D-Mo., who knew the facts of the matter because he was also a member of the Senate Armed Services Committee, which then had oversight of the CIA)?

THE TORRICELLI CASE. In 1995 Rep. Robert Torricelli, D-N.J., a member of the House Permanent Select Committee on Intelligence, wrote a letter to President Clinton accusing the CIA of having misled Congress about its activities in Guatemala and having had on its payroll a Guatemalan officer involved in human-rights violations. Torricelli also made his letter available to the *New York Times*. He admitted having leaked the information to the press but argued that his duty as a member of Congress to preserve the integrity of government was greater than the oaths to preserve secret information that he had taken as a member of the House and the Intelligence Committee. Torricelli also argued that he had not violated committee rules, since he had received the information from a State Department officer in his personal office, and that it was not clear to him that the information had been properly classified.

The chairman of the Intelligence Committee filed charges against Torricelli, which were adjudicated by the House Ethics Committee. This committee decided that House rules concerning the handling of classified information were vague and ordered that in the future members would have a positive obligation to ascertain the true classification of information before releasing it. The committee went on to say that, had this ambiguity been resolved at the time he released the information, Torricelli would have been guilty of violating House rules.

Torricelli believed that the information provided by the State officer, a former employee of his, revealed CIA duplicity. Having written to the president, was it necessary to release the information to the *New York Times* as well? Should he first have expressed his concerns to the committee leadership or his party's leadership?

Interestingly, the only person who was punished was the State officer, Richard Nuccio, who gave the information to Torricelli. A panel appointed by DCI Deutch decided that Nuccio had provided the information without proper authorization. Nuccio lost his clearances and resigned from the State Department, eventually returning to work on Torricelli's staff. Ironically, Torricelli could have saved Nuccio by saying that he had asked Nuccio for the information. But, by doing so, Torricelli would have undercut his argument that he had been the innocent recipient.

In 1998 the Intelligence Community Whistleblower Protection Act became law, after much debate in Congress and the executive branch. The law established procedures by which intelligence community employees may report a complaint or urgent concern. They must first do so through channels in the intelligence community but are free to inform the Intelligence Committees if the community has taken no action by a specific time. Even then, the employees must inform executive branch officials that they are going to Congress and must handle their information in accordance with proper security procedures. Reflecting the Torricelli case, the whistleblower law states, "A member or employee of one of the intelligence committees who receives a complaint or information . . . does so in that member or employee's official capacity as a member or employee of that committee."

THE MEDIA

Reporters and their various media outlets exist to publish stories. The First Amendment to the Constitution offers the press broad freedom: "Congress shall make no law . . . abridging the freedom . . . of the press."

The government has no way to prevent the media from reporting information that it has obtained. But freedom to publish is not the same as "the people's right to know," which is an interesting catch phrase but does not appear anywhere in the Constitution. The press's right to report also does not obligate government officials to provide information, especially classified information.

But what, if any, obligations does the press have when it obtains information with national security implications? Should press limits be self-imposed, or should the press operate on the premise of "finders keepers, losers weepers"? Just as ethics and morals change in other areas, so, too, they change in the media.

In the past the press has come upon intelligence activities and agreed not to write about them for the sake of national security. For example, reporters discovered Cuban exile training camps in Florida prior to the Bay of Pigs and also learned about the construction of the *Glomar Explorer*, built by the Hughes Corporation for the CIA to retrieve a sunken Soviet submarine.

In the post–Watergate era of "investigative journalism" (a wonderful redundancy, as all journalism is investigative), it is difficult to imagine that many reporters or media outlets would be willing to suspend publication or drop a story entirely. One has only to think about such scenes as U.S. television camera crews waiting onshore as the first U.S. troops landed in Somalia in 1993 to question the premise.

Still, the question remains. At what point, if any, should reporters put aside their professional and career interests for the sake of preserving the secrecy of some intelligence activity or information? What responsibilities, if any, does the press have for the results of a story it publishes?

CONCLUSION

Intelligence is not without its ethical and moral dilemmas, some of which can be excruciating. That these intelligence dilemmas exist also means that policymakers have choices to make that can have ethical and moral dimensions. Intelligence, perhaps more than any other government activity, operates on the edge of acceptable morality, occasionally dealing in techniques that would not be acceptable elsewhere in government or in private life. For most citizens, the trade-off between ethics and increased security is acceptable, provided that the intelligence community operates with rules, oversight, and accountability.

FURTHER READINGS

Barry, James A. "Covert Action Can Be Just." *Orbis* 37 (summer 1993): 375–390.
———. *The Sword of Justice: Ethics and Coercion in International Politics.* New York: Praeger, 1998.
Godfrey, E. Drexel. "Ethics and Intelligence." *Foreign Affairs* 56 (April 1978): 624–642; see also, the response by Art Jacobs in the following issue.
Lauren, Paul Gordon. "Ethics and Intelligence." In *Intelligence: Policy and Process.* Ed. Alfred C. Maurer et al. Boulder: Westview Press, 1985.
Masters, Barrie P. "The Ethics of Intelligence Activities." National Security Affairs Forum, National War College, Washington, D.C., (spring–summer 1976).
Powers, Thomas. *The Man Who Kept the Secrets: Richard Helms and the CIA.* New York: Knopf, 1979.
Sorel, Albert. *Europe under the Old Regime.* Trans. Francis H. Herrick. New York: Harper and Row, 1947.

Chapter 14

Intelligence Reform

Efforts to improve, alter, or reorganize the intelligence community are as old as the community itself. Richard Best, in a Congressional Research Service (CRS) study prepared for the House Intelligence Committee as part of its own review of intelligence community functions, IC21, examined nineteen major studies, reviews, and proposals, covering the period 1949 to 1996, for change in the intelligence community. For devotees and critics of the intelligence community, reform is something of a cottage industry. Like the caucus race in *Alice in Wonderland,* debates over intelligence reform seem to have neither a beginning nor an end.

A brief word is in order about the use of the word "reform." Intelligence reform is a catch-all phrase, used to connote any and all efforts to make significant changes in the intelligence community. However, in the mid-1970s, in the aftermath of the Church and Pike committees' investigations, reform had a more specific meaning, referring to efforts to prevent the reoccurrence of abuses of authority or illegal acts that had been uncovered by the committees and the earlier "Family Jewels" report, written at the direction of DCI James Schlesinger (1973), describing illegal CIA activities.

The use of the word "reform" remains problematic in that it can imply that something needs fixing, as opposed to simply being improved. In this chapter, "reform" will be used without quotation marks and in the broader, more benign sense of the word—improvement rather than correcting abuses.

THE PURPOSE OF REFORM

When one sifts through the various proposals for reform, a key question must be asked: What is the purpose of these reforms? Richard Best, in his CRS study, delineated three broad chronological categories of proposals:

- To improve the efficiency of the intelligence community in the context of the cold war
- In response to specific intelligence failures or improprieties, including the Bay of Pigs, the "Family Jewels," Iran-contra, and others
- Post–cold war efforts to refocus intelligence community requirements and structure

To some extent, we are still in this third phase, which has acquired new urgency and a slightly changed form since the terrorist attacks of September 2001.

Efforts to redress glaring failures or misdeeds are easy to understand. Efforts to "improve" intelligence per se are more difficult to assess. As noted above, there are few reliable guidelines for measuring intelligence, which makes it difficult to determine what constitutes efficiency or how to achieve it. Interestingly, this may be a bigger problem for analysis than it is for collection or operations. Assessing the latter two activities is more straightforward. Either you have the capability to collect against a target or you do not, and if you do, then the collection has either been accomplished or it has not. There may be extenuating circumstances, but the evaluation process for collection is rather simple. Similarly, for operations, the goals are either achieved or unmet. Some operations may go on without resolution, such as U.S. support to the contras, but the lack of resolution itself may be an important indicator of the likelihood of ultimate success. Analysis remains more elusive. There are few efficiencies to be had in what is essentially an intellectual process. Volumes of reports or "batting averages" are not useful measurements.

The terrorist attacks in 2001 brought renewed calls for intelligence reform, with some of the most persistent advocates arguing, "If not now, when?" Even so, the purposes of reform have not been entirely clear. Several different purposes, not all of which are mutually exclusive, can be discerned:

- To improve the intelligence community's ability to deal with terrorism overall
- To prevent further terrorist attacks against the United States
- To determine if the attacks occurred because of specific intelligence lapses, and, if so, who was responsible for them
- To use the attacks as an opportunity to push intelligence reform concepts, whether or not related to the attacks or the war on terrorism

One final factor that must be taken into account is the misperception that the advent of multiple round-the-clock news media makes the intelligence community redundant. Those who hold this view believe that the community must transform itself in order to be more competitive.

Journalism and intelligence have some interesting similarities: the need for reliable sources, the need to make complex stories comprehensible, the tyranny of deadlines. But there are also important differences. Deadlines may be even more tyrannical for the news media—both print and broadcast, but especially the latter—than they are for the intelligence community. News broadcasts must go on the air as scheduled, regardless of the quality of that day's events. Journalists accept this operating necessity and use updates, corrections, or retractions as necessary. Whenever possible, intelligence managers and analysts seek to delay reporting (sometimes too long) until they have the story correctly, or as correctly as collection will allow. Also, in an average non-crisis news broadcast over a twenty-four-hour period there is a great deal of filler and repetition. The intelligence community also needs to report, but not around the clock. This is a saving grace. Also, the intelligence community seeks to do more than report; value-added analysis is an essential part of its reporting. This happens much less frequently in the news media, particularly the broadcast media; when it does occur, analysis can spill over into opinion. Squabbles between the two twenty-four-hour news networks about which of them has a liberal or a conservative bias underscore the problem.

That said, the misperception persists, even among some policymakers, that round-the-clock news sources upstage the work of the intelligence community. The misperception that the two are in competition may reveal a less than firm understanding of their fundamental differences, although the news media may employ concepts, technologies, and approaches that would be of use to intelligence.

ISSUES IN INTELLIGENCE REFORM

Discussions about intelligence reform tend to fall into two broad areas: structure—or reorganization—and process. Both approaches have their advocates. Ideally, the issues should be approached together. Altered structure and unaltered process can become little more than moving boxes on the bureaucratic organization chart. Changing the process without changing structure would likely end in few, if any, meaningful results, as the old structure would probably resist the new processes. The following are some of the more frequently discussed issues in intelligence reform, some of which have been mentioned in preceding chapters.

THE ROLE OF THE DCI. This remains the most central issue in the management and functioning of the intelligence community: the gap between the responsibilities (extensive) and the authority (limited) of the DCI. Under Executive Order 12333 (1981), the DCI is "the primary adviser to the President and the NSC on national foreign intelligence." This designation includes "full responsibility for [the] production and dissemination of national foreign intelligence," which includes the authority to task agencies beyond the CIA.

This executive order notwithstanding, the DCI's authority remains limited. As previously noted, some 80 percent of intelligence agencies and their budgets are under the direct control of the secretary of defense. Any additional power granted to the DCI must come from the secretary of defense. It is a zero-sum game. Few, if any, secretaries of defense have believed that the DCI threatened their authority, although, as noted, the staff of OSD/C3I (the Secretary's intelligence managers) is a jealous guardian on two fronts: the actual authority of the secretary (often referred to as "Title 10 prerogatives," as spelled out in the U.S. Code) and concerns about intelligence support for military operations.

Much of the problem with the DCI's authority stems from the origins of the office and how the intelligence community developed and grew. The designation DCI predates the creation of the CIA. The first DCIs ran the Central Intelligence Group (CIG), which became the CIA in the National Security Act of 1947. It is important to remember that President Harry Truman's goal in creating the CIA, under the DCI, was to have a central organization that could coordinate the disparate analyses coming from the State Department and the military. No one envisioned the CIA's producing finished intelligence in its own right or conducting operations. Thus, the limited authority granted to the DCI was consistent with his role as coordinator.

However, as the CIA moved to fill both analytical and operational voids, and as the intelligence community grew and diversified with new agencies, the DCI's role took on divergent challenges. As director of the CIA, his bureaucratic base grew, but his ability to coordinate diminished. He has little or no real authority over NSA, DIA, the military intelligence units, or NIMA, and shares authority over the NRO.

There are two main arguments in favor of increasing the DCI's authority:

- To rationalize his authority with his responsibilities
- To manage the intelligence community better as an integrated whole, limiting duplication, internecine competition, and so forth

Some would grant such additional authority only if the DCI gave up control of the CIA, becoming (either *de facto* or *de jure*) a director of national intelligence. Others, particularly in the Defense Department, argue that such a change runs the risk of limiting intelligence support to military operations; that is, without direct Defense control, this intelligence support may be wanting. The likelihood of this happening seems rather small. It is difficult to believe that any DCI would run the political risk inherent in not giving full support to the military in peacetime or in war, if for no other reason than self-protection, to avoid being blamed for military setbacks or casualties.

Others, such as the IC21 report, have suggested enabling the DCI to function more as a chief executive officer of the intelligence community, with greater authority to give coherent general direction without sacrificing the independence of the various agencies. An existing model could be the way the secretary of defense runs his department, within which there are three distinct military departments (and four services).

Underlying any of these prescriptions is the question of budget program authority. Those wise in the ways of government know that true control and responsibility entail authority over budget programs. Thus, any significant change in the DCI's authority would also involve some expansion of his budget authority. The DCI or advocates of such a change will run into opposition not only from the Defense Department but also from the current program managers, whose autonomy derives largely from their budget authority.

REQUIREMENTS. The intelligence requirements process is widely recognized as being somewhat haphazard and static. A major problem here is that policymakers, who are the true hub of requirements, have little impetus to alter the process. The most frequent reform idea is some sort of mechanism that would foster—or mandate—greater involvement of policymakers in intelligence requirements. For example, the U.S. Commission on National Security/21st Century (also known as the Hart-Rudman commission, after its cochairmen, former senators Gary Hart and Warren Rudman) recommended, in February 2001, that the NSC be "continuously engaged" with the DCI to set strategic intelligence priorities by means of a new NSC strategic planning staff. However, as long as the policymakers' most pressing needs are covered by the intelligence community, which is usually the case, they see little or no reason to add to their own burdens. Short of levying some executive or legislative mandate for a document on formal intelligence requirements—which would likely take more time than is desirable and would also be very anodyne but not very substantive—there is little prospect for change.

STOVEPIPES. This shorthand term refers to agencies in similar or analogous lines of work (collection or analysis) that tend to compete with one another, sometimes to a wasteful and perhaps harmful extent.

The stovepipe issue is most often discussed in reference to the big three INTs—SIGINT, IMINT, and HUMINT and particularly the technical INTs—especially SIGINT and IMINT. Some have proposed putting at least the technical INTs (SIGINT, IMINT, MASINT) under a single agency with the authority to decide which INTs should respond to which requirements, thus limiting some collection that may not be optimal or necessary. This solution raises questions of its own:

- Who would run such an agency? Would it matter if that person were civilian or military?
- Would this new agency be manageable?
- Since the Defense Department now currently controls all the technical INTs, would this remain true? What are the implications either way?

The main goal here is some modicum of collection efficiency and improved resource management, but the suggested solution would create a rather large entity, one whose inherent power might rival that of the DCI.

It has also been suggested that the two HUMINT components—CIA/DO and DIA/DHS—be unified, also to avoid duplication. Along similar lines, some have proposed that the clandestine services (HUMINT and covert action) be a separate agency, either to improve management responsibility or to avoid "contaminating" analysis, or both.

In the area of collection, OSINT is a particular reform issue. As noted above, OSINT remains underutilized and has no strong organizational locus. Reformers have advanced several concepts to improve the role of OSINT, including creating an OSINT agency or office or contracting out stronger OSINT services. The common goal is to elevate OSINT to a full-standing INT that is readily available to all analysts, as opposed to the more random situation that currently exists.

Two final collection issues that are part of the reform debate have already been discussed above: the balance between HUMINT and the TECHINTs and the need for improved TPEDs.

Turning to analysis, a major issue of reform is the flexibility of the analytical corps. Reform advocates often refer to this as "agility." As noted above, there is no reserve or surge capacity in the analytical agencies. Analysis is still organized around two basic structures: regional and topical offices. These are not mutually exclusive, but no intelligence service around the world has discovered a third organizing principle.

The problem stems, in part, from the fact that analysts have to be expert in *something*, which necessarily defines and limits the issues on which they can work. Creating a corps of intelligence generalists is impractical and dangerous. They will likely know a little bit about a great many issues but not very much about any single issue. Successful intelligence analysis requires expertise, and long-term expertise is one of the major "value adds" of the intelligence community. Thus, the problem is to maintain some level of flexibility or surge within this body of experts.

Surge is most important during crises, especially in areas that had a low priority but are suddenly important. However, in giving a low priority to a particular issue or nation, the policy and intelligence communities have already decided not to allocate many resources to it. Short of either finding someone already on staff who actually has some working knowledge of the issue or dragooning others into working on it, there is not much that can be done internally. A frequently suggested reform proposal is the creation and use of an intelligence "reserve"—a body of experts, either former intelligence analysts or outside experts, who can augment analytical ranks during a crisis.

Congress actually created such a reserve in 1996, but the intelligence community has not fully implemented it. Several issues are involved, one of which is security. Many outside experts do not have security clearances and may be unwilling to accept the restrictions they impose. This either eliminates them as sources or requires the intelligence community to find ways to tap their expertise without revealing classified information. Although this is not an impossible task, those responsible for security are likely to raise some objections. Another issue is cost. The intelligence community does not budget for such contingencies—just as the Defense Department does not budget for actual wartime operations during peacetime. As with the military, budget mechanisms—reallocations, supplemental appropriations—are available. The main impediment appears to be attitudes within the intelligence community.

Finally, there is the issue of redundancy in the three all-source agencies—CIA, DIA, and State/INR. This intentional duplication stems from two fundamental operating principles of the intelligence community: the distinct intelligence needs of different senior policymakers and the concept of competitive analysis. Unless one is willing to give up either or both of these operating principles, one must accept the cost of this redundancy. It does not seem likely that either the executive branch or Congress will abandon either concept or accept the idea of having a single analytical agency, which has been among the more radical proposed alternatives.

INTELLIGENCE AND THE IT REVOLUTION. A major and growing source of reform ideas stems from the ongoing information technology revolution. Some of these ideas concern technology; others focus on process.

The IT revolution had an interesting effect on the intelligence community. For years, its home-grown technology—that is, technology developed entirely internally or with contractors—was much more advanced than that available on the open market. However, the advent of the computer revolution allowed the open market to leapfrog over the intelligence community, through no fault of its own. Unfortunately, the community's first reaction was to resist this externally developed technology in a classic case of the "not invented here" syndrome. Various reasons were cited, including special needs or security requirements.

This resistance phase has now passed, although the intelligence community (and the rest of the government) still has problems in bringing new technologies on board quickly. It is important to note that the word "technology" is being broadly used here, including computer technology, analytical tools and other software, and new information sources. The issue has actually become more difficult as the marketplace fills with many technologies and tools, all making competing claims about their capabilities. The intelligence community, like every other modern enterprise, seeks technologies that are best suited to its specific needs. What is needed is a good "scouting force" that can sample as many technologies as possible and make purchasing decisions quickly. In 1995 an IT industry expert noted that computer technology was changing every eighteen months, but that it took the intelligence community from two to five years to purchase a computer. Thus, at best, an analyst was getting a computer that was already six months out of date. The situation today may be better, but the rapid absorption of modern technology remains an issue.

Process is a more difficult issue. Some reform advocates suggest a looser intelligence structure, a community of networks and more flexible organizations. Again, "agility" becomes a key goal.

The applicability of these concepts to intelligence is uncertain. Greater flexibility in the analytical corps would be a tremendous improvement, but we are unlikely to move to an intelligence community that is completely free-form, relying on the analysts to provide its structure. There is much to be said for having the ability to bring together disparate and even physically distant analysts to work on pressing issues and then to disband them or to allow new groups to form as the issues change. However, this will not eliminate the need for some bureaucratic apparatus: supervisors who can relay requirements and oversee the meeting of deadlines, reviewers of analysis, and so on. The key is to find a way to provide the necessary structure without stifling analytical fluidity. Some will bridle at what seems to be a half-hearted solution, although it may prove to be more practical in the end.

It is important not to overburden these new technologies and concepts with more promise than they can deliver. The dot-com meltdown of 2001–2002 is instructive in this regard. Many prognosticators proclaimed a new economic age and the victory of virtual enterprises over bricks-and-mortar firms. Indeed, there has been a rapid and somewhat savage winnowing of the dot-coms, while the bricks-and-mortar firms go on. The problem here has been a confusion of means and ends. The IT revolution is not an end in itself, at least for intelligence. Rather, it is—or should be—a means by which the intelligence community can perform certain tasks more efficiently.

ADMINISTRATIVE REFORM. An important although seemingly minor issue is administrative reform. Because the intelligence community is composed of separate agencies, it has many distinct processes for security, personnel policies, training, and so on. To many, these seem wasteful and duplicative. No one would dispute the fact that there are significant differences in training a cryptanalyst, an imagery analyst, and a case officer. But personnel procedures and some training are to a certain extent generic. The disparate infrastructure systems impose unnecessary costs. For example, if a terrorism analyst at DIA seeks a better job at CIA, also covering terrorism, more is involved than a simple transfer. The analyst must apply to CIA, be revetted for security, and resign from DIA. Managing analysts as some larger integrated corps would be an improvement.

OTHER REFORM CONCEPTS. Among the many other proposals for intelligence reform, a "market-based" intelligence community has been advocated. Its proponents argue that intelligence currently exists as an essentially free benefit for policymakers, which undercuts its value to them. In part, this view may stem from the intelligence community's habit of referring to policymakers as "clients" or "customers." This usage represents an effort to indicate the closeness of the relationship, but it also implies a type of relationship that may not be apt. It may be that policymakers are more of a captive audience than they are customers. Market advocates take the term literally. They believe that if policymakers had a better understanding of the true costs of intelligence—in terms of collection, analysis, and so on—they could make more informed decisions about the specific intelligence they wanted, for which they would then be charged. Presumably, policy agencies would have intelligence expense budgets that could be spent as they saw fit. In a variant of this proposal, a "mixed economy" has been suggested: policymakers would receive a certain amount of intelligence without charge but would have to supply resources if greater intelligence support was desired.

Advocates of this idea have not yet fully developed it, so it may be unfair to consider all the questions it raises. There is an interesting underlying premise: market competition will make intelligence more efficient and more competitive. This might work in some respects for issues that are currently high on the policy agenda, but it is not clear how one would handle the sudden unexpected crisis or maintain some level of expertise on less pressing issues.

The market concept also flies in the face of some of the generic aspects of intelligence, especially for collection. It is very difficult, if not impossible, to determine the cost of collecting against specific issues. For example, a SIGINT or IMINT satellite over Iraq may be collecting intelligence for support to military operations or on proliferation or regional stability. Similarly, over Afghanistan one might collect for support to military operations or on terrorism or narcotics. How does one then determine the fair "cost" for any one issue?

CONCLUSION

There is an inconclusive aspect to the intelligence reform debate. This reflects both the difficulty of the issues and choices involved and the boundless enthusiasm of reform advocates, particularly those outside the intelligence community.

Few would argue that improvements cannot be made in intelligence, although it is uncertain how "efficient" an inherently inefficient and intellectual process can be. It is important to note the rather wide gulf that exists between government-based reviews of the intelligence community, which largely tend to accept the status quo, suggesting modest changes, and the more acerbic critiques offered by those wholly outside the system, many of whom are intelligence community veterans. Are these differences real, or do they reflect, to some extent, parochial prejudices? It is clear that the executive branch has rarely shown enthusiasm for major reforms. At least three factors explain this. First, many, if not most, policymakers believe that their most important needs are usually met, so they are not deeply dissatisfied. Second, many of the proposals for reform would require greater involvement of policymakers, which they would prefer to avoid if only because they already have more than enough to do. Third, many policymakers understand some of the fragility of the intelligence community and fear the possibility of making things worse.

It is also important to remember that intelligence is a government activity. Revolutionary proposals tend to be ignored or, at best, to be severely moderated before they are enacted.

What is certain is that the debate over intelligence reform will go on, largely on its own momentum, with heightened attention during crises or after incidents deemed to be intelligence failures.

FURTHER READINGS

Literature on intelligence reform is extensive but very uneven. There are many opinions and proposals, not all of which are practical, with quite a few hobbyhorses among them. The following readings include some of the more recent studies noted in the appendix and some of the more thoughtful and practical works by knowledgeable observers.

Berkowitz, Bruce, and Allen Goodman. *BEST TRUTH: Intelligence in the Information Age.* New Haven: Yale University Press, 2000.

Best, Richard A., Jr. *Proposals for Intelligence Reorganization, 1949–1996.* Congressional Research Service report, 1996. (Appendix to the IC21 report; see below.)

Betts, Richard K. "Fixing Intelligence." *Foreign Affairs* 81 (January–February 2002): 43–59.

Carter, Ashton. B. "The Architecture of Government in the Face of Terrorism." *International Security* 26 (winter 2001–2002): 5–23.

Council on Foreign Relations. *Making Intelligence Smarter: The Future of U.S. Intelligence.* New York: Council on Foreign Relations, 1996.

Eberstadt, Ferdinand. *Unification of the War and Navy Departments and Post-war Organization for National Security.* Report to Hon. James Forrestal, Secretary of the Navy. Washington, D.C., 1945.

Johnson, Loch. "Spies." *Foreign Policy* 120 (September–October 2000): 18–26.

Quinn, James L., Jr. "Staffing the Intelligence Community: The Pros and Cons of and Intelligence Reserve." *International Journal of Intelligence and Counterintelligence* 13 (2000): 160–170.

Treverton, Gregory F. *Reshaping National Intelligence for an Age of Information.* New York: Cambridge University Press, 2001.

U.S. Commission on National Security/21st Century. *Road Map for National Security: Imperative for Change.* Phase III Report. Washington, D.C., 2001.

U.S. Commission on the Roles and Responsibilities of the United States Intelligence Community. *Preparing for the 21st Century: An Appraisal of U.S. Intelligence.* Washington, D.C., 1996.

U.S. House Permanent Select Committee on Intelligence. *IC21: The Intelligence Community in the 21st Century.* Staff study. 104th Cong., 2d sess., 1996.

Chapter 15

Foreign Intelligence Services

Although this book focuses on the U.S. intelligence community, it is instructive to examine how intelligence in foreign countries operates, both as a means of examining alternative intelligence choices and of benefiting from the light they shed on the U.S. intelligence community. However, one encounters a problem with sources. No intelligence service, even those in other democracies, has undergone the same detailed scrutiny that the U.S. intelligence community has. The reliable literature on foreign intelligence services derives mostly from the press and from some of the more popular rather than scholarly histories.

Although virtually every nation has some type of intelligence service—if not both civilian and military, at least the latter—the services of five nations have been chosen for examination, based on their importance and breadth of activity: Britain, China, France, Israel, and Russia. As is the case with the United States, each nation's intelligence services are unique expressions of its history, needs, and preferred governmental structures.

BRITAIN

It is important to understand that, despite their similarities and obvious historical connections, the British and the U.S. governmental structures and civil liberties have significant differences, which are important in understanding their intelligence practices.

First, the Cabinet, which embodies Britain's executive, enjoys a supremacy beyond that of the U.S. president. The Cabinet has the right to make appointments and to take major actions (declare war, make peace, sign treaties) without referring to Parliament, where, by definition, the Cabinet enjoys a majority in the House of Commons. Second, the division between foreign and domestic intelligence is less stark in Britain than it is in the United States. Third, Britain does not have a written Bill of Rights protecting specific civil liberties (although Prime Minister Tony Blair has talked about creating one). In terms of intelligence, one of the most important differences is that the British government can enforce prior restraint on the publication of articles deemed injurious to national security.

There are three major intelligence components—MI5, MI6, and GCHQ—all of which now operate under statutory basis. MI5, also known as the Security Service, is a domestic intelligence service, responsible for providing security against a range of threats, including terrorism, espionage, WMD proliferation, threats to the economy, and also giving support to law enforcement agencies. MI5 focuses on "covertly organized threats." A major preoccupation has been combating Irish Republican Army (IRA) terrorism in Northern Ireland and Great Britain. In the 1990s MI5 won Parliament's approval to expand its mandate to include organized crime, narcotics, immigration and benefits fraud. This legislation includes authority to monitor telephones and mail (both of which require warrants from the home secretary) and to enter homes and offices of organized-crime suspects. MI5 operates under the authority of the home secretary, for whom there is no precise U.S. equivalent. (The Home Office is responsible for police, criminal justice, prisons, immigration, and other matters.) The Security Service Acts of 1989 and 1996 govern MI5.

MI6 is also known as the Secret Intelligence Service (SIS). Its activities are governed by the Intelligence Services Act of 1994, which also governs GCHQ. MI6 is charged with the collection (by means of HUMINT and TECHINT) and production of "information relating to the activities or intentions of persons outside the British Islands" and also performs other related tasks—a legal echo of the vague CIA charter in the National Security Act. MI6 comes under the authority of the foreign secretary (equivalent to the U.S. secretary of state).

GCHQ is the Government Communications Headquarters, always referred to by its initials. GCHQ is the British SIGINT agency, also operating under the foreign secretary. It is the British equivalent of NSA, with which it enjoys an extremely close working relationship. Like NSA, GCHQ has facilities at home and overseas. The function of the Communications Electronics Security Group (CESG) is reflected in its name.

There is also a Defence Intelligence Staff, under the chief of Defence Intelligence, who reports to the defence secretary. DIS controls the Defence Geographic and Imagery Agency (DGIA), which, like NIMA, produces both geographic and imagery products.

Executive control of British intelligence is based on the Cabinet structure and its supporting Cabinet Office. The prime minister is responsible for all intelligence and security issues, with the support of the Ministerial Committee on the Intelligence Services, which serves an oversight and policy review function. The prime minister chairs this committee;

other members are the deputy prime minister, the home, defence, and foreign secretaries and the chancellor of the exchequer (equivalent to the U.S. secretary of the Treasury). Each Cabinet ministry has a permanent under secretary, its senior civil servant, who has power over administrative and budget issues. The relevant permanent under secretaries make up the Permanent Secretaries' Committee on Intelligence Services, which is chaired by the Cabinet secretary. This committee provides periodic advice on collection requirements, budgets, and other issues. An intelligence coordinator (also chairman of the Joint Intelligence Committee) assists the permanent under secretaries in dealing with the intelligence budget.

A key component in British intelligence is the Joint Intelligence Committee (JIC), which is part of the Cabinet Office and has management, oversight, and production functions. It serves as a link between policymakers and the intelligence components to establish and order priorities, which are then approved by the ministers. The JIC also periodically reviews agency performance in meeting established requirements. The JIC's Assessments Staff produces intelligence assessments on key issues, which are roughly equivalent to U.S. NIEs. The JIC also has a monitoring and warning role in terms of threats to British interests.

All three intelligence components are also overseen by Parliament's Intelligence and Security Committee, established in 1994. This oversight includes budget, administration, and policy, but it is not as powerful as the oversight exercised by U.S. congressional committees. The Intelligence and Security Committee reports annually to the prime minister; this report is later released after sensitive portions have been deleted. Interestingly, the government then issues a response to the report.

The extremely close intelligence relationship between Britain and the United States is most evident in the GCHQ/NSA relationship, but it exists elsewhere. Britain's independent IMINT capability is restricted to airborne platforms, but it receives satellite imagery from the United States. There is also a range of shared intelligence products, both collection and analytic. British HUMINT does not completely overlap that of the United States, with Britain having some advantages in Commonwealth countries.

During the cold war, British intelligence suffered several Soviet espionage penetrations. The most famous was Kim Philby, who, with four other Cambridge University associates, began spying for the Soviet Union in the 1930s. Philby became the MI6/CIA liaison, an invaluable position for a Soviet spy. Others included George Blake, an SIS officer, and Geoffrey Prime, a GCHQ employee. As noted, most known British spies did so for ideological rather than monetary reasons. Interestingly, there were allegations that Sir Roger Hollis, a director general of MI5, was a spy, but he was cleared after an investigation in 1974.

The British services do not conduct assassinations. However, British special forces units, the Special Air Service (SAS) and Special Boat Service (SBS), have taken part in antiterrorist activities against the IRA that some people have charged were assassinations. The most famous case occurred in March 1988, when the SAS killed three IRA members in Gibraltar. The British government claimed that the IRA members were on "active service," planning a series of bomb attacks. The SAS has conducted special operations for MI6.

CHINA

In the past few years, much has been written in the press about Chinese intelligence, stemming largely from allegations of espionage activities against the United States. As in all communist states, Chinese intelligence has a twofold purpose: internal security activities against dissidents and foreign intelligence operations.

Chinese intelligence is run by the Ministry of State Security. As with all other security issues in China, however, the most powerful body in the state is the Central Military Commission of the Communist Party, which has much greater influence than its title would imply. The following Ministry of State Security bureaus are of greatest importance in intelligence:

- Second Bureau: intelligence collection abroad
- Fourth Bureau: technology development for intelligence gathering and counterintelligence
- Sixth Bureau: counterintelligence, primarily against Chinese communities overseas

Although much controversy surrounds allegations of Chinese espionage, its existence is not in doubt. China clearly has a well-developed HUMINT program that relies on overseas Chinese. For example, Larry Wu-tai Chin was a Chinese spy who worked for the CIA for decades before being discovered in the 1980s. A more controversial, and ultimately inconclusive, case was that of Wen Ho Lee, a Los Alamos Laboratory scientist who downloaded thousands of pages of sensitive material. Chinese espionage apparently puts special emphasis on scientific and technology targets, both civil and military. These activities were the major focus of the Cox committee report (1999), especially allegations that China had stolen an array of information about nuclear weapons and satellite-related technology.

In addition to HUMINT, China has an array of Earth-based SIGINT platforms and is in the process of developing an imagery satellite that it plans to launch in the next several years.

The U.S.-Chinese intelligence relationship is an interesting barometer of the larger political relationship. The United States and China were hostile until President Richard Nixon's overture to China in the 1970s. That event, plus the shared fear of growing Soviet power, led to some level of intelligence cooperation. Gaining access to sites in far western China, the United States was able to recover capabilities it had lost in Iran to track Soviet missile tests. China and the United States also cooperated on the operational level, both supporting the Mujaheddin against the Soviet Union in Afghanistan in the 1980s. The collapse of the Soviet Union led to new fears on the part of China about U.S. hegemony, leading to a deterioration in relations. Chinese assertiveness prompted the prolonged captivity of a U.S. reconnaissance plane crew, which was forced to land in China after colliding with a Chinese military jet. This incident occurred after the bombing of China's embassy in Belgrade, Serbia, in May 1999— a mistake caused by the use of outdated information on that city, which did not record the embassy's new location. In January 2002 news reports alleged that the United States had planted multiple listening devices in a plane being outfitted in the United States prior to delivery to China's president. This time China played down the reports, bolstering the view that such intelligence incidents were largely a means of expressing official attitudes about the relationship with the United States. According to subsequent press reports, some U.S. analysts believed that the listening devices were Chinese in origin, part of an internal power struggle.

FRANCE

The main French intelligence organization is the DGSE (Directoire Générale de la Sécurité Extérieure—General Directorate for External Security), which reports to the minister of defense. DGSE, created in 1982, is the latest in a series of French intelligence organizations.

The four major directorates largely define the DGSE mission:

- Strategic: responsible for establishing intelligence requirements with policymakers, especially the Foreign Ministry, and also conducting intelligence studies
- Intelligence: responsible for intelligence collection, particularly HUMINT, and the dissemination of this intelligence
- Technical: collects SIGINT, largely through a number of ground sites
- Operations: responsible for clandestine operations

The DRM (Directoire du Renseignement Militaire—Directorate of Military Intelligence) was organized in 1992, combining a number of

TECHINT entities. As its name indicates, the DRM is responsible for military intelligence and imagery analysis. France has an independent satellite imagery capability. According to some reports, DRM has branched out into political and strategic intelligence areas where DGSE has been responsible.

The DPSD (Directoire de la Protection et de la Sécurité de la Défense—Directorate for Defense Protection and Security) handles military counterintelligence and maintains, in a uniquely French function, political surveillance of the military, with a view to its political reliability. This function goes back to the French Revolution, when "representatives on mission" served as political commissars, looking over the shoulders of French commanders. It also reflects the occasional intrusion—or threatened intrusion—of the military into French political life, although this has not happened since the Algerian war in the 1960s.

France has independent IMINT and SIGINT capabilities, which, as previously noted, led France to disagree with U.S. assertions about Iraqi troop movements, leading the Clinton administration to send a warning to Iraq by means of a cruise missile attack in 1996. France has also played a central role in European efforts to build an independent imagery capability.

The Operations Division of the DGSE has had much greater latitude in its activities than do the clandestine services of the United States and Britain. This includes the use of violence against certain targets. The most famous case was the sinking, in July 1985, of the *Rainbow Warrior*, a boat being used by the Greenpeace organization to protest ongoing French nuclear tests in the South Pacific. French agents planted a bomb on the *Rainbow Warrior* while it was in the harbor at Auckland, New Zealand, which resulted in the death of one person on board. France initially denied responsibility but then admitted it, leading to the resignation of the defense minister and the firing of the head of the DGSE.

The DGSE is also active in economic espionage, including activities against U.S. firms. The targets appear to be firms that compete with major French firms, reflecting the semistatist nature of parts of the French economy. In a response to apparent French economic espionage, in 1993, the Hughes Aircraft firm announced it would not take place in the prestigious Paris air show.

In the late 1990s, according to press accounts, a U.S. NOC (nonofficial cover agent) in Paris was discovered. The agent's area of concentration was also economics. As former DCI James Woolsey noted in his article on ECHELON, there are two main U.S. economic intelligence concerns: foreign bribery intended to give their firms unfair economic advantages, and economic counterintelligence.

ISRAEL

Israeli intelligence proceeds from the premise that the state is, essentially, under siege. There are two major intelligence services: Mossad and Shin Bet. Mossad (Ha-Mossad Le-Modin Ule-Tafkidim Meyuhadim—Institute for Intelligence and Special Tasks) is responsible for HUMINT, covert action, and counterterrorism, as well as a series of intelligence reports. Shin Bet (Sherut ha-Bitachon ha-Klali—General Security Service) has both counterintelligence and internal security functions. A third component, Aman (Agaf ha-Modi'in—Military Intelligence), is distinct from the intelligence components of each of the services, producing a series of intelligence reports, including national estimates. The Foreign Affairs and Security Committee of the Knesset (Parliament) oversees Israeli intelligence.

Israeli intelligence activities have become both legendary and controversial. Over the years, a number of successful HUMINT penetrations into Egypt and Syria have been conducted. However, one of these operations against Egypt in the early 1950s was discovered, resulting in the deaths of four Israeli agents and the prolonged incarceration of several others. This became known as the Lavon affair, after the defense minister at the time, Pinhas Lavon.

A more recent controversy involved a U.S. naval intelligence analyst, Jonathan Pollard. He appears to have been a walk-in, motivated by concerns that the United States was not sharing vital intelligence with Israel. However, Pollard also accepted cash and gifts in exchange for the intelligence he provided, including intelligence reports, imagery, and information about weapons systems. In 1985 he was arrested outside the Israeli Embassy and in 1987 was sentenced to life imprisonment. Some people felt that the sentence was too harsh, although successive reviews of Pollard's case have upheld the initial concerns that prompted this sentence.

Israel initially attempted to pass off the case as a rogue operation, but in early 1998 admitted that Pollard had been working as a regular agent. He had also been granted Israeli citizenship. The Pollard case became a constant irritant in U.S.-Israeli relations, not only because of the ill will it engendered but also because of constant Israeli attempts to get Pollard released. Most significantly, Israeli prime minister Benjamin Netanyahu raised the Pollard issue at the Wye Island peace talks in 1998, and President Clinton appeared to be receptive to releasing him. DCI George Tenet reportedly threatened to resign if Pollard was pardoned and released to Israel, whereupon Clinton dropped the issue. (Pollard supporters constantly bring up the fact that the United States traded Soviet spy Rudolf Abel for U-2 pilot Francis Gary Powers in the 1960s, asserting that this created a precedent. They fail to comprehend that the United States is willing to repatriate a foreign spy in exchange for a U.S. intelligence officer, but that it does not trade U.S. citizens convicted of espionage.) The Pollard case is a classic example of a successful penetration whose political costs may far outweigh any intelligence that was obtained.

In addition to its emphasis on HUMINT, Israel has also developed an independent satellite imagery capability and is at the forefront of imagery cooperation between nations. Press reports cite Turkey and India as two of its partners.

Israeli intelligence has conducted a variety of covert operations abroad, including both kidnapping and assassination. The most famous kidnapping was of the Nazi official Adolf Eichmann, who was abducted in Argentina in 1960. Eichmann had been responsible for the implementation of Hitler's "final solution," the extermination of the Jews. He was brought to Israel, where he was tried and executed. In 1986 Israeli intelligence abducted Mordechai Vanunu, who had worked at Israel's secret nuclear installation at Dimona. A year after leaving Dimona, Vanunu published details about Israel's nuclear weapons program in the London *Sunday Times*. Lured from London to Rome, Vanunu was abducted and returned to Israel, where he was sentence to eighteen years in prison.

Israeli assassinations have targeted terrorists outside of Israel or the occupied territories. These have included the terrorists responsible for the capture and death of Israeli athletes at the 1972 Munich Olympics, although one innocent Arab in Norway was misidentified and also killed by Israeli agents. More recently, Israel has killed a number of terrorists during the unrest in both occupied and Palestinian-controlled areas. Israel refers to these as "targeted killings," or "interceptions," rather than assassinations or military reprisals. They appear to have been carried out by either intelligence or military forces.

Like the United States and the Soviet Union, Israel has also suffered a major strategic intelligence failure. In 1973 Egypt and Syria achieved strategic surprise in the opening phase of the Yom Kippur War. In a still-controversial postwar investigation, the Agranat commission primarily faulted the military leadership and Aman for the surprise. The commission found that, although there were many indications of an impending attack, the military was overly committed to an indications and warning concept that led them to downplay the indicators they were seeing because not all of the conceptual indicators had been seen. In other words, they had created an I&W model and refused to react to the indications they were seeing because these very real Arab actions did not completely fit the I&W concept. Thus, even with an indications and warning model, the threshold had been set too high. This experience provided a valuable lesson on the possibility of surprise. Commenting on it nine years after the war, the staff director of the Knesset committee responsible for oversight of intelligence said: "The United States [during the cold war] has to watch every part of the globe. We know who our enemies are. We only have to watch six or seven countries—and still we were surprised."

RUSSIA

More has been written about Russian intelligence than about any other except for that of the United States. Russian intelligence capabilities probably most closely parallel those of the United States, although the KGB and the CIA were not directly comparable during the cold war.

The now defunct KGB (Komitet Gosudarstvennoi Bezopasnosti—Committee of State Security) was the last in a long line of Russian and Soviet intelligence services whose primary responsibility was to combat internal dissent. The following KGB directorates had foreign intelligence roles:

- First Chief Directorate (Foreign): responsible for all nonmilitary intelligence, foreign counterintelligence, HUMINT, foreign propaganda, and disinformation
- Eighth Chief Directorate (Communication): SIGINT, both offensive and defensive, the latter role shared with the Sixteenth Directorate (Communications Security)

One can question the KGB's effectiveness in its broader and more important internal security role. KGB leadership was involved in the abortive 1991 coup against Gorbachev that led to the demise of the Soviet Union. Moreover, the KGB clearly misread—or failed to report—the depth of anticommunist discontent in both the satellite states and the Soviet Union itself.

The GRU (Glavnoye Razvedyvatelnoye Upravnie—Main Intelligence Administration) was and remains the military intelligence organization, tasked with the collection of a large array of intelligence related to military issues. The GRU has HUMINT, SIGINT, and IMINT capabilities. During the cold war the Western services viewed the GRU as an occasional rival of the KGB. (Oleg Penkovsky was a GRU officer.)

As with any other HUMINT enterprises, the records of the KGB and GRU are mixed. The various successful penetrations of U.S. and British services have previously been noted. At the same time, however, Western services were also successful in recruiting spies in the Soviet Union and, apparently, the post-Soviet state. Oleg Penkovsky is among the best known. It should also be noted that the damage done by Aldrich Ames—and perhaps Robert Hanssen simultaneously—

involved at least twelve U.S. agents. Moreover, Hanssen's arrest apparently came as a result of information supplied by a U.S. intelligence source in Russia.

Like so much else in what was the Soviet Union, the intelligence services have been forced to undergo an unplanned transition. The KGB's First Chief Directorate emerged as the SVR (Sluzhba Vneshnei Razvedki—External Intelligence Service). It is responsible for intelligence liaison, industrial espionage, and HUMINT, and included the handling of Aldrich Ames and Robert Hanssen, carry-over assets from the KGB period. The SVR has made much of the fact that it has reduced its overseas presence, attempting to portray itself as a more benign organization than its predecessor. Some observers believe this may be largely cosmetic. Russia is now more open and accessible than was the Soviet Union, making it easier for the SVR to have contacts with agents in Russia rather than overseas.

The KGB's counterintelligence function reemerged as the FSB (Federal'naya Sluzba Besnopasnoti—Federal Security Service), which is responsible for internal counterintelligence, civil counterespionage, and internal security. Vladimir Putin headed the FSB from July 1998 until his elevation to the position of acting prime minister in August 1999.

FAPSI (Federalnoe Agenstvo Gravitelstvennoi Sviazi I Informatsii—Federal Agency for Government Communications and Information) is the successor to the KGB's Eighth Chief Directorate, responsible for cryptography, SIGINT, and the Communications Troops. These functions are parallel to those of NSA, but FAPSI also controls internal electronic communications, again making comparisons imprecise.

Russia's TECHINT capabilities come closest to those of the United States, although there have been persistent reports of deterioration in these capabilities since the demise of the Soviet Union. Numerous press reports have noted financial constraints affecting these collection assets, in terms of both the number of satellites in orbit and problems affecting ground facilities.

In October 2001 President Putin announced that Russia would close its major SIGINT facility at Lourdes, Cuba. Located within 100 miles of U.S. territory, the Lourdes complex reportedly could intercept telephone, microwave, and communications satellite traffic and was also reportedly used to manage Russian spy satellites. It was a major irritant in U.S.–Russian relations and an added difficult aspect of the U.S.–Cuban relationship. The closing appears to have been motivated primarily by economics. Russia paid Cuba $200 million annually for the use of the site—a sum that one Russian general said could be better used to buy "twenty communications and intelligence satellites and 100 modern radars." Two other factors that may have prompted the decision were the deterioration of the

Russian spy satellite fleet, limiting the importance of Lourdes in that role, and the steady shifting of U.S. communications from microwave to fiber-optic cable. Interestingly, some Russian officials expressed the hope that the United States would reciprocate by closing some ground-based SIG-INT facilities on the Russian periphery, particularly the one at Vardo, Norway. At the same time, Russia also announced the closing of its base at Cam Ranh Bay, Vietnam, which had been a major U.S. base during the Vietnam War. Soviet and Russian forces used it as a base for reconnaissance aircraft and a SIGINT facility targeting China.

The Soviet intelligence apparatus conducted assassinations, or what they termed "wet affairs." The most famous was the assassination of Josef Stalin's former rival, Leon Trotsky, in Mexico City in 1940. Some analysts believed that the Soviet Union was behind the attempted assassination of Pope John Paul II in 1981, but no conclusive proof has been uncovered. It is not known if Russian policy on assassinations has changed.

It is safe to say that the Russian intelligence capability is less formidable than it was during the height of Soviet power, although it is still not a benign or powerless service. If nothing else, there reposes in former Soviet intelligence archives—and in the minds of current or former Russian intelligence officers—a great deal of intelligence about U.S. sources and methods. In an interesting parallel to the "loose nukes" issue (former Soviet nuclear weapons or nuclear expertise being used in other WMD proliferation programs), concerns have been expressed about how some former Soviet intelligence officers—whose status, like that of nuclear scientists, has fallen greatly—might seek to profit from this knowledge. This intelligence issue may be even more difficult to track than "loose nukes."

The Russian services have also lost important former liaison partners. The intelligence services of former Soviet satellites served, in effect, as subcontractors. The East German and Czechoslovakian services both had contacts with guerrilla and terrorist groups. The Polish service was used for industrial espionage in the West. The Bulgarian service was occasionally used for assassinations. Bulgaria also assassinated one of its own dissidents, Georgi Markov, in London in 1978. The East German state no longer exists; Poland and the Czech Republic are now part of NATO.

CONCLUSION

An important factor to keep in mind in assessing different intelligence services is that most have liaison relationships with other services, thus increasing their capabilities. The degree to which these relationships complement or overlap one another is important.

As should now be evident, comparing intelligence services with one another is an inexact and perhaps not very useful endeavor. Each service is—or should be—structured to address the unique intelligence requirements of its national policymakers. Some of the structures will also reflect each nation's distinctive national and political development. Skills and capabilities will also vary from service to service. The key issue in assessing any intelligence service is the one that has pervaded this book: does it provide timely, useful intelligence to the policy process?

FURTHER READINGS

Literature on foreign intelligence services is uneven at best. The works cited below emphasize the current status of these organizations rather than historical treatments, although some of these have been cited as well. In addition, the Federation of American Scientists' Web site, www.fas.org, contains useful information on all of the services discussed in this chapter and others as well.

Britain

National Intelligence Machinery. London: The Stationery Office, 2000.
Smith, Michael. *New Cloak, Old Dagger: How Britain's Spies Came in from the Cold.* London: Gollancz, 1996.
Security Service (MI5), *www.securityservice.gov.uk* (This is the official web site of the United Kingdom's security intelligence agency.)
www.five.org.uk (This is not an official site. The site is actually hostile to intelligence services but has some useful information on the legal basis of the British services.)

China

Eftimiades, Nicholas. *Chinese Intelligence Operations.* Annapolis: Naval Institute Press, 1994.
U.S. House Select Committee on U.S. National Security and Military/Commercial Concerns with the People's Republic of China. Report. 3 vols. Washington, D.C. 105th Cong., 2d sess., 1999. [Cox committee report]

France

Direction Générale de la Sécurité Extérieure, *www.dgse.org* (Despite its title, this is an unofficial but useful site, in French.)
Porch, Douglas. "French Intelligence Culture: A Historical and Political Perspective," *Intelligence and National Security* 10 (July 1995): 486–511.

Israel

Black, Ian, and Benny Morris. *Israel's Secret Wars: A History of Israel's Intelligence Services.* New York: Grove Weidenfeld, 1991.

Katz, Samuel M. *Soldier Spies: Israeli Military Intelligence.* Novato, Calif.: Presidio Press, 1992.

Raviv, Dan, and Yossi Melman. *Every Spy a Prince: The Complete History of Israel's Intelligence Community.* Boston: Houghton Mifflin, 1990.

Thomas, Gordon. *Gideon's Spies: Mossad's Secret Warriors.* New York: St. Martin's, 1999.

Russia

Albats, Yevgenia. *The State within a State: The KGB and Its Hold on Russia—Past, Present, and Future.* Trans. Catherine A. Fitzpatrick. New York: Farrar, Strauss and Giroux, 1994.

Albini, Joseph L., and Julie Anderson. "Whatever Happened to the KGB?" *International Journal of Intelligence and Counterintelligence* 11 (spring 1998): 26–56.

Andrew, Christopher, and Oleg Gordievsky. *KGB: The Inside Story of Its Foreign Operations from Lenin to Gorbachev.* New York: HarperCollins, 1991.

Knight, Amy. *Spies without Cloaks: The KGB's Successors.* Princeton: Princeton University Press, 1996.

Waller, J. Michael. *Secret Empire: The KGB in Russia Today.* Boulder: Westview Press, 1994.

Appendix 1

Additional Bibliographic Citations and Web Sites

This bibliography, arranged topically, provides readings additional to those listed after each chapter. It is not a comprehensive bibliography of intelligence literature. Rather, the works have been chosen based on their relevance to and amplification of the themes developed in the book. Some works, although older, remain highly useful.

The list of Web sites was originally compiled by the late John Macartney, a career intelligence officer (U.S. Air Force) and a long time scholar and teacher of intelligence, who passed away in 2001.

REFERENCE

Lowenthal, Mark M. *The U.S. Intelligence Community: An Annotated Bibliography.* New York: Garland, 1994.

U.S. Congress. House Permanent Select Committee on Intelligence. *Compilation of Intelligence Laws and Related Laws and Executive Orders of Interest to the National Intelligence Community, as amended through January 3, 1998.* 105th Cong., 2d sess., 1998.

Watson, Bruce W., et al., eds. *United States Intelligence: An Encyclopedia.* New York: Garland, 1990.

GENERAL WORKS

Dearth, Douglas H., and R. Thomas Goodden, eds. *Strategic Intelligence: Theory and Approach.* 2d ed. Washington, D.C.: Defense Intelligence Agency, Joint Military Intelligence Training Center, 1995.

Hilsman, Roger. *Strategic Intelligence and National Decisions.* Glencoe, Ill.: Greenwood, 1956.

Kent, Sherman. *Strategic Intelligence for American World Policy.* Princeton: Princeton University Press, 1949.

Krizan, Lisa. *Intelligence Essentials for Everyone.* Washington, D.C.: Joint Military Intelligence College, 1999.

Laqueur, Walter. *A World of Secrets.* New York: Basic Books, 1985.

HISTORIES

Andrew, Christopher. *For the President's Eyes Only.* New York: Harper Perennial Library, 1995.

Montague, Ludwell Lee. *General Walter Bedell Smith as Director of Central Intelligence: October 1950–February 1953.* University Park: Pennsylvania State University Press, 1992.

Ranelagh, John. *The Agency: The Rise and Decline of the CIA.* New York: Simon and Schuster, 1987.

Troy, Thomas F. *Donovan and the CIA: A History of the Establishment of the Central Intelligence Agency.* Frederick, Md.: Greenwood, 1981.

U.S. Senate Select Committee to Study Governmental Operations with Respect to Intelligence Activities [Church Committee]. *Final Report,* Book IV: *Supplementary Detailed Staff Reports on Foreign and Military Intelligence.* 94th Cong., 2d sess., 1976. [Also known as the Karalekas Report, after author Anne Karalekas.]

ANALYSIS—HISTORICAL

McAuliffe, Mary S., ed. *CIA Documents on the Cuban Missile Crisis 1962.* Washington, D.C.: Historical Staff, U.S. Central Intelligence Agency, 1992.
Price, Victoria S. *The DCI's Role in Producing Strategic Intelligence Estimates.* Newport: U.S. Naval War College, 1980.

COVERT ACTION—HISTORICAL

Aguilar, Luis. *Operation Zapata.* Frederick, Md.: University Publications of America, 1981. [Bay of Pigs]
Bissell, Richard M., with Jonathan E. Lewis and Frances T. Pudlo. *Reflections of a Cold Warrior.* New Haven: Yale University Press, 1996.
Blight, James G., and Peter Kornbluh, eds. *Politics of Illusion: The Bay of Pigs Invasion Reexamined.* Boulder: Lynne Rienner Publishers, 1998.
Draper, Theodore. *A Very Thin Line: The Iran-Contra Affairs.* New York: Hill and Wang, 1991.
Persico, Joseph. *Casey: From the OSS to CIA.* New York: Viking, 1990.
Thomas, Ronald C., Jr. "Influences on Decisionmaking at the Bay of Pigs." *International Journal of Intelligence and Counterintelligence* 3 (winter 1989): 537–548.
U.S. Senate Select Committee to Study Governmental Operations with Respect to Intelligence Activities [Church Committee]. *Alleged Assassination Plots Involving Foreign Leaders.* 94th Cong., 1st sess., 1975.
Wyden, Peter. *The Bay of Pigs: The Untold Story.* New York: Simon and Schuster, 1979.

INTELLIGENCE WEB SITES

SEARCHABLE DATABASES

- *http://intellit.muskingum.edu/intellsite/index.html* (Clark, J. Ransom; "The Literature of Intelligence: A Bibliography of Materials, with Essays, Reviews, and Comments," 2002)

MULTIPLE SITE LINKS

- *http://www.loyola.edu/dept/politics/intel.html* (Strategic Intelligence)
- *http://www.columbia.edu/cu/libraries/indiv/dsc/intell.html* (U.S. Government Documents/The U.S. Intelligence Community)
- *http://www.kimsoft.com/kim-spy.htm* (Kim-spy Intelligence and CounterIntelligence)

ARMED FORCES JOURNAL INTERNATIONAL

- *http://www.afji.com*

CENTRAL INTELLIGENCE AGENCY

- *http://www.odci.gov/csi* (Center for the Study of Intelligence)
- *http://www.foia.ucia.gov* (Freedom of Information Act documents)

NATIONAL SECURITY ARCHIVE

- *http://www.gwu.edu/~nsarchiv* (declassified documents)

NEW YORK TIMES CIA PAGE

- *http://www.nytimes.com/library/national/cia-diningmain.html*

SENATE SELECT COMMITTEE ON INTELLIGENCE

- *http://www.senate.gov/committee/intelligence.html*

HUMINT

- *http://www.fas.org/irp/wwwspy.html* (Federation of American Scientists)
- *http://www3.theatlantic.com/issues/98feb/cia.htm (Atlantic Monthly)*

IMINT

- *http://www.fas.org/irp/wwwimint.html* (Federation of American Scientists)
- *http://www.fas.org/irp/imint/kh-12.htm* (Federation of American Scientists)

MASINT

- *http://www.fas.org/irp/program/masint—evaluation—rep.htm* (Federation of American Scientists)
- *http://www.fas.org/irp/congress/1996—rpt/ic21/ic21007.htm* (Federation of American Scientists)

OSINT

- *http://www.oss.net* (Open Source Solutions)
- *http://www.fas.org/irp/eprint/oss980501.htm* (Federation of American Scientists)
- *http://www.fas.org/irp/wwwecon.html* (Federation of American Scientists)

SIGINT

- *http://www.fas.org/irp/wwwsigin.html* (Federation of American Scientists)

Counterintelligence

- *http://www.nacic.gov* (National Counterintelligence Center)
- *http://www.fbi.gov/ansir/ansir.htm* (Federal Bureau of Investigation)
- *http://www.dtic.mil/dodsi/researc2.html* (Defense Security Service)
- *http://www.loyola.edu/dept/politics/hula/hitzrept.html* ("Abstract of Report of Investigation, the Aldrich H. Ames Case: An Assessment of CIA's Role in Identifying Ames as an Intelligence Penetration of the Agency," October 21, 1994)

Covert Action

- *http://www.nytimes.com/library/national/cia-invismain.html (New York Times)*

Information Operations

- *http://www.infowar.com*

Current News Articles

- *http://cryptome.org (Cryptome maintained by John Young)*

Intelligence Reform of 1996

- *http://www.access.gpo.gov/int/report.html* ("Report of the Commission on the Roles and Capabilities of the United States Intelligence Community" [Les Aspin/Harold Brown])
- *http://www.access.gpo.gov/congress/house/intel/ic21/ic21—toc.html* ("The Intelligence Community in the 21st Century," Staff Study, Permanent Select Committee on Intelligence, House of Representatives, 104th Cong. [IC21])

Business (Competitive) Intelligence

- *http://www.lookoutpoint.com/index.html* (Real-World Intelligence Inc.)
- *http://www.scip.org* (Society of Competitive Intelligence Professionals)
- *http://www.stratfor.com* (Stratfor)
- *http://www.opsec.org* (Operations Security Professionals Society)
- *http://www.pcic.net* (Professional Connections in the Intelligence Community)
- *http://www.fas.org/irp/wwwecon.html* (Federation of American Scientists)

Foreign Intelligence Services

- *http://www.pro.gov.uk/releases/soe-europe.htm* (United Kingdom, Special Operations Executive)
- *http://www.mi5.gov.uk* (United Kingdom, MI-5)
- *http://www.gchq.gov.uk* (United Kingdom, Government Communications Headquarters)

- *http://www.csis-scrs.gc.ca* (Canadian Security Intelligence Service)
- *http://www.cse.dnd.ca/cse/english/home—1.html* (Canada, Communications Security Establishment)

SPECIAL REPORTS

- *http://www.carnegie.org/deadly/0697warning.htm* ("The Warning-Response Problem and Missed Opportunities in Preventive Diplomacy," Carnegie Commission on Preventing Deadly Conflict, 1997)
- *http://www.fas.org/irp/congress/1998_cr/s980731-rumsfeld.htm* ("The Rumsfeld Commission Report," *Congressional Record*,U.S. Senate, July 31, 1998)
- *http://www.seas.gwu.edu/nsarchive/news/19980222.htm* ("Inspector General's Survey of the Cuban Operation and Associated Documents," CIA report on Bay of Pigs)
- *http://www.fas.org/irp/cia/product/jeremiah.html* (Comments of Adm. David Jeremiah on his investigation into actions taken by the intelligence community leading up to the Indian nuclear test of 1998)
- *http://www.fas.org/irp/cia/product/cocaine2/index.html* ("Report of Investigation: Allegations of Connections between CIA and the Contras in Cocaine Trafficking to the United States," CIA inspector general)
- *http://www.washingtonpost.com/wp-srv/national/longterm/drugs/front.htm* ("Special Report: CIA, Contras and Drugs: Questions Linger," *Washington Post*)

PRIVATE ORGANIZATIONS

- *http://www.afio.com* (Association of Former Intelligence Officers)
- *http://www.nmia.org* (National Military Intelligence Association)
- *http://www.oss.net* (Open Source Solutions)
- *http://www.aochq.org* (Association of Old Crows)
- *http://www.opsec.org* (Operations Security Professionals Society)
- *http://www.afcea.com* (Armed Forces Communications and Electronics Association)
- *http://www.cloakanddagger.com/dagger* (Cloak and Dagger Books)
- *http://intelligence-history.wiso.uni-erlangen.de* (International Intelligence History Association)

Major Intelligence Reviews
of Proposals

This appendix, which lists some of the most important reviews or proposals for change in the intelligence community, is based on a 1996 Congressional Research Service report, *Proposals for Intelligence Reorganization, 1949–1996*, by Richard A. Best Jr. This brief synopsis offers some insight into the major concepts that have been debated or proposed over the years. It does not capture the many proposals made by individuals.

Eberstadt Report, 1945. Laid the basic groundwork for what became the National Security Act of 1947, creating the National Security Council (NSC), a de jure director of central intelligence (DCI), and the CIA. It also created a unified defense structure, as opposed to separate War and Navy Departments.

First Hoover Commission, 1949. Raised concerns about the lack of coordination among the CIA, the military, and the State Department, resulting in duplication and some biased estimates. Urged a more central role for the CIA in national intelligence.

Dulles-Jackson-Correa Report, 1949. Recommended that the DCI concentrate on community-wide issues, with a subordinate running day-to-day CIA operations.

Doolittle Report, 1954. Urged more effective espionage, counterespionage, and covert action to deal with the Soviet threat and noted the need for technical intelligence to overcome impediments to HUMINT in the Soviet bloc.

Taylor Commission, 1961. An assessment of the Bay of Pigs invasion that criticized all agencies involved, the planning and concept of the operation, and the plausibility of deniability. Made recommendations regarding future planning and coordination for covert action.

Kirkpatrick Report, 1961.   An internal CIA review of the Bay of Pigs, which also criticized the operation's planners.

Schlesinger Report, 1971.   Questioned the increased size and cost of the intelligence community in contrast with little apparent improvement in analysis; the cost of "duplicative" collection systems; and insufficient planning for future resource allocations. Recommended strengthening the role of the DCI in these areas.

Murphy Commission (Commission on the Organization of the Government for the Conduct of Foreign Policy), 1975.   Raised the issue of the DCI's responsibility versus authority but did not recommend increasing the DCI's line authority to agencies beyond the CIA. Argued for the DCI to spend more time on community-wide issues, delegating CIA's management to a deputy.

Rockefeller Commission (Commission on CIA Activities within the United States), 1975.   Formed in the wake of revelations about improper or illegal CIA activities (the Family Jewels report); focused largely on proposals to prevent a recurrence and to focus CIA solely on foreign intelligence activities.

Church Committee (Senate Select Committee to Study Governmental Operations with Respect to Intelligence Activities), 1976.   Senate investigation after the Family Jewels revelations, recommended legislative charters for all intelligence agencies, spelling out roles and prohibited activities. Also recommended statutory recognition of the DCI's role as principal foreign intelligence adviser, with authority to establish national intelligence requirements, the intelligence budget, and guidance for intelligence operations. National intelligence budget should be appropriated to the DCI rather than to agency directors. Recommended banning assassinations.

Pike Committee (House Select Committee on Intelligence), 1976.   House counterpart to the Church Committee, its recommendations exist not in a final approved release but only as leaked to the *Village Voice* newspaper. Recommended separating the DCI from the CIA to focus on community-wide issues, a ban on assassinations in peacetime, greater congressional oversight of covert action, charter legislation for the National Security Agency (NSA), publication of the overall intelligence budget figure, and abolition of the Defense Intelligence Agency (DIA), with its functions divided between the Defense Department and CIA.

*Tower Commission (Report of the President's Special Review Board),
1987.* Formed after initial revelations about Iran-contra, recommended
improvements in the structure and functioning of the NSC staff, more
precise procedures for the restricted consideration of covert action, and a
Joint Intelligence Committee in Congress. Also raised concerns about the
influence of policymakers on the intelligence process.

Boren-McCurdy, 1993. Recommendations of the chairmen of the
Senate and House Intelligence Committees (Sen. David Boren and Rep.
Dave McCurdy, respectively), including creation of a director of national
intelligence (DNI), with budgetary programming authority across the
intelligence community; two deputy DNIs, one for analysis and estimates
and one for intelligence community issues; a separate director of the CIA,
subordinate to the DNI; and consolidation of analytical elements under a
deputy DNI.

*Aspin-Brown Commission (Commission on the Roles and Capabilities of
the U.S. Intelligence Community), 1996.* A study of the future of the intelligence community after the cold war. Said the intelligence community
needed to function more as a true community, overcoming agency barri-
ers. Recommendations included a closer tie between intelligence and policy to improve direction of roles, collection, and analysis; a second deputy
DCI for the intelligence community; a fixed six-year term for the deputy
DCI responsible for the CIA; realignment of the intelligence budget under
"discipline managers" reporting to the DCI; transfer of DHS's clandestine
recruitment role to CIA/DO.

IC21: The Intelligence Community in the Twenty-first Century, 1996. A
study by the staff of the House Permanent Select Committee on Intelligence, contemporaneous with Aspin-Brown. Sought to create a more corporate intelligence community, with the DCI acting as a chief executive
officer. Recommendations included DCI concurrence in the secretary of
defense's appointments of NFIP defense agencies; increased DCI pro-
grammatic control over NFIP agency budgets and personnel; creation of
a second deputy DCI for community management; consolidation and
rationalization of certain management and infrastructure functions across
the intelligence community; creation of a Technical Collection Agency to
manage SIGINT, IMINT, and MASINT; creation of an intelligence community reserve.

*Council on Foreign Relations Independent Task Force (Making Intelligence
Smarter: The Future of U.S. Intelligence), 1996.* Recommended improve-

ments in the requirements and priorities process; less emphasis on long-term estimates on familiar topics and broad trends; greater use of open sources; increased influence of the DCI over intelligence components; creation of an intelligence reserve.

Hart-Rudman Commission (U.S. Commission on National Security, Twenty-first Century), 2001.   Phase II of this study recommended that the National Intelligence Council devote resources to the issues of homeland security and asymmetric threats; the NSC should establish a strategic planning staff, one of whose roles would be to establish national intelligence priorities; the DCI should emphasize recruitment of HUMINT sources on terrorism; the intelligence community should place new emphasis on collection and analysis of economic and science and technology security concerns and should make greater use of OSINT, with budget increases for these activities.

Author Index

Subject Index